Matthew Edwards.

GW00381294

DICKENS AND OTHER VICTORIANS

Dickens and other Victorians

Essays in Honour of Philip Collins

Edited by
JOANNE SHATTOCK

Lecturer in English
University of Leicester

MACMILLAN
PRESS

First published 1988

Published by
THE MACMILLAN PRESS LTD
Houndmills, Basingstoke, Hampshire RG21 2XS
and London
Companies and representatives
throughout the world

Typeset by Wessex Typesetters
(Division of The Eastern Press Ltd)
Frome, Somerset

Printed in Hong Kong

British Library Cataloguing in Publication Data
Dickens and other Victorians: essays in honour
of Philip Collins.
1. English literature—19th century
—History and criticism
I. Shattock, Joanne   II. Collins, Philip
820.9'008   PR461
ISBN 0–333–44708–5

For Philip Collins

Contents

List of Plates

Editor's Preface

This collection of essays in honour of Philip Collins originated with a conference held in July 1986 at the Victorian Studies Centre, University of Leicester, to mark his retirement. To it came colleagues and former colleagues, students and former students, and a large number of academic associates from many parts of the world. The conference became an academic reunion of a unique kind. It was, on the one hand, a family occasion for eminent Dickensians from Britain, North America, Europe and Japan. It was also a reunion of a group of scholars who had been closely associated with the emergence of Victorian studies as a distinctive academic activity some 25 years previously. Both groups reflected the wide-ranging academic and scholarly activities of the conference's guest of honour and both are represented in this volume.

The world of Dickens studies, by virtue of its central subject, can never remove itself entirely from the social, cultural and political milieu in which the books were written. Dickens scholarship has long been a particularly vigorous companion to Victorian studies, a fact which is ably demonstrated by the contributors to the first part of this book.

George Levine finds nineteenth-century science or, more precisely, the theories of natural theology, thermodynamics and evolution, informing the structural principles and the fabric of *Little Dorrit*. Sylvère Monod accounts for the uncharacteristically disparaging attitude towards children which Dickens displays in *Sketches by Boz*. Andrew Sanders looks in detail at the legendary 'cartloads of books' which Dickens had to hand while writing *A Tale of Two Cities* and also places the novel in the context of Dickens's crowded work schedule in 1859. K. J. Fielding speculates on the meaning of the phrase the 'Dickens world', so beloved of Dickens scholars, and adds some new reflections on the complex relationship between fiction and the 'world' of its author. Graham Storey argues for closer connections between the Dickens of the novels and Dickens the letter writer, and traces in the letters a change in the tone of Dickens's much heralded radicalism, the introduction of a more personal anger and a growing concern with areas of experience below the social and political. U. C. Knoepflmacher explores the complex attitudes to women demonstrated by Dickens's two autobiographical heroes, David Copperfield and Pip, attitudes founded, he argues, on Dickens's latent anger. Finally, John Sutherland writes on the vogue for serialised fiction sparked off by Dickens's phenomenal early successes, presenting an intriguing sub-stratum of nineteenth-century fiction, all of it in the shadow of the 'great inimitable'.

The contributors to the second part of this book turn to some of Dickens's major contemporaries, placing them in the context of Victorian politics, religious thought, ideas about the family and notions about literary tradition. Isobel Armstrong's case for rereading Victorian poetry is that it is the most sophisticated poetry of the last 200 years and that, despite overshadowing by the Romantic and the Modernist movements, Victorian poets were fully aware of their modernity and their complexity. R. K. Webb traces many of the themes in Mrs Gaskell's novels to currents of thought prevalent in mid-nineteenth-century Unitarianism, which she encountered first in childhood and which were strengthened and reinvigorated through her marriage to the Reverend William Gaskell. Michael Slater argues that while *Gryll Grange* has many recognisable characteristics of its unVictorian author, it also demonstrates signs of its origins as a novel of the early 1860s. A. R. Humphreys asks some of the same questions about the ability of a writer to recreate his society, or his 'world', with reference to Thackeray, as are posed by K. J. Fielding with reference to Dickens. Michael Wolff links nineteenth-century attitudes to the family, and the tensions between the family and the individual, particularly women, to the central struggles of three of George Eliot's major heroines – Maggie Tulliver, Romola and Gwendolen Harleth. The powerful inheritance left by Victorian writers is demonstrated by Gillian Beer, who traces the literary and cultural ancestry of Virginia Woolf.

These two groups of essays, though varied in approach, have an underlying unifying principle. Their authors determinedly place their texts in the wider context of nineteenth-century thought and culture, tacitly acknowledging the Victorian refusal to compartmentalise literature, science, theology, politics, history or ideas about society, and choosing rather to see each as part of an undivided cultural stream. It is a principle which has informed Philip Collins's own work, most notably in his two early books, *Dickens and Crime* (1962) and *Dickens and Education* (1964), but also in later works as varied as his monograph *Reading Aloud: A Victorian*

Metier (1972), his edition of Dickens's *Public Readings* (1975) and his
two collections of *Interviews and Recollections*, on *Dickens* (1981) and
on *Thackeray* (1983). Both implicitly and explicitly these essays pay
tribute to the enormous contribution made by Philip Collins, both to
Dickens studies and to Victorian studies. To him this volume is
affectionately dedicated.

                                                              J.S.
Leicester

Notes on the Contributors

Isobel Armstrong is Professor of English at the University of Southampton and formerly Senior Lecturer in English at Leicester University. Her publications include *The Major Victorian Poets: Reconsiderations* (1969), *Victorian Scrutinies* (1972), *Robert Browning* (1974) and *Language as Living Form in Nineteenth-Century Poetry* (1982). She is currently writing a critical history of Victorian poetry.

Gillian Beer is a University Lecturer at Cambridge and a Fellow of Girton College. Her publications include *Meredith: A Change of Masks* (1970), *Darwin's Plots* (1983), *George Eliot* (1986) and several essays on Virginia Woolf.

K. J. Fielding is Emeritus Professor and University Fellow of the University of Edinburgh; editor of *The Speeches of Charles Dickens* (1960); associate-editor and co-editor of the Pilgrim Edition of Dickens's *Letters*, vols I and V; author of *Charles Dickens: A Critical Introduction* (1965) and of *Studying Charles Dickens* (1986); co-editor of *Carlyle Past and Present* (1976) and of the Duke-Edinburgh Edition of the Carlyle *Letters* (1970–   ).

A. R. Humphreys is Emeritus Professor of English at Leicester University. His publications include *The Augustan World* (1954), editions of *Henry IV Pts I and II* (1960 and 1966) and *Much Ado about Nothing* (1981) for the Arden Shakespeare, *Henry V* (1968) and *Henry VIII* (1971) for the New Penguin Shakespeare Editions, and introductions to *Tom Jones* (1962), *Joseph Andrews* (1962), *Jonathan Wild* (1964) and *Amelia* (1973) for Everyman's Library, and *Melville* (1962).

U. C. Knoepflmacher is the author of a number of books and articles on Victorian literature and culture, including *Religious Humanism and the Victorian Novel* (1965), *George Eliot's Early Novels* (1968), *Laughter and Despair* (1971) and *Nature and the Victorian Imagination* (with G. B. Tennyson, 1977). He is currently finishing a study entitled *Ventures into Childland*, which looks at fantasies for children written by Ruskin, Thackeray, MacDonald, Carroll, Ewing, Ingelow and Christina Rossetti. He teaches at Princeton University.

George Levine is Kenneth Burke Professor of English at Rutgers University. A former editor of *Victorian Studies*, he is author of *The Boundaries of Fiction* (1968) and *The Realistic Imagination* (1981), and is currently editor of the new series on science and literature for the University of Wisconsin Press. He is completing a full-length study of the impact of Darwinian ideas on Victorian fiction.

Sylvère Monod, C.B.E., Hon.D.Litt. Leicester, is Emeritus Professor of English at the University of the Sorbonne Nouvelle. He is a past president of both the Dickens Society and the Dickens Fellowship. He has written several books and many articles on Dickens, including *Dickens Romancier* (1953) and has edited both *Bleak House* (with George Ford, 1977) and *Hard Times* (1980) for the Norton Critical Editions series. He is currently editing the fiction of Dickens and Conrad in French translation.

Andrew Sanders is a Lecturer in English at Birkbeck College, University of London. He is the author of *The Victorian Historical Novel, 1840–1880* (1978) and of *Charles Dickens: Resurrectionist* (1982) and has edited *Romola* for the Penguin English Library and *Sylvia's Lovers* and *Barry Lyndon* for the World's Classics. He has written a chapter on 'The High Victorians' for the *Oxford Illustrated History of English Literature* (1987) and his Companion to *A Tale of Two Cities* (Allen & Unwin) will be published shortly. He is at present working on a study of Victorian attitudes to the eighteenth century, and on an edition of *Tom Brown's Schooldays*.

Joanne Shattock is a Lecturer in English and bibliographer at the Victorian Studies Centre, University of Leicester. She has edited, with Michael Wolff, *The Victorian Periodical Press: Samplings and Soundings* (1982), has written articles and contributed to volumes on Victorian publishing, the periodical press, travel writing, nineteenth-century editors and the literary journal. She is currently writing a book on quarterly reviews in the early Victorian period.

Michael Slater is Reader in English at Birkbeck College, University of London. He was honorary editor of *The Dickensian* (1968–77) and has published and edited a number of works related to Dickens including *Dickens 1970* (1970), *Dickens on America and the Americans* (1978) and *Dickens and Women* (1983). He is co-editor, with Michael Baron, of two novels by Peacock, *Headlong Hall* and *Gryll Grange*, for the World's Classics series, and has edited Dickens's *Christmas Books* and *Nicholas Nickleby* for the Penguin English Library.

Graham Storey is a Fellow of Trinity Hall and Reader in English at the University of Cambridge. He is joint general editor with Kathleen Tillotson of the Pilgrim Edition of *The Letters of Charles Dickens*, of which vol. vi was published in 1987. He has recently published a short critical study of *Bleak House* (1987) for Cambridge University Press. He completed the late Humphry House's edition of G. M. Hopkins's *Journals and Papers*, has edited Hopkins's poems and is the author of *A Preface to Hopkins* (1981).

John Sutherland is Professor of Literature at the California Institute of Technology. He undertook his undergraduate and postgraduate education at the University of Leicester, 1964–7. He is the author of *Thackeray at Work* (1975), *Victorian Novelists and Publishers* (1976), *Fiction and the Fiction Industry* (1978) and *Best Sellers: Popular Fiction of the 1970s* (1981). He is currently completing a companion to Victorian fiction and a life of Mrs Humphry Ward.

R. K. Webb is Professor of History at the University of Maryland, Baltimore County, U.S.A. He has also served as Professor of History at Columbia University and as editor of the *American Historical Review*. Among his books are *The British Working-Class Reader, 1790–1848: Literacy and Social Tension* (1955), *Harriet Martineau: A Radical Victorian* (1960) and *Modern England* (1969, 1980). He is at present working on a history of English Unitarianism.

Michael Wolff is Professor of English at the University of Massachusetts, Amherst, and a founding editor of *Victorian Studies* and the *Victorian Periodicals Review*. He has been co-editor of and contributor to *1859: Entering an Age of Crisis* (with Philip Appleman and William A. Madden, 1959), *The Victorian City: Images and Realities* (with H. J. Dyos, 1973), *The Waterloo Directory of Victorian Periodicals* (with John North and Dorothy Deering, 1976) and *The Victorian Periodical Press: Samplings and Soundings* (with Joanne Shattock, 1982).

Part One

Part One

1

Little Dorrit and Three Kinds of Science

GEORGE LEVINE

In what follows I am going to be thinking about what I take to be the strangeness of *Little Dorrit* in relation to three overlapping and occasionally opposed scientific theories: natural theology, thermodynamics and evolution. The strangeness of *Little Dorrit* can be registered in its self-contradictions: the most religious of Dickens's novels, it most relentlessly explores the unredeemed secularity of human society. With much of the abundance and extravagance characteristic of the big 19-part novels, it implies a world austere and restrictive. It manifests a diminishing faith in the authenticity and value of selfhood, and initiates a series of studies of the artificiality and ultimately the breakdown of the self, such as we find in *Great Expectations*, *The Tale of Two Cities* and *Our Mutual Friend*. To be sure, *Little Dorrit* provides its Dickensian share of eccentrics and characters, yet most of these sustain their identities through willed retreat from nature and time. While it seems to condemn the absence of will of William Dorrit and the society he represents, it attempts to dramatise the redemptive capacity of this absence. I want to focus on this breakdown of selfhood, and the contradictions that impel it in relation to the conflicting ground plans of reality that contemporary scientific thought was drawing up.

One does not usually think of Dickens in relation to science at all, and I do not want to claim that it importantly influenced his writing. I do, however, want to argue that seeing Dickens in the context of contemporary science is a valuable enterprise. What I will be accounting for in one way will, surely, be accounted for in others, as well. But, tenuous as some of my arguments may seem, it is worth trying to catch at the edges of discourse the difficult but important relation between Victorian writers' imagination of the real, and the possibilities intimated by the science that was so authoritatively

3

reconstructing reality. Rereading *Little Dorrit*, I was astonished at
the energetic preoccupation of its prose with disorder and loss of
energy. That preoccupation appeared consonant with the
developments in the 1840s and 1850s, when thermodynamics was
acquiring its essential formulation and radically changing the way
scientists and lay people thought about the nature of the physical
world.[1] Thermodynamics came rapidly to my mind as an
appropriate metaphor for what I was finding in the novel. Of
course, the novel seems to want to deny the absence of energy that it
uses and exposes; at its most literal, it attempts, like most of
Dickens's earlier work, to affirm a world of abundance, growth and
multiplicity, a world far closer to Darwin's than to Helmholtz's. But
in its strangeness and self-contradictions, *Little Dorrit* enacts an
almost irreconcilable conflict between two mythic structures, which
I will identify with thermodynamics and Darwinian theory, for
control of a world Dickens was trying to save for order, stability and
God.

I do not want to suggest that Dickens was directly influenced by,
say, the work of Charles Lyell, Robert Chambers, James Prescott
Joule and William Thomson, although to a degree this *is* possible.
While the implications of Helmholtz's critical formulation of
thermodynamic theory of 1847[2] probably did not reach the level of
popular exposition in England until the late 1850s or early 1860s, the
idea of the conservation of force, that energy could not be
destroyed, and that energy within a closed system never increased
without the introduction of new force into that system, was
becoming part of scientific consciousness and was unsystematically
making its way in the world. I am assuming that the changes in ways
of imagining the world expressed and implied by scientific
developments in biology and physics reflect and are reflected by
more general cultural changes that would manifest themselves even
in popular literature. Science, of course, lives within the same
cultural complex as literature. As Robert Young has put it, 'At the
heart of its science we find a culture's values.'[3]

Just as my moment-to-moment sense of what the world is – this
room, this podium, my green flashing word-processor – depends
rather helplessly on second- and third-hand science that has trickled
through the culture, so for the Victorians, their moment-to-moment
sense of their lives, even their sense of what a good story is, was
partly dependent on how science was renaming and reshaping the
world. Yet at the same time, it is possible to imagine that the way the

culture tells stories, that is, imagines its life, subtly shapes the way science asks questions, arrives at the theories that reshape the culture that formed them.

Little Dorrit is, in a way, my test of this notion, in part because it is sufficiently concerned with science to suggest the kind of metaphorical extension of analysis I am proposing. Alexander Welsh warns us not to underestimate Dickens's knowledge of science. Less flatteringly, Ruskin called Dickens a 'pure modernist – a leader of the steam whistle party *par excellence*'.[4] His distrust of the past led him to look to the new as a way out of the decadent mess he was finding all about him, from Tom All Alone's to Bleeding Heart Yard. At the very centre of *Little Dorrit* Daniel Doyce with his new invention is posed against the worn-out traditions of aristocratic order embodied in the totally disordered Circumlocution Office, that principle of entropy bureaucratised.

Although much of my argument will be conducted at the level of this last metaphor, I should like to begin with at least a little caution by suggesting that scientific models are not really alien to Dickens's way of thinking: *Household Words* is the best place to look, and it was full of science – if almost always in domestic terms. Articles on natural history, on cell theory, on the chemical history of candles and beer are impressively meticulous about the science, but punctuated regularly with comments that remind us of the application of the science to domestic life. 'Nature's Greatness in Small Things' (1857) tells us of the unity of type that underlies all variation among living organisms, echoing Schleiden's views on cell theory and Richard Owen's on comparative anatomy. On the point of thermodynamics, 'The Mysteries of a Tea-Kettle' (1850) tells us many of the same things that Joule – another important figure, with Helmholtz, in the development of thermodynamic theory – told his audiences in his important lecture 'On Matter, Living Force, and Heat' in 1847, or that Tyndall, in the major English popularisation of thermodynamics, was to tell in his *Heat: A Mode of Motion* (1863).[5] *All the Year Round*, of course, began after *Little Dorrit* was completed, but it is worth noting that only months after publication of *The Origin of Species*, it carried two very generous review-essays of that book.

In any case, one need not strain metaphors to find in Dickens the first 'science' I want to impose on *Little Dorrit*: natural theology was the framework for all popular natural history, and for most science in England.[6] It is, of course, not really a science at all, but a theology. Although the famous Bridgewater Treatises of the early 1830s were the last deep breath of that constricting and optimistic tradition, the need to read nature within the context of established religion remained strong enough to inhibit Darwin from publishing his theory until 1859. It perpetuated the endangered tradition of reading matter as evidence of spirit, a tradition whose presence we can feel in Dickens's uncannily intense registration of particulars. One could be a physicist or even a Darwinian and retain the natural-theological belief in the evidences of the creator, although that often entailed some strategic manoeuvring, of the sort that, say, brought epicycles into the Ptolemaic scheme. All natural phenomena could be described, as Darwin often described them himself, as 'contrivances', with the implication of guiding intelligence. However rationalistic its sources and methods, natural theology implied behind matter a world spiritually alive. Its science had to be teleological; all of its nature told or implied stories, and stories with happy endings. A more sophisticated version of the tradition is at work in Owen's idealist anatomy, which infers the divine hand from the unity of type that pervades all organisms. *Household Words* put it this way:

> beyond and above the law of design in creation, stands the law of unity of type, and unity of structure. No function so various, no labours so rude, so elaborate, so dissimilar, but this cell can build up the instrument, and this model prescribes the limits of its shape. Through all creation, the microscope detects the handwriting of oneness of power or of ordnance. It has become the instrument of a new revelation in science, and speaks clearly to the soul as to the mind of man.[7]

The second of my sciences is thermodynamics. In England, there was no immediately recognised incompatibility between thermodynamics and religious faith, as witness the very religious James Prescott Joule, or William Thomson, later Lord Kelvin. Yet thermodynamics, particularly the second law, seemed to run counter to the optimistic 'progessivist' directions of most contemporary science, particularly evolution. Not long before *Little Dorrit*, Thomson was foreseeing the death of the sun.

The third of the sciences is evolutionary biology. While unestablished scientifically before Darwin, it was, as we all know, very much in the air. Chambers's notorious *The Vestiges of Creation* (1844) had been very popular in spite of violent scientific and religious objections. In most versions, evolution, or development or transmutation theory, was progressivist. Chambers needed spontaneous generation as Darwin was to need Malthusian overpopulation, but the direction – with some losses at least for extinction – was onward and upward. Given what we can see in *Household Words* and of Owen's friendly participation in it, Dickens was probably an Owenite. Yet certain elements of *Little Dorrit* suggest a break with pre-Darwinian ways of looking. Darwin's theory deprives life of its spiritual ancestry and subjects everything to natural law (just as Chambers did). But the progressivist direction of evolutionary thought was easily adaptable by some scientists and clerics to teleology and design,[8] while the degenerationist directions of thermodynamics, which also applied theories of energy source and expenditure to the human body, led to the bleakness of vision we find, say, in Huxley's *Evolution and Ethics* 40 years later.

These three sciences suggest three different versions of the world: one, a world rational, just, divinely meaningful; one a world fallen from a golden age; one a world moving toward that golden age. The myths are, however, more complicated than that and pose different sorts of threats for Dickens and his audience. Evolutionary theory and thermodynamics came into conflict directly, when Thomson deprived Darwin of the time he needed for natural selection to create the organic world we know. Moreover, thermodynamics – at least its second law – came to suggest a tragic narrative, evolution a comic one. The theories would seem to agree, however, in their emphasis on time. While Darwin defines all things by their continuing and evanescent movement through time, thermodynamics is almost equally important in thrusting time into 'natural law'. The formulas of Newtonian mechanics worked with equal effectiveness backwards or forwards. But the second law of thermodynamics introduces the irreversible arrow of time, the inevitable movement from warmer to colder, from order to disorder, from concentrated to dissipated energy.

But even here there is a radical difference. While Darwin's time may entail loss, it tends to transform loss into gain and implies movement from lower to higher forms of order. Gillian Beer has emphasised that Darwin's theory implied abundance, excess, multitudinousness; but thermodynamics is a rather stingy theory. If energy does not perish, it does not increase, and is only redistributed. For every gain there must be a loss, and inefficiency is universal; the quantity of heat never translates into work without some loss. Evolution is profligate and tends to be read as progressive; thermodynamics has something of the severity of the austere Calvinist world which almost crushes Clennam, which imprisons his mother, which punishes inexorably every spontaneous outburst of feeling, every excess.

But the ostensible incompatibility between thermodynamics and evolution is probably of less significance than the incompatibility between natural theology and both thermodynamics and evolution. The positivist extension of the claims of scientific knowledge to primacy in all areas of knowledge depended in part on the development of sciences that could extend natural law to human behaviour. For scientific explanation to achieve its authority, it had to discover, as Darwin did for biology, 'uniformity of law and natural causes' in operation everywhere.[9] Although Joule believed that his argument about the indestructibility of living force could have been derived *a priori* on the strength of our knowledge of the Creator, material explanations of behaviour gradually removed the necessity to invoke God or design or intention. The loopholes for spirit were closing rapidly.

The second law not only seems to exclude design, but reduces, perhaps eliminates, the possibility of human intervention in its relentless processes. Thomson managed to remain a progressivist and a believer only by positing the possibility of action *outside* the system of nature as we now understand it. Such a move, Darwin would have argued, is a betrayal of science and would have been, as he seemed to like to say, fatal to his own theory. Although, Thomson says, 'mechanical energy is *indestructible*, there is a universal tendency to its dissipation. . . . The result would inevitably be a state of universal rest and death, if the universe were finite and left to obey existing laws.'[10] Thomson, that is to say, continues the strong early century tradition which saw science and religion as complementary. Yet there is a difference. Unlike Paleyan thinkers, Thomson was not arguing for divine intelligence *in* the laws of nature. He affirms the divine presence by giving the game away to positivism: religion and science take parallel paths in which their mutual claims do not conflict or converge.

> It is impossible to conceive a limit to the extent of matter in the universe. . . . Science points rather to an endless progress, through an endless space, of action involving the transformation of potential energy into palpable motion and thence into heat. . . .

It is also impossible to conceive either the beginning or the continuance of life without an overruling creative power; and therefore no conclusions of dynamical science regarding the future condition of the earth can be held to give dispiriting views as to the destiny of the race of intelligent beings by which it is at present inhabited. (p. 350)

The intellectual dead end has its narrative counterpart. What separates both thermodynamics and evolutionary theory from natural theology is their mutual readiness to read all experience in inhuman but non-divine terms. Human life is determined by its intake and expenditure of energy. The laws that govern the expiration of a candle, govern the expiration of human life.[11] Together thermodynamics and evolution offer themselves as modes of explanation which omits what Dickens would think of as the distinctively human; and they pose two threats: that a moral, voluntarist reading of experience is no longer possible, and that the meanings constructed by narrative resolution will be arbitrary human impositions on forces that owe allegiance only to the laws of matter, not of spirit.

We take for granted George Eliot's concern with the large impersonal forces, social and psychological, by which the individual will is bent to the service of its primary animal nature and constrained by the weblike, irrational and powerful community. The bleakness of *Middlemarch* reflects the power of what she once called 'undeviating law', and the apparent powerlessness of individuals not only in increasingly complex social structures but against the unconscious strategies of their own psyches. Given the representative status of *Middlemarch* it is easy to assume that the Victorian novel, as a form, is consistently struggling with such impersonal constraints. Yet even with Scott and Thackeray, and a remarkable series of his own novels behind him, Dickens did not have available a fully developed tradition of this kind. Through most of his earlier work, he had celebrated exuberantly the powers of innocence, of good intentions, of change of heart, although he had always been uneasy about strong will. In *Little Dorrit*, there is far more uneasiness, and no celebration. It manifests Dickens's deep distrust of institutions, but also of the wills and consciousnesses that internalise the system. Strong will becomes ineffectual. Energy dissipates and landscapes fragment into disorder.

In *Little Dorrit*, Dickens makes discoveries that subvert his intentions: faith in energy and free choice is partly denied at the moment it is affirmed. Choosing to see nature from within the context of natural theology, he reveals a threatening disorder that does not disguise ultimate design; the web of connections determining modern life is reckless of individual will and entails a reimagination of 'character'; the pressures of the impersonal assert themselves in the self and threaten identity; the mystery required formally to sustain Dickensian narratives and thematically to construct a new urban world no longer legible even to its most familiar citizens is not so obviously penetrable. Choice begins to lose its significance, and the natural world threatens to mean nothing but itself. We find in *Little Dorrit* ambivalences about modern, particularly urban life, with its enormous potential for creative change and its apparently inevitable move to decay. These shadow forth a crisis of selfhood and personality, later celebrated by D. H. Lawrence, but here uneasily wavering between religious and secular forces, and echoing the contentions among the scientific theories I have been laying out here.

We might trace the development of these ambivalences and contradictions from Dickens's initial conception of the novel. The original title was to be 'Nobody's Fault', and its central character was to be a man 'who should bring about all the mischief, lay it all on Providence, and say at every fresh calamity, ". . . nobody was to blame".'[12] Its central idea as proposed in the notebooks was 'The people who lay all their sins negligences and ignorances on Providence'. The title, of course, was to be ironic, and in Gowan's cynical stance we have the sort of thing Dickens must originally have intended. But Dickens had great difficulties with the conception. The problem, Harvey Sucksmith argues, was that 'the central idea he had chosen for the novel was incapable of organizing the material into an integrated and meaningful structure and vision' (p. xviii). My emphasis would be different. Dickens was finding that the initiating idea was becoming literal rather than ironic. The world he was constructing was making individual choice, or action, almost impossible. Action is largely exaggerated passivity, particularly with Arthur Clennam, possibly, too, with Little Dorrit herself. Dickens, that is to say, had moved into a world where 'nobody's fault' had become an almost inevitable reading of experience, where the power of the will was indeed in question, where the voluntaristic model of behaviour was put to the test.[13]

In what follows, I want to suggest how some of these pervasive difficulties, intimated by reiterated images and motifs, can be seen as reflections of the new thermodynamic model of nature, and how the efforts to reject this model by reaffirming the design and meaning of natural theology lead to creative incoherences in the way Dickens imagines 'character', self and the action of the will.

The science of *Little Dorrit* is implicit in its images. Taken together, they imply an argument: that the primary force in the world is a mysterious nature that creates its own impersonal plot of entropic decline and cuts like fate itself across the conventional narrative through which characters and narrator alike aspire to meaning. More repressive than society itself, because more embracing, nature manifests itself particularly through ineluctable time. As Thomson invoked the infinite to deny the authority of the thermodynamic laws he formulates, Dickens attempts to make the natural and the divine compatible. But the option of timelessness, intimated through a natural theological view of the laws of nature and through the prison bars not of society but of nature itself, is unavailable. The risk and the power of *Little Dorrit* is in Dickens's ultimate dramatisation of the primacy of the secular: the protagonists must re-engage in time. Despite the ultimate convergence in love between Amy and Clennam, only on the margins of the narrative, perhaps in Doyce, certainly in Physician, is there the suggestion of a world less austere, where the irreversible arrow does not inevitably point downward.

The primary physical feature of this world is entropic decline: the novel is full of fragmented land- and city-scapes, from the 'Babel' of foul-smelling Marseilles, to the dissonance and soot and death carts of Clennam's plague-ridden London, to the ruins of Rome, through the Alps, where there was loveliness without but 'dirt and poverty within', to Venice, with its mouldering rooms and fading glories. Matter, objects, ominously symbolic in the texture of the prose, resist the meanings to which they are assigned, do not seem evidence of the power, goodness and wisdom of the Creator. The sun that beat down on Marseilles that August day is raw, oppressive energy, exhausting all it touches, signifying nothing but itself – it 'was no greater rarity in Southern France then, than at any other time, before or since' (p. 39).

Each book begins with extreme images of disorder. The powerful Marseilles sun beats down on dust, disharmony, fatigue and prison, which itself holds a cluster of heterogeneous and waste objects, and

vermin, human and rodent. The second book opens at the Great St
Bernard, in a chaos of cold, of mules biting each other, of men racing
about; and

> In the midst of this, the great stable of the convent, occupying the
> basement story and entered by the basement door, outside where
> all the disorder was, poured forth its contribution of cloud, as if
> the whole rugged edifice were filled with nothing else, and would
> collapse as soon as it had emptied itself, leaving the snow to fall
> upon the bare mountain summit.   (p. 484)

I have not time to recount the book's excessive preoccupation with
such scenes, which extend to such places as Fanny's theatre, or the
neighbourhood around Miss Wade's house, or Mrs Clennam's
house, or, metaphorically, the house of Merdle.

The images of disorder, while suggesting a moral condition, are
also couched in the language of mystery that renders them objects
intrinsically meaningless. We expect of Dickens, especially after
Bleak House, that he will build his narrative around mysteries, whose
secrets will be revealed either gradually or abruptly. But the world of
Little Dorrit is all mystery, and its secrets oppress and overwhelm.
The Circumlocution Office is the obvious comic–satiric expression of
the institutional source and power of this mystery. But perhaps the
richest figure for it comes in a passage which registers Clennam's
perceptions as he walks through the city:

> As he went along, upon a dreary night, the dim streets by which
> he went seemed all depositories of oppressive secrets. The
> deserted counting-houses, with their secrets of books and papers
> locked up in chests and safes; the banking-houses, with their
> secrets of strong rooms and wells, the keys of which were in a very
> few secret pockets and a very few secret breasts; the secrets of all
> the dispersed grinders in the vast mill, among whom there were
> doubtless plunderers, forgers, and trust-betrayers of many sorts,
> whom the light of any day that dawned might reveal; he could
> have fancied that these things, in hiding, imparted a heaviness to
> the air. The shadow thickening and thickening as he approached
> its source, he thought of the secrets of the lonely church-vaults,
> where the people who had hoarded and secreted in iron coffers
> were in their turn similarly hoarded, not yet at rest from doing
> harm; and then of the secrets of the river, as it rolled its turbid tide

between two frowning wildernesses of secrets, extending, thick and dense, for many miles, and warding off the free air and the free country swept by winds and wings of birds.[14]

To wrench images and passages from context to build my argument risks loss of the sense of full context, and in this passage, of course, we are dramatically located in Clennam's consciousness at a moment when he is preoccupied with secrets and particularly with secrets about money. But this cluster of apocalyptic images offers, even in context, no religious alternative. And part of my whole argument is that there is a tension in the novel between its actual achievement and its overt direction, which is in part an opening of Clennam to love and to a less bleak, less Calvinist vision of reality. London is dramatically shown to be precisely the kind of city Clennam here is imagining it to be. And amid such secrecy, it might be fair to say of Clennam that whatever it is, it is not his fault. It is, as it were, precisely the 'nobody's fault' that Dickens was attempting to deny. Unlike *Bleak House*, *Little Dorrit* goes out of its way to keep secrets obscure. It does not offer interpretable clues, such as the likeness of Esther to the portrait. The characters are swept up unable to retreat or to understand. The natural world that seems an alternative in this passage is elsewhere no alternative. Secrecy, death, absence of self-definition are linked as conditions of life. As the conventional self disintegrates under the pressure of the impersonal forces which diminish it to a spot in the landscape, or to a Clennam-like 'nobody', so the conventional narrative unfolding toward a clarifying revelation is put under extreme pressure. The plot of nature resists Dickens's plot.

The takeover, as it were, by natural law moving toward a merely material and determined universe such as that implied by thermodynamic theory, is further developed in the narrative's fatalistic language. We might expect Dickens to dismiss fatalistic language as belonging precisely to those figures 'who lay all their sins negligences and ignorances on Providence', that is, to the ironic objects of the original title, 'Nobody's Fault'. Yet that is not how it works. True, Miss Wade, the most wilful of characters, announces the motif first: 'In our course of life we shall meet the people who are coming to meet *us*, from many strange places and by many strange roads . . . and what it is set to us to do to them, and what it is set to them to do to us, will all be done' (p. 63). But several chapters later, when Clennam first sees Amy, it is the narrator who talks about 'the destined interweaving of their stories' (p. 140). Rigaud talks of 'destiny's dice-box' (p. 175). Yet, in discussing Mrs Clennam's time-locked room and the candle burning in it, the narrator echoes him:

> Strange, if the little sick-room fire were in effect a beacon summoning some one, and that the most unlikely some one in the world, to the spot that *must* be come to. Strange, if the little sick room light were in effect a watch-light, burning in that place every night until an appointed event should be watched out! Which of the vast multitude of travellers, under the sun and the stars, climbing the dusty hills and toiling along the weary plains, journeying by land and journeying by sea, coming and going so strangely, to meet and to act and react on one another; which of the host may, with no suspicion of the journey's end, be travelling surely hither?
>
> Time shall show us.   (p. 221)

Such ominously naturalistic language emphasises the powerlessness of the will to effect change. So Clennam, translating himself into nobody, looks down the road as he walks with Gowan and thinks: 'Where are we driving, he and I, I wonder, on the darker road of life? How will it be with us, and with her, in the obscure distance' (p. 367).

This language, however reverberant with mystery, invokes again the irreversible arrow of time and is fully consonant with that self-conscious elimination of the divine towards which science was moving. So, for example, at a meeting of the Geological Society of London in 1852, William Hopkins, noting the irreversible loss of heat through geological time, put it flatly: 'I am unable in any manner to recognize the seal and impress of eternity stamped on the physical universe.'[15]

The thermodynamic movement through time into ruin implied by the dominant images of the book runs counter to the normal Dickensian structure of narrative, which usually implies a meaningful end, or telos. It seems to emphasise both deterministic restriction on free human action and the likelihood that after all what is to happen is not foreknown or planned: it is merely inevitable.

We return then to the way the images affirm nature's power over any human resistance. Characteristically, the novel's fatalistic images are also road images.[16] Jerome Beaty notes that the first image of the book is not the prison, but the sun. And nature swirls in the breezes that touch even the Marshalsea, floods under the iron bridge, rises with the sun. It manifests itself in the prisons in Marseilles and London, in the creaking timbers of Mrs Clennam's house, over the streets of London at Little Dorrit's party. If you granted the sun 'but a chink or keyhole' 'it shot in like a white-hot arrow' (p. 40). But nature is not unremittingly oppressive. It often becomes the only source of joy outside human love that the novel allows. While nature images emphasise the smallness of the human and the social, they also imply an unwonted expansiveness. In a move characteristically self-contradictory, Dickens seems to turn to the very nature which constrains, which limits meaning and the possibility of action, to provide the way back beyond the merely natural to a more traditionally natural-theological nature.

The dream of the world outside the Marshalsea, 'the free air' and 'the free country', is an aspect of the prison metaphor. Amy spends her free hours on the iron bridge watching the river, the only occasions of solitude and peace in her Marshalsea life. (The river, though viscid and mysterious for Clennam, on the whole serves to suggest the possibility both of movement with change, and of regularity and order, and Little Dorrit's instinctive attraction to it implies the book's commitment to or quest for these qualities through the figures of nature.) Enclosed and restricting, the Marshalsea still participates as all life must in the natural world, and its static image is in part created by its constant juxtaposition to the motions of nature itself. So,

> The equinoctial gales were blowing out at sea, and the impartial south-west wind, in its flight, would not neglect even the narrow Marshalsea. While it roared through the steeple of St George's Church, and twirled all the cowls in the neighbourhood, it made a swoop to beat the Southwark smoke into the jail; and, plunging down the chimneys of the few early collegians who were yet lighting their fires, half suffocated them.   (p. 130)

The stasis and unnaturalness of prison and city[17] are regularly countered by bursts of wind and rushing clouds, as at Little Dorrit's 'party'. For the inhabitants of the Marshalsea, the fields of Surrey intimate joy and freedom. The world is larger than any character's imagination of it, and connections extend out endlessly. In its vastness and in the sureness of its movement, it seems indifferent to human ambition. Regardless of the arbitrariness and violence of human action, nature continues its regular movement, has its own plot, as it were, which inevitably crosses with and absorbs the human plot.

Even in its aspiration beyond material law, the book tends unsentimentally to imply the meaninglessness of the world that science was discovering. In counterpointing the narrow lives of the characters, who are shut up in dark rooms or in prisons, or at dinner parties, blind in Venice to the constant movement of the waters, huddled against the chill of the Alps, nature affirms the reality they try to deny. Nature is not a moral model of spiritual generosity and indulgence. Thermodynamically and Calvinistically unsympathetic to the characters' feelings, it is a fact they ignore at their peril. It crosses their lives, betrays their ambitions, ages and kills them. Or, like the stars over the rubble of the Clennam ruins, it speaks of a larger world.

Dickens's ambivalence about nature, and an ultimate commitment to the secular, is evident even when the language reaches for spiritual meaning. The last double number returns to the sun, but gives us a very different image of it as it rises in London:

> Far aslant across the city, over its jumbled roofs, and through the open tracery of its church towers, struck the long bright rays, bars of the prison of this lower world.

Here, the language seems to shift from the aggressively secular metaphors of the opening passage to an emblem traditionally sacred. But the 'jumble' of roofs reasserts the pervasive secular disorder; the juxtaposed tracery of the church towers, ostensibly different, implies disorder in two ways, first in the incongruity of its relation to the jumble, second in its containment by the 'bars of the prison of this lower world', the bars of nature itself. Tentativeness about the religious implications of such passages is appropriate. 'Lower world' implies a higher one, but we are given only the lower. The laws of nature are determining for both the secular and the religious.

Through the clustered images, nature asserts itself primarily in time and movement with their figuring in the road. It is a commonplace that although William Dorrit takes to the road, he is always in prison: he denies the past and lives in a stasis similar to that of other prominent figures. The most obvious of course is Mrs Clennam, who remains locked in her room and in the unforgiving self she has invented, and enacts the consequences of the refusal of nature; certainly, her house does. The ignored creaking sounds that do so much work of mystery are the material signs of time's arrow: stasis itself is an artificial construction of identity, but only a temporary stay against, or, more accurately, a disguise of the movement of time toward the collapse of order in the dissipation of energy. 'I am not subject to change', says Mrs Clennam (p. 389). In less melodramatic versions, we have the absurdity of Flora, pretending to be a young lover, of the patriarch, Mr Casby, glowing contentedly, unwithered by time. More painfully, we have the stop-time of poor Maggie, who believes she is ten years old. Against the artificiality of stasis and fixed identity are the images of road and street, into which, appropriately, Clennam and Little Dorrit descend in the last page of the novel. Time is, simply, natural, and the characters who live in it must accede to its power. Change, which is movement in time, thus becomes essential to whatever possibilities the austere world of *Little Dorrit* will allow. But acquiescence in time undermines selfhood. Time breaks down the artificially constructed character (such as Mrs Clennam) whose rigid self denies the inevitabilities of thermodynamic or evolutionary movement.

But there are negentropic forces in the novel. Dickens's ambivalence toward nature is most particularly evident in his handling of the representatives of 'true' science. These figures have the quality of saviours, even though they are confined to dramatically marginal roles. I mean, of course, Daniel Doyce and the figure called 'Physician'.

With the 'scientists' the languages of religion and of nature cross. Doyce, to be sure, belongs in the thermodynamic schema as the book's one principle of both energy and order. Pitted in a losing battle against the overwhelming entropic force of the parasitical Barnacles and the Circumlocution Office, he has something oddly otherworldly about him. Dickens has put his faith in science, but, consistent with the contradictions I have been locating, he thinks of science as entirely compatible – in the mode of natural theology – with the world of spirit. He deliberately gives to the word 'practical' some of the same mystique Caleb Garth gives to the word 'business' in *Middlemarch*. So the negentropic Doyce is, in his reversal of the irreversible arrow of time, also a spiritual figure.

> He never said, I discovered this adaptation or invented that combination; but showed the whole thing as if the Divine artificer had made it, and he had happened to find it; so modest he was about it, such a pleasant touch of respect was mingled with his quiet admiration of it, and so calmly convinced he was that it was established on irrefragable laws.   (p. 570)

There is, nevertheless, a tricky ambivalence here: the 'Divine artificer' may be read as an invention of Doyce himself. Tricky or not, the language assimilates science and religion: like Paley finding a watch that evidences design, Doyce *finds* the 'irrefragable laws' – principles of order and stability – that Dickens seeks in both science and religion. The tradition of natural theology, like science itself, valorises what the narrator calls the 'regularity and order' (p. 736) that the rest of the novel cannot find. (One should note here in passing that even the 'good man' refuses to make claims for the self or to claim responsibility.)

If there is some slight uncontrolled ambiguity about the religious implications of what Doyce represents, there is none in regard to 'Physician'. It is he who counters disorder and decay, not through denial but through frank recognition of the realities of nature. As scientist, he is given the burden of peace, stability and spirit. A figure who would seem to belong to the cluster of impersonal caricatures who are aspects of the systemic decline the book traces, Physician emerges as almost divine. The extravagance of the praise is astonishing and suggests how thoroughly Dickens relied on science as he worried the problem of the relation of the physical to the moral and religious world:

> Many wonderful things did he see and hear, and much irreconcilable moral contradiction did he pass his life among; yet his equality of compassion was no more disturbed than the Divine Master's of all healing was. He went, like the rain, among the just and the unjust, doing all the good he could, and neither proclaiming it in the synagogues nor at the corner of streets.   (p. 768)

The indifference of nature and of society itself becomes here a spiritual condition, akin to that of Amy Dorrit. Dickens requires something like an allegorical figure to express this pre-Darwinian conjunction of science and religion. Here the confusion of the novel that I have been intimating, between a selflessness which reflects merely secular failure of will and the ideal of Christian selflessness, is most clearly figured. Here, too, there is a kind of Darwinian extension of the laws of nature to the laws of human nature, and to the physical possibilities of human life. Like nature, and yet also like Christ, Physician is the most explicit expression of the saving possibility of the power to accept the natural without disguising the facts of one's physical being – even, as it might turn out, one's apelike ancestry.

Dickens accedes to the irreversible arrow of time. Before Darwin and against the grain of the great sages who refused the full implications of science's descent into time, Dickens saw the ideal of permanence as vicious, change as the condition for life. Better to move with time at the sacrifice of clear and willed identity, than to deny it, as Mrs Clennam and the whole of aristocratic society do.

Yet if life is determined not by religious energy from outside the system, but by the system itself, reliance on time as redeemer is belied by the second law of thermodynamics. But there was a secular alternative: evolution. Only a culture released from an Aristotelian position that identifies permanence with the divine, and change with corruption, could have been ready for the Darwinian argument. And although *Little Dorrit* shows us a Dickens divided on the question, his desire for peace, stability, 'the hearth', is countered by his instinct for change, and life.

The moral language remains in *Little Dorrit* in spite of the evidence that time will run us all down and nobody will be at fault. At the end, Dickens attempts to transform the meaningless sun into an intimation of the divine, while the imprisoned characters seem all, as Edward Eigner suggests, to burst into rebellion against imprisonment – Affery, Pancks, Frederick Dorrit, Mrs Clennam herself.[18] These splendidly and traditionally conceived 'characters' all renounce the prisons of their imposed identities, although each rebellion is not realistically accounted for. Similarly, as the novel struggles to a conventional ending, it is thoroughly unconvincing in explaining the powerfully imagined mysteries. The tradition of natural theology reasserts itself against the new imprisoning systems which reduce all experience to the terms of natural law. We have seen Kelvin's evasion of the problem; through Mrs Clennam's confession, Dickens resorts to forced imposition of meaning on an experience too complicated to be resolved through these narrative means.

Finally, then, the contradictions in *Little Dorrit* are significant of its courage. The narrative seeks signs of the Creator in the forced conventions of an earlier conception of character and plot, but follows the direction of its images elsewhere. These images, I have tried to suggest, reflect a world irredeemably secular, in which the self has lost its identity as well as its powers. The text is at the intersection of positivist and what I have been calling natural-theological ways of knowing and imagining. But following the logic of its own vividly registered sense of the material world it almost chooses to find its way inside the positivist structure and it does so by turning to the way of seeing that was to inform Darwin's great work. Dickens clearly could not have sustained unmodified the thermodynamic structure so potently, pervasively at work in the book's images. Neither could he deny the force of its vision. Redemption entailed looking within time, but away from the model of the irreversible arrow moving toward disorder and the dissipation of energy. Clennam and Little Dorrit may be inseparable and blessed as they move into the streets, and into movement, and into the stream of time, and the sun may finally shine on them 'through the painted figure of Our Saviour on the window' (p. 894), but they go *down*. *Little Dorrit* itself is a descent into time, and in the course of the descent, Dickens loses firm control over at least three central aspects of his art: first, over the centrality of character, with all the adhering notions of selfhood and moral responsibility; second, over the narrative connection between action and responsibility; third, over the *meaningful* movement of narrative time (that is, from the image of time as water, obeying universal laws, and thus universally significant even in its temporality, to time as the image of the movement on the streets, among the arrogant, and the froward, and the vain, which is continuous and unredeemable).

The secular/scientific way out of the crisis was evolutionary science, whose arrow pointed upward and whose direction could be understood as designed. If evolution and thermodynamics presented a radical difficulty for the traditional conception of character, evolution could at least suggest not decline, but growth and improvement. This arrow, too, moves through nature, despite the prisons and the urban and claustrophobic texture of so much of the novel. Nature counterpoints the stasis of will that characterises the society of *Little Dorrit* and determines our understanding of it. Unsentimentally, and erratically, nature introduces into the novel the possibility of change in a negentropic direction. Like society itself, impersonal and indifferent to the individual needs of the protagonists, nature is nevertheless the possibility of life: it becomes at the end not a road to inevitable decline, but a very secular street chancily, vitally leading to the possibility of joy and love.

In so far as he could return to the religious interpretation of nature, as is partly implied by the late images of the sun (seeming rather fatigued, however, without the secular energy of the opening pages), Dickens could avoid temporarily, at least, many of the bleak scientific implications of what his imagination was revealing to him. The courage of *Little Dorrit* is in its confrontation of the possibility that the religious account could not stand against the pressure of those irrefragable laws, denying both God and self, that he wanted to celebrate, and his willingness to risk that the arrow of 'time' would point at last beyond his own imagination of character and narrative to life and regeneration.

Notes

1. For an excellent survey of the contributions to the thermodynamic theory by Carnot (a book of 1824), Joule, Mayer (with major papers in 1842 and 1845), Clausius (a book of 1850), and Helmholtz (with a definitive paper in 1847), see Charles Coulston Gillispie, *The Edge of Objectivity: An Essay in the History of Scientific Ideas* (Princeton, N.J.: Princeton University Press, 1960) pp. 352–405.
2. See 'The Conservation of Force: a Physical Memoir', in Russell Kahl (ed.), *Selected Writings of Hermann von Helmholtz* (Middletown, Conn.: Wesleyan University Press, 1971).
3. Robert Young, *Darwin's Metaphor: Nature's Place in Victorian Culture* (Cambridge: Cambridge University Press, 1985) p. 125.
4. Letter to Charles Eliot Norton, 19 June 1870; *The Complete Works of John Ruskin*, ed. E. T. Cook and Alexander Wedderburn, 39 vols (London: George Allen, 1909) vol. 37, p. 7.
5. 'The Mysteries of a Tea-Kettle', *Household Words*, 2 (16 Nov. 1850) 176–81; James Prescott Joule, 'On Matter, Living Force, and Heat',

reprt. in *Science before Darwin*, ed. Howard Mumford Jones and I. Bernard Cohen (London: André Deutsch, 1963) pp. 173–87. The tea-kettle essay was one of several written by Percival Leigh, at the suggestion of Dickens, based on lectures that Faraday delivered at the Royal Institution. Dickens clearly wanted his readers to understand the materials ot their lives in terms of the most advanced science available to them. While there is a quality of 'believe-it-or-not' about some of the facts explained, the essay provides wonderfully lucid characterisations of 'latent heat', and, more important, comfortably demonstrates the complexity of the ostensibly simple materials of ordinary life. The world of the tea-kettle is a world of transformations, in which no energy or matter is destroyed. Joule's essay also aspires to a clarity necessary for the intelligent lay audience, and he makes the overall thesis that points to the law of the conservation of energy much more overt. He does it, moreover, by making physical law compatible with divine:

> We might reason, *a priori*, that . . . absolute destruction of living force cannot possibly take place, because it is manifestly absurd to suppose that the powers with which God has endowed matter can be destroyed any more than that can be created by man's agency; but we are not left with argument alone, decisive as it must be to every unprejudiced mind. . . . How comes it to pass that, though in almost all natural phenomena we witness the arrest of motion and apparent destruction of living force, we find that no waste or loss of living forces has actually occurred? . . . Experiment has shown that wherever living force is apparently destroyed or absorbed, heat is produced. (pp. 178–9)

6. See Lynn Barber, *The Heyday of Natural History* (Garden City, N.Y.: Doubleday, 1980): 'Victorian natural history books were written with the aim of encouraging their readers to see evidence of God's existence and attributes in the natural organisms around them, by means of natural theology. And on this basis it was quite legitimate to pass over any facts which did not immediately illustrate God's goodness or wisdom.' Although a very popular account, it is sensible and reliable and makes no claim to consideration of the more serious scientific work of the time. *Household Words*, although it often attempted fuller accounts of natural history, often presented essays full of theo- and anthropocentric readings of nature, and fully confirms Barber's general account of popular versions of natural history.
7. 'Nature's Greatness in Small Things', *Household Words*, xvi (28 November 1857) 513. The attribution to Ernest Hart is in Anne Lohrli's enormously useful *Household Words: A Weekly Journal: 1850–1859, Conducted by Charles Dickens: Table of Contents, List of Contributors, and their Contributions* (Toronto: University of Toronto Press, 1973).
8. See James R. Moore, *The Post-Darwinian Controversies: A Study of the Protestant Struggle to Come to Terms with Darwinism in Great Britain and America, 1870–1900* (Cambridge: Cambridge University Press, 1979).

Dickens was ready for Darwin's *Origin of Species*, when it arrived, but he was not ready for the way Darwin relied on a refusal of the argument from design to make his own case. The kind of Darwinism Dickens might have subscribed to was like Robert Chambers's in his notorious *Vestiges of Creation*, or that of Asa Gray, who very quickly adapted Darwin's argument – against Darwin's objections – to teleology and design in an essay entitled 'Natural Selection Not Inconsistent with Natural Theology': see Asa Gray, *Darwiniana: Essays and Reviews Pertaining to Darwinism* (New York: Appleton, 1884). In a popular exposition of the theory in December 1860, Henry Fawcett argues: 'Those who, like Mr Darwin, endeavour to explain the laws which regulate the succession of life, do not seek to detract one iota from the attributes of a Supreme Intelligence. Religious veneration will not be diminished, if, after life has been once placed upon this planet by the will of the Creator, finite man is able to discover laws so simple that we can understand the agency by which all that lives around us has been generated from those forms which life first dawned upon' (*Macmillan's Magazine*, vol. III, December 1860, no. 145–6).

9. See Neal C. Gillespie, *Charles Darwin and the Problem of Creation* (Chicago, Ill.: University of Chicago Press, 1979) p. 10. Using the basic argument of Gillespie's book for my purposes here, I would suggest that *Little Dorrit* is a text at the intersection of two competing ways of knowing, the 'creationist', and the positivist. Dickens's narrative seeks signs of the creator but is constrained by the condition of a world that seems irredeemably secular.

10. William Thomson, 'On the Age of the Sun's Heat' (1862, *Popular Lectures and Addresses*, vol. I, p. 349.

11. Ann Wilkinson points out how the death of Krook in *Bleak House* is partly based on ideas Dickens had come across through the lectures Faraday developed into *A Chemical History of a Candle* (see Ann Y. Wilkinson, '*Bleak House*: from Faraday to Judgment Day', *ELH*, 12 (1967) 225–47). This excellent and imaginative use of contemporary physics to read *Bleak House* is a model of the sort of analysis I am attempting to use here. Much that Wilkinson says about *Bleak House* applies equally well to *Little Dorrit*.

12. 'Introduction', *Little Dorrit*, ed. Harvey Peter Sucksmith (Oxford: Oxford University Press, 1979) p. xiii.

13. Of course, we do not need science for this: there are more obvious places to turn, as, for instance, to Calvinism and bureaucracy, two of the targets of Dickens's anger in *Little Dorrit*. At the time of the writing of *Little Dorrit* Dickens was both enraged and depressed at the failures of British institutions. Edgar Johnson has shown how the horrifying official ineptness during the Crimean War, the failures to effect Parliamentary and administrative reform, the conditions in England itself, and the developing disasters of his own marriage helped feed his imagination of uncontrollable disorder. See Edgar Johnson, *Charles Dickens: His Tragedy and Triumph*, 2 vols (New York: Simon & Schuster, 1952) vol. II, ch. 6. A man of action, Dickens was finding England a great Circumlocution Office, teaching daily how not to do it. And he

found in all around him, and as a worrying inkling in himself, a failure of will to change. As Lionel Trilling argued, in his well-known essay on the novel, it is about 'the will and society'; 'at the time of *Little Dorrit* [Dickens] was at a crisis of the will which is expressed in the characters and forces of the novel' (see Lionel Trilling, *'Little Dorrit', The Opposing Self* (New York: Viking Press, 1955) pp. 57, 63).

14. *Little Dorrit*, ed. John Holloway (Harmondsworth, Middx: Penguin, 1973) pp. 596–7.
15. See Gerald Holton and Stephen G. Brush, *Introduction to Concepts and Theories in Physical Science* (Princeton, N.J.: Princeton University Press, 1985) p. 287. Hopkins's presidential address might well have been available to Dickens, as would Thomson's paper on the sun. Certainly, the general positions, with Hopkins's rather ominous application of it, would have been available to the lay reader.
16. It is the movement of time that is central to *Little Dorrit*'s narrative meaning, and, as Beaty says, 'Human life in time is like . . . the road' (see Jerome Beaty, 'The "Soothing Songs" of *Little Dorrit*: New Light on Dickens's Darkness', in Clyde de L. Ryals (ed.), *Nineteenth-Century Literary Perspectives* (Durham, N.C.: University of North Carolina Press, 1974) p. 229).
17. The full context of the novel reminds us, of course, that neither prison nor city are solid and unchanging. In the preface to the 1857 edition, Dickens addresses the question of whether 'any portions of the Marshalsea Prison are yet standing'. Some, it turns out, are – including the room Little Dorrit was born in! One can, to be sure, stand on 'the very paving stones of the extinct Marshalsea', but the entire Preface frames the novel in change (pp. 35–6), and Dickens gives the description of the place to a boy 25 years too young to have seen the Marshalsea as it was supposed to have been at the time of the novel.
18. Edward Eigner, *The Metaphysical Novel in England and America* (Berkeley, Calif.: University of California Press, 1978): 'If, as virtually every reader has noted, imprisonment is the controlling metaphor of the first eighteen numbers of the book . . ., then the final double number is characterized by a succession of stunning jailbreaks' (p. 116).

2

Revisiting *Sketches by Boz*

SYLVÈRE MONOD

Revisiting Leicester is always a joy. Revisiting *Sketches by Boz* may be regarded as more of a mixed blessing, but it has been my fate to do so repeatedly in connection with a French edition of that work, the first complete one ever, that was published in 1986, the year of its 150th anniversary.

In a short essay, I cannot hope to do justice to such a complex work as *Sketches by Boz*. I shall therefore merely list a few possible directions for exploration, and then concentrate on one point which became apparent to me only lately; I shall altogether omit the theatrical aspect, which is of considerable interest: but one doesn't carry coals to Newcastle, or deal here, in Collinsland, with the theatrical Dickens.

Among the other points a conscientious revisitor of *Sketches by Boz* could not afford to bypass are, of course, young Dickens's humour, his satirical attitude to most of his characters, the melodrama and even bathos toning down the general exuberance and alacrity of the narrative or description, the importance given to places (especially streets and houses), the irresistible power of the writer's imaginative and story-making faculties. Also of interest, of course, are the astonishing textual and publishing histories of the *Sketches* between 1833 and 1839.

To a lesser extent, the critical fortune or heritage of Dickens's earliest book is fascinating to contemplate. The critical debate about the value of the collection, or the placing in the oeuvre as a whole, begins with the disagreement between Dickens and Forster. Forster believed Dickens to have underrated his earliest book. It is true that the author's prefaces to the successive editions of the *Sketches,* if they vary in approach from the heavily jocular to the dismissively perfunctory, have two features in common: they are uniformly mediocre, and they are consistently apologetic. Forster makes a number of valid remarks about the merits of the *Sketches*; they suit his book, in that they confirm his view that the early Dickens was the great Dickens, that his innate, spontaneous genius was on the whole preferable to his later more ambitious, more laboured inventions. Few readers of our own time would unreservedly agree with Forster about that point, but it remains an interesting historical fact that the *Sketches*, in book-form, as the work of a very young and completely unknown writer, achieved a considerable measure of success. The two volumes of February 1836 were hailed as a work of genius by several reviewers. Then, for several months, while the first numbers of *Pickwick Papers* appeared, the *Sketches* held their own against that new rival. And when they sank into comparative oblivion, it was because they had been eclipsed by the still more phenomenal triumph of their own successor. Boz alone had been able to outshine the author of the *Sketches*.

I should now like to focus attention on one detail. Without forgetting that in so far as the book has one central theme, it is human gullibility as a consequence of snobbish ambition – that, surely, is the obvious target of most of the 'Characters' and 'Tales' – at the same time one may be struck by the author's surprising attitude to children. When describing Dickens's interest in children, it may be opportune to specify that we are dealing with Mr Charles, not Mr Geoffrey Dickens. Charles Dickens's reputation is, among other things, that of a novelist who had a profound knowledge and love of children. That reputation rests mostly on *David Copperfield* and *Great Expectations*, since Oliver, Nell and Paul are not particularly child-like. It is probably true that Charles Dickens, as author of *David Copperfield*, showed extraordinary powers of searching the childish mind and sensibility, of identifying himself with a child – though it might be contended that the author of *Copperfield* appears to be mostly a lover, knower and understander of himself, of the child he had been, of his own childhood. In any case, Boz, as author of the *Sketches*, turns out to have been anything but a lover of children.

Statistics about the number of children present in the *Sketches* are difficult to provide with anything like accuracy. Starting from the Cruikshank illustrations may help. Out of 39 etchings, 26 show no children at all; the other 13 have one or more each; the first two happen to contain 15 each, thus accounting for 30 out of the total of 65 depicted by Cruikshank; many of them are characteristic of Cruikshank's manner, in that they are often ugly, cramped, deformed, prematurely adult, and yet lively or pathetic (in three of the etchings, vivid pathos is extracted from a view of a poor child's back). A sense that Cruikshank's representation of children is warped and unreal will be dispelled by a glance at a collection of photographs taken by Dr Barnardo of the young inmates of his 'Homes': Dr Barnardo's camera vindicates Cruikshank's pencil; of the two, the camera is by far the more satirical and bathetic instrument.

It is impossible to provide a similar count of the children mentioned in the text of the *Sketches*, because the word *children* is often found in the indefinite plural, usually with a pejorative connotation, because children become harmful by being numerous. The general impression produced by the *Sketches* is that there are too many children in too many places, even though there are a few all-adult stories and scenes; children are to be found, for instance, in gin-shops (if only as part of 'the throng of men, women, and children'[1]), at the pawnbroker's (at least one 'ragged urchin' who makes a nuisance of himself and becomes 'the unfortunate little wretch'[2]), at Newgate ('fourteen boys were under fourteen years of age', 'and fourteen such terrible little faces we never beheld. – There was not one redeeming feature among them'[3]), in the police van (a girl prisoner of fourteen and 'hardened boys of ten'[4]), and of course at the hospital ('a child enveloped in bandages, with its body half-consumed by fire'[5]). All of which is, to say the least, unlovely. And here are three typical phrases referring to children in the *Sketches*: 'infantine scavengers',[6] 'a diminutive specimen of mortality',[7] 'a damp earthy child'.[8]

The impression grows upon the reader (or revisitor) that having children is a mistake, a ridiculous thing, and also a social sin, since children are a permanent encumbrance and a potential source of catastrophes. It is all very well to enjoy the lisping prattle of a well-bred child, but when they lisp in numbers, in large numbers, children soon become tiresome; it is not safety, but danger that lies in numbers. It seems that in that world boys will be boys with a vengeance, that they are inherently vicious (more so than girls, though even girls seem to be forever, from an early age, tottering on the edge of prostitution, but they have better capabilities in them, while Boz speaks frankly of 'the viciousness of boys as a rule'[9]).

Of course, poverty is the condition that makes children particularly undesirable. But the spoilt child or children of the rich are no more agreeable; witness the offspring of 'Mr Brook Dingwall, M.P.', about whom Boz's comments must be seen to be believed. Even then, the caricature of that family is so excessive that the uninformed reader would think Dickens had never seen a live M.P.; the truth being, of course, that it was through seeing hundreds every day for years that he developed a lifelong allergy to the genus. In two pages and perhaps ten minutes, the M.P.'s nameless boy, first defined as 'one of those public nuisances, a spoiled child', manages: to run away with a lady visitor's chair 'as fast as it was placed for her', to 'fall out of an armchair with an awful crash', to stand upon the aforesaid lady's 'most tender foot', to demonstrate his high spirits by 'in the excess of his joyousness breaking a pane of glass, and nearly precipitating himself into an adjacent area' (nearly, but unfortunately, Boz seems to think, not quite); after that last exploit, the child is expelled or carried away screaming and kicking violently. Meanwhile, just in case the reader might disbelieve in the existence of such an accomplished little monster, Boz makes him real by describing his face with one of his truly inimitable touches: it 'looked like a capital O in a red-lettered play-bill!'[10]

Boz's fairly consistent treatment of children in the *Sketches* can be seen in more than one way. One approach is that of S. J. Newman in his interesting critical volume entitled *Dickens at Play*. Newman sees Boz as giving evidence of 'almost paedophiliac' interest in children (would Mr Charles have exposed himself to the strictures of Mr Geoffrey, one wonders). At this point I would like to read three brief quotations in quick succession; namely: Boz on a young child; Newman on Boz on the child; and myself on Newman on Boz on the child (like the house that Jack built, as Mr Skimpole would have said). Here is Boz in 'The Steam Excursion' describing one of the two children who have been scandalously smuggled into the party: 'attired for the occasion in a nankeen frock, between the bottom of which, and the top of his plaid socks, a considerable portion of two small mottled legs was discernible. He had a light blue cap with a gold band and tassel on his head, and a damp piece of gingerbread in his hand, with which he had slightly embossed his countenance.'[11] Without pausing to wonder whether we do not find here Boz, or even Dickens, at his humorous descriptive best, I now give you S. J. Newman: he sees here that Dickens 'moves with almost paedophiliac absorption to the exposed legs – except that "mottled" complicates the sexuality with hints of brawn, cannibalism and death'; Newman later adds that 'the gilding on the gingerbread is the closest Dickens goes to "golden lads"'.[12] And here are some unkind comments in a review which I permit myself to quote from now, because I am reasonably sure nobody read it,

since it was published in a weekly other than the *TLS*, not in one of
those scholarly journals that everybody reads: 'Apart from the fact
that there is no gilding on the gingerbread but a gold band on the
cap, this is the kind of analysis that will make literature and criticism
more and more austere if it is to become generalised. Poor little boy
of four! Poor little Boz of twenty-four!'[13]

I called my earlier comments unkind, and they may well have
been unfair as well. One advantage of revisiting the *Sketches* has
been the chance of using new angles of vision. When one is on the
look-out for paedophiliac Boz, one finds – not very much, but things
like 'Scenes xv, Omnibuses', which begins with an elaborate, and
perhaps laborious, demonstration of the inferiority of stage-
coaches. One of the drawbacks of stage-coaches is illustrated by an
experience: 'We have also travelled occasionally, with a small boy of
a pale aspect, with light hair, and no perceptible neck, coming up to
town from school, and directed to be left at the Cross Keys till called
for'.[14] This is another example of Boz's descriptive and evocative
powers; it is also interesting in that the smelly boy appears as an
Ur-David Copperfield (and the *Sketches* are full of such *Ur*-
characters). Boz seems to have had insuperable and clearly
obsessive objections to boys in public conveyances. In his earliest
known sketch, Mr Minns is exposed to the importunities of a 'little
dear' whose 'little fat legs were kicking, and stamping, and twining
themselves into the most complicated forms, in an ecstasy of
impatience' when he, Mr Minns, boarded a coach. Later on, it
appears that 'Playfulness was agreeably mingled with affection in
the disposition of the boy', who kept 'scraping his drab trousers
with his dirty shoes, poking his chest with his mamma's parasol,
and other nameless endearments peculiar to infancy'.[15] Besides, the
quotation I have just read results from a toning down of the first
version! So, apart from the 'little fat legs', which one might call
suspiciously appetising, there is more paedophobia than
paedophilia here. But if we revert to the pale boy in the omnibus, the
point is that the narrator adds to his description, at once: 'This is,
perhaps, even worse than rum-and-water in a close atmosphere.'
Rum-and-water refers to an adult fellow-traveller, a stout man, who
drank a great deal on the stage-coach. Various questions arise: are
boys naturally ill-smelling? Did Boz breathe, inhale boys? Was Boz
after all afraid of boys? Or of the attraction they had for him? In the
next paragraph of 'Omnibuses', the whole thing is turned into a
joke, and the superiority of the omnibus appears; for children 'are not

often to be found in an omnibus; and even when they are, if the vehicle be full, somebody sits upon them, and we are unconscious of their presence'. If it is a joke, it may appear as a sick one, and one might even contend that Dickens's flaunted enmity to children is but a disguise which he uses to fight, and hide even from himself, a disturbing attraction to them. I do not really believe that to be the case, but I now recognise that the case can be made by someone who cares to do so. For the time being, I am not dealing in the unconscious.

And at the conscious level, the same story ('The Steam Excursion') shows mainly that children are an infliction. It begins with an innocuous allusion to the sights of Gray's Inn Square gardens, which include 'town-made children, with parenthetical legs'[16] (another of those wonderfully terse phrases which constantly surprise and delight the reader or revisitor of *Sketches by Boz*). Then it shows that a happy party must needs be a party of adults: 'What a shame to bring children!' said everybody, 'how very inconsiderate!'[17] Punishment must be inflicted for this lack of considerateness on the part of the children's parents; but it must also be inflicted on the children, through a holy alliance of the other adults in the party. In the rest of the story, even a parent's legitimate alarm is made to sound theatrically ridiculous. Our friend the little boy of four is duly terrified by the professional wag of the party, who then brazenly denies his guilt, so that the boy will be further punished 'for having the wickedness to tell a story'.[18] When bad weather sets in, the two children on board the steamer scream continuously and remain unheeded. It should be noted that the two children in that tale are unnecessary appendages, being irrelevant to the central point of the story (which is about a certain Captain Helves, an impostor and a crook who takes in everybody, and resembles Horatio Sparkins, or Captain Walter Waters in 'The Tuggs's at Ramsgate', or any number of decoy ducks for tuft-hunters in the *Sketches*).

At the conscious level also, the most representative figure in his attitude to children is Mr Dumps, the bachelor godfather at 'The Bloomsbury Christening', whose fictional career deserves a glance, for the tale is crucial. Dumps at first appears to resemble Mr Minns, the sorry hero of the first tale ever published by Dickens. Dumps has a hatred of children and that fundamental attitude of his is described at length and assumes original forms, such as his worship of 'King Herod for his massacre of the innocents';[19] but Dumps distinguishes himself from Minns in being far less passive; he often takes the offensive; he is the aggressor, not the victim; he strikes terror into an expectant father's soul (his nephew's) by depicting with relish and with imaginary details the deadly accidents to which infancy is prone. The difficulties of getting anywhere in London are referred to in the sequel of the story, but it is in another tale that one finds the revealing analytical sentence: 'There are three classes of animated objects which prevent your driving with any degree of comfort or celerity through streets which are but little frequented – they are pigs, children, and old women.'[20] Yes, in that order, pigs, children, and old women. That belongs to the narrator of Watkins Tottle's sentimental adventure. But the feeling is distinctly Dumpsish: Dumps might have omitted women, for whom, young or old, he has little use, but the alliance between children and pigs, with the pigs perhaps slightly above the children, is quite in his line. Disagreeable as he is, Dumps is probably right to resist the conventional ecstasies and general silliness engendered by the appearance of a baby in society. Incidentally, the baby's appearance at the christening party occasions one narratorial remark which might bring grist to Mr Newman's mill: '"Oh! What dear little arms!" said a fourth [young lady], holding up an arm and fist about the size and shape of the leg of a fowl cleanly picked.'[21] I am no authority on the possible link between paedophilia and paedophagy, but the latter phenomenon, advocated by Swift, must have shown at least an oral fondness for its objects. Yet, to be fair, the edible character of human beings is not the exclusive privilege of babies; the child's mother, in fact, had been referred to as 'one of those young women who almost invariably, though one hardly knows why, recall to one's mind the idea of a cold fillet of veal'.[22] One hardly knows why, indeed! Nor does one particularly wish to enquire.

Dumps, however, really comes into his own later on when he makes a speech at the christening 'sit-down supper'. He is given an unexpected talent for speechifying: 'he was always a pretty good hand at a speech',[23] the reader is told; this is not quite in character, and brings him suspiciously near to his creator. So we may wonder whether Dumps is not to a certain extent speaking with the voice of Boz when he outlines the trials that may lie in wait for the baby's parents. All *may* go well, Dumps admits, but it is as well to be prepared for 'premature decay', 'lingering disease', and especially for a child's ingratitude when he goes to the bad in later life: 'Should he not be what we could wish – should he forget in after times the

duty which he owes to [his parents] – should they unhappily
experience that distracting truth, "how sharper than a serpent's
tooth it is to have a thankless child"'!²⁴ Like the Devil, Dumps can
quote the Shakespearian Scripture for his own purposes. Dumps
will not wholly succeed in his attempt at deterrence; his nephew and
niece will never again choose a misanthropic and speechifying
godfather, but they are in for a large family (thus illustrating the
ostrich-like silliness of human beings: they suppress the
denunciation and encourage the evil). But Dumps had only harped
on one of the favourite and indeed obsessive themes of *Sketches by
Boz*.

To Boz's enmity to children (especially of the male kind), there is
one brilliant, revealing and indeed delightful exception in the sketch
called 'Astley's'.²⁵ There one sees a large family party with nine or
ten children. The whole picture is charming. With the exception of
the eldest boy, who is an adolescent, everybody here is happy and
loving, even the girls' governess, who is very much looked down
upon; the parents are complacent, and not a little ridiculous, but
they naturally like their children and are proud of their large family.
The enjoyment of the little ones at the show is shared by father and
mother, and sympathised with by the writer. It is altogether one of
the happiest pieces in the whole volume. One might add to it as a
kind of companion piece the Christmas dinner²⁶ which evokes an
Ur-Tiny Tim, and is again full of children who are also loved, loving
and fully integrated in the scene. The Astley sketch includes one
interesting character to whom the conclusion of this essay will revert
in a moment: that is, the adolescent eldest child in the large family.

Meanwhile, however, the characteristic attitude and dominant
mood of *Sketches by Boz*, where children are concerned, are to be
found, not at Astley's, but in 'The Bloomsbury Christening'. Dumps
is not merely a close cousin of Mr Minns; he illustrates the view that
children are on the whole an infliction, and a disappointment,
sometimes tragic. The child for whom a fond mother sacrifices
herself and who goes to the bad, reappears again and again in the
Sketches. He (incidentally, it is always a boy) is to be found in
Monmouth Street, or, rather than found, deduced from a collection
of old clothes, which goes to show that the observer is far from
passive and projects his obsessions on to the scenes that meet his
eye. In Monmouth Street, Boz imagines the widowed mother
feeding her lad and practising 'the refusal of her own small portion,
that her hungry boy might have enough'.²⁷ The poor woman has

misgivings (or Boz imagines that she has them, so that the picture is twice unreal, and yet compelling); she entertains 'the thought, almost too acute to bear, that as he grew to be a man his old affection might cool, old kindnesses fade from his mind, and old promises be forgotten'; of course, the misgivings turn out to have been justified (or, again, since all this is visionary, they turn out to be imagined to have been justified – and Boz exclaims: 'We could imagine that coat – imagine! We could see it'); that boy becomes dissipated and inflicts upon his mother 'the brutish threat, nay, even the drunken blow'. A bad son becomes a bad husband and father; the end of the story is inevitable: 'A prison, and the sentence – banishment or the gallows.' How that would have gladdened the heart of Mr Dumps, by proving him right!

A similar character appears in 'Criminal Courts', when a boy of 14 or 15, on being released from prison, is met by his mother: 'Their little history was obvious.'[28] The mother had sacrificed herself to the boy's welfare; but there had come 'dissolute connections; idleness had led to crime' and prison. That particular boy is unique in that he shows some compunction and eventually and edifyingly 'burst[s] into tears'. Then there is the son of the woman in 'The Black Veil'; the reader does not seem him alive, but only after he has been hanged; yet his history is told and it 'was an everyday one': and again we are in for the widowed mother denying herself 'necessaries to bestow them on her orphan boy'. He, on his side, is 'unmindful of her prayers' and 'plunge[s] into a career of dissipation and crime'.[29]

And the last sketch of all 56 supplies only a slight variant, together with an intriguing anomaly. It is 'The Drunkard's Death'; the variant is that here it is the mother who dies early, in an appallingly unreal scene of children piously kneeling around her sick bed (they 'mingled low bursts of grief with their innocent prayers'), while the father reels instead of kneeling, reels back to his pub. All three of his sons become criminals as a matter of course, but that is, thank God, when they are 'children no longer'. The anomaly is that the drunken widower cannot even count his orphaned chickens: the reader is told of 'the three children who were left to him',[30] and when Boz goes into the details, the three turn out to have been four, one daughter and three sons. A kind of drunkard's double vision in reverse.

Sketches by Boz, then, with phrases like 'the vices of the boy had grown with the man',[31] express the Wordsworthian view of human life gone sour. And the sentence about the vices of the boy is applied to the imaginary figure in Monmouth Street. Heaven does not quite lie about us in our infancy if we are citizens of Bozland, but certainly men move farther and farther away from the purity and happiness of childhood into dissipation and crime, and life *is* a process of deterioration and a forgetting.

Boz himself, however, is perhaps most closely to be identified with the eldest child of the Astley-going parents, the adolescent boy who sits unhappily between two chairs and two worlds, the two worlds of childhood and adulthood. At any rate, the boy's *malaise*, his *difficulté d'être*, are brilliantly analysed. He is first introduced as 'a boy of fourteen years old, who was evidently trying to look as if he did not belong to the family';[32] then the reader is told that this George 'carried a dress cane and was cultivating whiskers' and that he disliked 'having his name repeated in so loud a voice at a public place', which justifiably makes his parents and his siblings laugh heartily, so that poor George 'assumed a look of profound contempt'. Later again, he is referred to as 'the exquisite in the back of the box, who, being too grand to take any interest in the children, and too insignificant to be taken notice of by anybody else, occupied himself, from time to time, in rubbing the place where the whiskers ought to be, and was completely alone in his glory'. Boz is poking fun at that adolescent, but it is not unsympathetic fun. Boz knows that being 'an exquisite of fourteen' can make one suffer exquisitely, that whiskers, however assiduously cultivated, may refuse to grow at that age (or later, if we take George to be an *Ur*-Fledgeby), and mainly that adolescence, that is, etymologically, the process of becoming adult, is a painful one. There are in the *Sketches* other figures of premature manhood, and others again of prolonged childishness; there is an *Ur*-Dodger, for instance, of great brilliancy, and there are miserable youthful workers (chimney-sweeps and the like), or 'small office-lads in large hats, who are made men before they are boys'.[33] The *Ur*-Dodger, that is, the juvenile delinquent in 'Criminal Courts',[34] happens to be one of the liveliest and least dislikable of boys in the whole volume. Master Billsmethi, in 'The Dancing Academy', on the other hand, an *Ur*-Hinfant Phenomenon, is really young, precocious and promising.[35] Boz, then, expresses dislike and distrust of children, but explores with a kind of fascination the borderland at the end of childhood.

I should like now to propose my tentative explanation of this little phenomenon. In February 1836 and in the three previous years, Boz had, of course, no children of his own. The children he knew or remembered best were his siblings. In 1833 and even in 1836 he was still very young; and he was at an age when childhood had to be repudiated, if only in order to assert one's own manhood finally (whether or not one had doubts about one's manliness). In other words, Charles Dickens, though certainly not lacking in generosity and sentiment (of which he gives plentiful evidence in the *Sketches*) *is* himself in some important respects an adolescent still in those years. Also, he is a member of a large family; too large, he thinks, and he wishes to stand as far apart from it as he can, 'evidently trying to look as if he did not belong to the family'. One should remember that John and Elizabeth Dickens had eight children all told, of whom seven survived into adulthood; that Charles was the second, that he thus witnessed six of his mother's pregnancies, the last coming as late as 1827, when he himself was 'an exquisite of fifteen' and that must have been, even in a pre-Victorian family, a traumatic experience to a lad who was trying to find his feet in the world of adulthood. It would, or might, tend to make him recede into infancy.

With regard to my main point in this essay, I should like to summarise my conclusion by saying that, like one other famous act perpetrated in English fiction of the nineteenth century, Boz's treatment of children in *Sketches by Boz* was 'done because we are too menny'.

Notes

1. 'Scenes', xxii, p. 186. All the references to *Sketches by Boz* are given in this simplified form, with the title of the section, the number of the sketch within its section, and a page number in the *Oxford Illustrated Dickens* (1966 reprint of 1957 edition, with Introduction by Thea Holme).
2. 'Scenes', xxiii, pp. 191–2.
3. 'Scenes', xxv, p. 207.
4. 'Characters', xii, pp. 273–4.
5. 'Characters', vi, p. 242.
6. 'Scenes', vi, p. 74.
7. 'Scenes', ix, p. 95.
8. 'Scenes', x, p. 102.
9. 'Scenes', ii, p. 54.
10. See 'Tales', iii, pp. 325–6.
11. 'Tales', vii, p. 394.

12. S. J. Newman, *Dickens at Play* (London: Macmillan, 1981) pp. 28–9.
13. S. Monod, *The Literary Review*, vol. 2, no. 39 (August 1981) p. 22.
14. 'Scenes', xvi, p. 138.
15. 'Tales', ii, p. 317.
16. 'Tales', vii, p. 382.
17. Ibid., p. 393.
18. Ibid., p. 397.
19. 'Tales', xi, p. 467.
20. 'Tales', x, ii, p. 446.
21. 'Tales', xi, p. 479.
22. Ibid., p. 475.
23. Ibid., p. 481.
24. Ibid., p. 482.
25. 'Scenes', xi.
26. 'Characters', ii.
27. 'Scenes', vi, p. 76.
28. 'Scenes', xxiv, p. 197.
29. 'Tales', vi, p. 381.
30. 'Tales', xii, p. 486.
31. 'Scenes', vi, p. 77.
32. 'Scenes', xi, pp. 105–6.
33. 'Scenes', i, p. 51.
34. 'Scenes', xxiv.
35. 'Characters', ix.

3

'Cartloads of Books': some Sources for *A Tale of Two Cities*

ANDREW SANDERS

In his Preface to *A Tale of Two Cities* Dickens tells his readers of two distinct influences on the plot of his novel – Wilkie Collins's drama *The Frozen Deep* and Thomas Carlyle's *The French Revolution*. This essay will show that there were other published sources, some major, some minor, all of which went into the making of, in Dickens's terms, an exceptionally carefully moulded narrative.

Dickens claimed in his Preface that 'the main idea of the story' came to him when he was acting in Collins's play with his children and friends. This may not be a precise enough claim. *The Frozen Deep* was first publicly performed at the novelist's London residence, Tavistock House, on 6, 8, 12 and 14 January 1857, with a cast which did indeed include his children and his close friends.[1] His sons, Charles junior and Alfred, and his daughters Kate and Mary took leading roles and the cast also included his sister-in-law, Georgina Hogarth, and his old friends Mark Lemon, Augustus Egg, and the author of the piece, Wilkie Collins. The play was performed again in London on 11, 18 and 25 July 1857 and was then revived, with a significantly changed cast, for three charity performances at Manchester. What Dickens does not mention in his Preface is that at some point in that Spring he almost certainly got wind of the plot of the Irish dramatist Watts Phillips's as yet unperformed play, *The Dead Heart*, a plot which bears certain striking similarities to that of *A Tale of Two Cities*.[2] Given his likely knowledge of this French Revolutionary drama, in which characters exchange places before an execution, it would seem probable that the 'main idea' of the prospective novel came to Dickens either during the July performances of *The Frozen Deep*, or, yet more probably, during the Manchester performances in August 1857.

The three stagings of Collins's play in Manchester on 21, 22 and 24 August have considerable biographical importance for Dickens. For these performances professional actors were employed, presumably because the novelist's children and friends were not quite equal to the extra demands made of them by the transfer of the play to the new Free Trade Hall at a time when Manchester was attracting influential visitors to the great Art Treasures Exhibition. These professional actors included three members of the Ternan family. Mrs Ternan took over the role of the psychic Nurse Ellen from Mrs Wills; her daughter Maria the part of Clara from Mamie Dickens, and her younger daughter, Ellen, the part of Lucy Crayford from Georgina Hogarth. As had happened with his first cast, Dickens had problems with the emotional disturbance occasioned in some of his actors by the force of his own remarkable performance as Richard Wardour. Maria Ternan, for one, had to be carefully coached but still managed to weep profusely as Wardour died in her arms in the performance on 21 August.[3] The character of Richard Wardour, a disappointed lover who dies sacrificially, clearly lies behind that of Sydney Carton, an aspect of the characterisation which is reaffirmed by the fact that in the manuscript of the novel Dickens originally allotted the Christian name 'Dick' to Carton.[4] The connection with the novelist's own surname need not be dwelt upon. Significantly too, Dickens transferred the name 'Lucy' from the character played in Manchester by Ellen Ternan to the heroine of the new novel. He may well have retained a fondness for his childhood sweetheart, Lucy Stroughill, as Michael Slater has argued,[5] but Lucie Manette also bears a striking physical resemblance to Ellen Ternan. As her friend, Helen Wickham, noted, Ellen shared 'that curious, intent, rather strained look' which seemed part of her nature and which was 'a somehow pathetically earnest gaze at times'.[6]

If then, we can date the 'main idea' of the story to the August of 1857 there may well be a further significance in the long delay before Dickens actually began work on his novel in January 1859. During this period the novelist separated from his wife, broke with his publishers, Bradbury and Evans, terminated *Household Words*, and began his public reading tours. Although he had evidently noted down the notion of the Lion/Jackal relationship of Stryver and Carton as early as 1855[7] and had studied the effects of long-term solitary confinement during his American tour of 1842,[8] he seems to have pondered the nature of his story from its 'growing inclinations' of 27 January 1858 to the actual beginning of work a full year later.[9]

Dickens arrived at the present title of the novel by 11 March 1859, a title which he considered fitted his opening 'to a T'.[10] He had, however, already been working at that opening for a month or so, and on 21 February he wrote to Forster announcing that he could not please himself with it and that he could not 'in the least settle to it or take to it'.[11] It would seem probable that this inability to 'settle' to the new story was the result of an unease about his command of details of the historical background. The novel's opening chapter, with its general commentary on the contradictions inherent in any view of an historical period, clearly draws much of its rhetoric from Carlyle's 'wonderful book' *The French Revolution*. The play in the first paragraph with the terms 'times', 'age' and 'epoch' appears to reflect Carlyle's ironic account of the debates in France concerning the state of society in the years preceding the Revolution and perhaps the opening of the earlier essay, *Signs of the Times* of 1829. The opening chapter also draws heavily on the volumes of the *Annual Register* for 1775 and 1776, which formed part of the run of a hundred odd volumes of that invaluable historical source in his collection at Gad's Hill.[12] It was from the 1775 volume that he extracted details of 'daring burglaries by armed men, and highway robberies', including attacks on City tradesmen by a disguised fellow-tradesman, the robbery of the Norwich stage, and the mugging of the Lord Mayor himself at Turnham Green. Here too he found an account of a prison riot in Southwark, the dispatch of troops into St Giles, and the stealing of Lord Stormont's St Andrew's Cross at a reception at St James's Palace. In other cases Dickens seems to have inserted telling anecdotes without checking sources. The case of the 'prophetic private in the Life Guards', for example, refers both to a 'crazy prophet' (not a soldier) who had indeed predicted that Deptford and Greenwich were to be swallowed up by an earthquake in February 1775, and to the earlier incident when in April 1750 a 'crazy lifeguardsman' had started a panic by prophesying the end of the cities of London and Westminster. This 'prophetic private' had been confined in Bedlam and had been the subject of an article in the *Gentleman's Magazine* and of wry comment in Horace Walpole's *Letters*.[13] The reference in the fourth paragraph of the first chapter to the sentencing of a French youth 'to have his hands cut off, his tongue torn out with pincers and his body burned alive, because he had not kneeled down in the rain to do honour to a dirty procession of monks' recalls a *cause célèbre* of 1766 taken up by

Voltaire. It is likely that Dickens knew of the sad case of the young Chevalier de la Barre from Voltaire's two published protests of 1766 and 1775 which he possessed in his 70-volume edition of the philosopher's *Oeuvres Complètes*.[14]

As can be seen, the novel's new title fitted its opening 'to a T' because it captured both the balance of opposites in the first paragraph and the juxtaposition of examples of English and French disorder, lunacy and barbarity in the remainder of the chapter. It is noticeable, however, that English instances somewhat outweigh French ones. Dickens's unease expressed itself in a letter to Carlyle in mid-March in which he requested assistance with sources of information about French life both before and during the Revolution. Carlyle responded promptly with what Dickens was later whimsically to describe as 'two cartloads of books' from the London Library.[15] The novelist gratefully acknowledged the loan on 24 March:

> I cannot tell you how much I thank you for your friendly trouble, or how specially interesting and valuable any help is to me that comes from you. I do not doubt that the books received from the London Library, and suggested by you, will give me all I want. If I should come to a knot in my planing, I shall come back to you to get over it.[16]

Dickens's image of 'planing' here suggests that Carlyle had provided what he needed in terms of finishing his design once the mechanics of cabinet-making were complete. The design of the novel seems to have been clear in his head, including the precise relationship between his fictional and the historical events; what was lacking was a further authority which one can only call anecdotal. It was this that the 'cartloads' of books provided.

Before attempting to identify those books, and estimating Dickens's debts to them, it is useful to re-stress the extent of the novelist's obligation to Carlyle's narrative masterpiece *The French Revolution*.[17] According to the 'Inventory of the Books' at 1 Devonshire Terrace, drawn up when the house was let during the Dickenses' sojourn in Italy in May 1844, there was a copy of the three-volume first edition of *The French Revolution* in the novelist's collection. In July 1851 he claimed to be reading 'that wonderful book' for the 500th time.[18] He evidently mislaid that first edition for, at the time of his death, the edition listed in the Catalogue of the

Gad's Hill library is the two-volume issue of 1857. This would seem to be the copy that Dickens used in preparing the ground for his novel and to which he referred regularly during the process of composition. His intimate knowledge of the *History* can be largely taken for granted, though, as the novelist stressed in his Preface, he hoped merely 'to add something to the popular and picturesque means of understanding that terrible time', and not to supplement the 'philosophy' readily available to readers in 'Mr Carlyle's wonderful book'. Carlyle provided him both with authority and chronology; he also offered some justification for Dickens's choice of perspective. *A Tale of Two Cities* has frequently been censured by unsympathetic critics for its narrow view of the Revolution and for its emphasis on the destinies of private individuals inexorably caught up in events beyond much of their control. In an important way Dickens seems to be deliberately leaving the 'philosophy' – in the sense of 'the knowledge of things and their causes' – to Carlyle's narrative while, at the same time, borrowing that historian's distinctive use of individual voices. *The French Revolution* is at many points a dazzling amalgam of eye-witness report, retrospective memoir, and a telling use of ephemera. To many contemporaries it seemed, as it seemed to Kingsley's Alton Locke, 'that great prose poem, the single epic of modern days'.[19] Whereas Carlyle incorporates many voices into his multifarious epic, Dickens attempts the 'popular and picturesque' in concentrating on the destinies of select, and fictional, observers, Dickens's narrative, with its eschewal of sub-Carlylean philosophy, ought to be seen as an alternative to Carlylean epic-history.

It is with this proviso in mind that we can best consider Dickens's use of historical events in his fiction, most notably the storming of the Bastille. As a rule, the great set pieces of Carlyle's narrative – the entry of the Royal Family into Paris, the Flight to Varennes, or the execution of the king, for example – are not repeated in *A Tale of Two Cities*. In the case of the fall of the Bastille and the murder of Foulon, it is notable that in the first instance our attention is directed to the actions of Defarge, and in the second to those of Mme Defarge. Dickens's larger obligation lies in his occasional summaries of the progress of events, such as that in Book III, chapter 4, when he seeks to remind his readers of the passage of time. He evidently checked his own fictional time-scheme against Carlyle's historical scheme. The manuscript of the novel reveals that Darnay was originally to have left for France at the end of Book II in the winter of 1792–3.

Once Dickens realised that this would deprive him of having Darnay in Paris at the time of the September massacres, and indeed might have suggested that Darnay would have been signally foolish to embark on a trip to France at this juncture, he moved events back to the late summer of 1792 and revised all mention of the season in the long chapter entitled 'Drawn to the Loadstone Rock'.

The third and final book of *A Tale of Two Cities*, which is exclusively set in Revolutionary Paris (apart from its retrospect, in Dr Manette's testament, to the 1750s), reveals a considerable debt to the wealth of ordinary detail in Carlyle's narrative. Dickens shows himself to be aware of Revolutionary terminology and symbolism, to the vagaries of costume and new nomenclature, and to the new sights of Republican Paris.[20] He refers to the Black Flag announcing the proclamation of 'La Patrie en Danger', to the execution of the Girondins, to Samson the headsman, to the barges moored on the Seine on which military equipment was forged, and to the unswept streets of the summer of 1793. In one case, however, he seems to have jumped to a wrong conclusion, or simply to have misremembered, an aspect of a particularly unpleasant incident during the prison massacres of September 1792. In Book III, chapter 2 ('The Grindstone') Mr Lorry and Dr Manette observe a group of men involved in the massacres sharpening their weapons at a grindstone set up in the adjacent courtyard. The men are disguised with 'false eyebrows and false moustaches'. There can only be one source for this detail – Carlyle's account of the brutal murder and dismemberment of the Princesse de Lamballe at La Force on 3 September 1792. Other eye-witnesses, or contemporary reporters, of the prison massacres, to whose accounts Dickens may have had access, make no mention of false hair.[21] Carlyle describes the Princess's murder and subsequent multilation somewhat differently:

> She shivers back, at the sight of the bloody sabres; but there is no return: Onwards! That fair hind head is cleft with the axe; the neck is severed. That fair body is cut in fragments; with indignities, and obscene horrors of moustachio *grands-lèvres*, which human nature would fain find incredible, – which shall be read in the original language only.[22]

Dickens clearly did not pursue the reference, though he seems to have had an important French source to hand at this stage in the composition of the novel, Louis-Sébastien Mercier's *Nouveau Paris*:

> Lorsque les assassins se furent partagé les morceaux sanglans de son corps, l'un de ces monstres lui coupa la partie virginale et s'en fit des moustaches.[23]

As Carlyle's careful avoidance of particularity in this instance suggests, the circumstances of Mme de Lamballe's murder were not unfamiliar, nor inaccessible, to some of his perceptive or inquisitive readers. It is likely that Dickens's misreading of the evidence stems from a basic purity of mind on which Philip Collins has elsewhere remarked.

Dickens's failure to check a French source at this point leads us back to the 'two cartloads of books' sent to him from the London Library in March 1859. In his Preface to his novel he is insistent that 'whenever any reference (however slight) is made here to the condition of the French people before or during the Revolution, it is truly made, on the faith of the most trustworthy witnesses'. One can make informed guesses as to who these witnesses were. Carlyle's own footnotes to *The French Revolution* represent the best guide, for it would seem likely that he recommended to Dickens volumes he himself had used in his own pursuit of local colour, vivacity and 'trustworthiness'. It is scarcely surprising to find that of some thirty odd publications of contemporary anecdotes, journals, letters and memoirs which figure prominently as sources of *The French Revolution* all are listed in the 1842 and 1847 catalogues of the London Library.

We have long been able to identify the most significant of Carlyle's recommendations, Louis-Sébastien Mercier's earlier series of volumes entitled *Le Tableau de Paris*, published in Amsterdam between 1782 and 1788. In a letter to Bulwer-Lytton, printed in Forster's *Life of Charles Dickens*, the novelist attempts to justify his stark picture of the pre-Revolutionary aristocracy and their oppression of the peasantry:

> If there be anything certain on earth, I take it that the condition of the French peasant generally at the day was intolerable. No later enquiries or provings by figures will hold water against the tremendous testimony of men living at the time. There is a curious book printed at Amsterdam written to make out no case

whatever, and tiresome enough in its literal dictionary-like minuteness; scattered up and down the pages of which is full authority for my marquis. This is Mercier's Tableau de Paris.[24]

Dickens drew a vast deal of information from Mercier's 12-volume work and from its sequel, *Nouveau Paris* (1797). His debt is especially in evidence in the seventh chapter of Book II, 'Monseigneur in Town', an account of the Marquis Saint Evrémonde's attendance at the Paris salon of 'one of the great lords in power at the Court'. The four men who serve Monseigneur his chocolate, and the fact that the chief lackey wears two watches, derives from Mercier's essay, 'Domestiques. Lacquais', in his second volume. The same essay is the source of the sharp comments about the matrimonial alliances of rich Farmers-General, and of the information that such men were able to keep 30 horses in their stables, 24 male domestics and six waiting-women.[25] From the short chapters on Abbés (I.xc) and Bishops (I.xci) stem Dickens's references to 'brazen ecclesiastics', while the comments on 'military officers destitute of military knowledge' and the 'doctors who made great fortunes out of dainty remedies' derive from the essays on Officers (II.cvi) and Doctors (II.cxxxv). The 'Projectors', the 'Unbelieving Philosophers' and the 'Unbelieving Chemists', all of whom are present at Monseigneur's levée, are readily related to Mercier's 'Faiseurs de Projets' (I.lxxiii) and to his essays on the 'Chercheur de la Pierre philosophale' (IX.dclxxxv) and on 'Athéisme' (VII.dxcv). The 'Spies among the assembled devotees' come from 'Hommes de la Police' (I.lxi).

By far the most substantial borrowing, and one that has long puzzled readers of the novel who have not consulted Mercier, concerns the members 'of a fantastic sect of Convulsionists' and those attached to a sect 'which mended matters with a jargon about "the Centre of Truth"'. The Convulsionists clearly fascinated Dickens most for he was later to commission an article on these charismatic Jansenists for *All the Year Round*, drawing parallels between past and present religious 'revivals'.[26] The passage in *A Tale of Two Cities* dwells, however, on the three followers of the so-called 'Philosophe Inconnu', Louis-Claude de Saint Martin. These three guests of Monseigneur hold

that Man had got out of the Centre of Truth – which did not need much demonstration – but had not got out of the Circumference, and that he was to be kept from flying out of the Circumference, and was even to be shoved back into the Centre, by fasting and seeing of spirits. Among these, accordingly, much discoursing with spirits went on – and it did a world of good which never became manifest.

Dickens's final sardonic remark firmly suggests where the narrator stands in relation to this gobbledegook. He has in fact lifted it almost verbatim from Mercier's essay 'Amour de Merveilleux':

> Une secte nouvelle, composée surtout de jeunes gens, paroît avoir adopté les visions répandues dans un livre intitulé *les Erreurs & la Verité*, ouvrage d'un mystique à la tête echauffée, qui a néanmoins quelques éclairs de génie. Cette secte est travaillée d'affections vaporeuses. . . . Selon cette secte, l'homme est un être dégradé, le mal moral est son propre ouvrage; il est forti du *centre de verité*; Dieu par sa clémence le retient dans la *circonférence*, lorsqu'il auroit pu s'en éloigner à l'infini; le *cercle* n'est que l'explosion du *centre*: c'est à l'homme de se rapprocher du *centre* par la *tangente*. (II.cxci)

As I have suggested elsewhere, Dickens appears to have got the clue to his introduction of the Marquis's reckless driving away from the reception from Mercier's comments on the dangers to pedestrians in the streets of Paris.[27] The incident of the running-over of a child playing by a Paris fountain derives only indirectly from Mercier's essay 'Gare! Gare!' (I.xxxix), an essay which appears to have stirred the novelist's memory of a similar aristocratic accident recounted in the letters of the German visitor to England, Prince von Pueckler-Muskau.[28] Mercier does, however, remind his readers of the celebrated accident which occurred to Jean-Jacques Rousseau during one of his solitary walks in the Paris region in 1776. Rousseau makes much of the incident in the second section of the *Rêveries du Promeneur Solitaire* (1792).

In his letter to Bulwer-Lytton, Dickens cites Rousseau as his authority 'for the peasant's shutting up his house when he had a bit of meat'. It would seem most unlikely that Rousseau's works were included amongst the books recommended by Carlyle, but the novelist evidently found that his memory of earlier reading, or at least his recall, of an often-cited anecdote from the *Confessions*, was of use to his overall concept of life in France in the 1750s (even though the event to which Rousseau referred took place in 1732). In

Dr Manette's testament (Book III, chapter 10, 'The Substance of the Shadow') the dying brother of the abused girl tells the doctor that he and his class were 'pillaged and plundered to that degree that when we chanced to have a bit of meat, we ate it in fear, with the door barred and the shutters closed, that his people should not see it and take it from us'. This example of aristocratic oppression and excessive taxation derives, somewhat erratically, from Rousseau's account of his brief stay in the house of a peasant during his return journey to Switzerland from Paris:

Je priai celui-ci de me donner à diner en payant. Il m'offrit du lait écrèmé et de gros pain d'orge en me disant que c'étoit tout ce qu'il avoit. Je buvois ce lait avec délices et je mangeois ce pain, paille et tout; mais cela n'étoit pas fort restaurant pour un homme épuisé de fatigue. Ce paysan qui m'examinoit jugea de la vérité de mon histoire par celle de mon apetit. Tout de suite après m'avoir dit qu'il voyoit bien que j'étois un bon jeune honnête homme qui n'étois pas là pour le vendre, il ouvrit une petite trape à côté de sa cuisine, descendit, et revint un moment après avec un bon pain bis de pur froment, un jambon très apetissant quoiqu'entamé, et une bouteille de vin dont l'aspect me réjouit le coeur plus que tout le reste. On joignit à cela une omelette assez épaisse et je fis un diné tel qu'autre qu'un piéton n'en connut jamais. Quand ce vint à payer, voila son inquietude et ses craintes qui le reprennent; il ne vouloit point de mon argent; il le repoussoit avec un trouble extraordinaire, et ce qu'il y avoit de plaisant étoit que je ne pouvois imaginer dequoi il avoit peur. Enfin il prononça en fremissant ces mots terribles de Commis et de Rats-de-cave. Il me fit entendre qu'il cachoit son vin à cause des aides, qu'il cachoit son pain à cause de la taille, et qu'il seroit un homme perdu si l'on pouvoit se douter qu'il ne mourut pas de faim. Tout ce qu'il me dit a ce sujet, et dont je n'avois pas la moindre idée, me fit une impression qui ne s'effacera jamais. Ce fut là le germe de cette haine inextinguible qui se developpa depuis dans mon coeur contre les vexations qu'éprouve le malheureux peuple et contre ses oppresseurs.[29]

As Rousseau himself proclaims, the incident was the beginning of the philosopher's hatred for the oppression of the poor. Both he and Dickens blame the tax-man, and, by extension, aristocratic privilege, but Dickens misreads the circumstances in his insistence in *A Tale of Two Cities* on the extremity of peasant poverty. Rousseau's peasant has good bread, ham and wine for a privileged guest, but he chooses to hide them until he has proved that his visitor is not an exciseman. He is oppressed but he has a better diet than his oppressors suppose. Dickens's peasant merely chances to have meat on occasions, and then is afraid that it will be taken away.

In his letter to Bulwer-Lytton Dickens was responding to criticism of his treatment of society under the *ancien régime* and claiming that the picture he offered in *A Tale of Two Cities* had an authenticity which derived from documented sources. Even if Carlyle had recommended Rousseau's *Confessions* together with the ten volumes of Mercier's *Tableau de Paris* we would still not seem to be approaching the 'two cartloads' of books Dickens was later to claim he had received. The most likely addition we can make is a major source of information about life in Revolutionary Paris, Mercier's second series of studies entitled *Le Nouveau Paris* published in six volumes in Paris in 1797. From these essays Dickens may well have supplemented information already available to him in *The French Revolution* on such matters as the September Massacres (see above), on Trees of Liberty,[30] on Samson the executioner,[31] and on the use of the term 'Citoyen' as a compulsory form of address.[32] It would also seem very probable that Dickens consulted what has remained a standard source for the state of the French countryside in the period immediately preceding the Revolution and in the first two years of the upheaval, Arthur Young's *Travels in France during the Years 1787, 1788 and 1789* (1792, 2nd edn 1794). Arthur Young's two volumes partly justify the long-held English supposition that the French peasant was grossly undernourished by comparison with his English equivalent, but they also suggest the extent of the disruption caused by outbreaks of *jacquerie* in 1789 and 1790. Young's Appendix, 'The Revolution in France', of 1792, appears to have given Dickens the clue to his complaint in Book II, chapter 24 that French emigrés, and their conservative British sympathisers, saw the Revolution simply as 'the only harvest ever known under the skies that had not been sown'. The comment: 'as if observers of the wretched millions in France, and of the misused and perverted resources that should have made them prosperous, had not seen it inevitably coming, years before, and had not in plain words recorded what they saw' seems likely to be a reference to Young's book.[33]

There is firm evidence that Dickens read through the first section of another of Carlyle's most useful sources, the two-volume compilation of reminiscences of certain victims of the Terror, *Mémoires sur les Prisons* (Paris, 1823). These volumes contain, amongst others, the prison-memoirs of the playwright, Caron de Beaumarchais, though Dickens appears to have drawn most from the account of his imprisonment offered by Honoré de Riouffe. From this source the novelist took details for his description of the inside of La Force and the Conciergerie and the activities of prisoners. Here too he found the term 'sheep of the prisons', which Carton applies to the spy, Barsad,[34] and the whimsical phrase 'the Evening Paper' for the list of prisoners to be tried before the Tribunal.[35] It would also seem likely that the reference to 'the customary prison sign of Death – a raised finger', shared between the condemned leaving the Tribunal, and those still awaiting trial, derives from the action of Mme Roland as described by Riouffe:

> Après sa condamnation, elle repassa dans le guichet avec une vitesse qui tenait de la joie. Elle indiqua par un signal démonstratif qu'elle était condamnée à mort.[36]

As Dickens later cites Mme Roland's famous speech at the foot of the scaffold, he was, like so many other commentators on the Revolution, clearly drawn to this particular figure.[37]

All of the books that Dickens consulted on Carlyle's advice are either anecdotal or are written in the first-person as journals, letters or memoirs, thus justifying his claim in the preface to the novel that he was reliant 'on the faith of the most trustworthy witnesses'. We can, however, add two final published sources which Dickens had come across long before he started work on *A Tale of Two Cities*, one factual, one fictional. An early, and singularly abusive critic of the novel, Sir James Fitzjames Stephen, first remarked on the parallels between the trial for treason at the Old Bailey of Francis Henry de la Motte and that of Charles Darnay.[38] De la Motte was accused, like Darnay, of 'divers overt acts of a treasonable connection with the French court to destroy the naval power of this country'; he was convicted on the evidence of a spy and, unlike Darnay, was condemned to be hanged, drawn and quartered as a traitor. Dickens must have known of the case both from his own collection of *State Trials* and from the report of the case sandwiched between a record of the trial of Lord George Gordon and certain letters from Gordon to Lord North in the volume of the *Annual Register* for 1781.[39] The fictional source is Alexandre Dumas's popular novel *Le Comte de Monte Cristo* (1844–5). Dickens seems to be referring to this novel in his essay, 'A Flight' (republished in *Reprinted Pieces*) in which he dreams of being a 'prisoner of state' attempting to escape from a French fortress. In *A Tale of Two Cities*, the incarcerated Manette takes the ink with which he writes his testament from 'soot and charcoal from the chimney, mixed with blood'. This invention closely resembles the discovery of the Abbé Faria in *Le Comte de Monte Cristo*:

> Il y avait autrefois une cheminée dans mon cachot . . . tout l'intérieur en est donc tapissé de suie. Je fais dissordre cette suie dans une portion du vin qu'on me donne tous les dimanches, cela me fournie de l'encre excellente. Pour les notes particulières et qui ont besoin d'attirer les yeux, je me pique les doigts et j'écris avec mon sang.[40]

In some significant ways *A Tale of Two Cities* contains the echoes of many voices. Those echoes have gone into shaping both its tight plot, of which Dickens was inordinately proud, and its historical background. If the spirit and the detailing of Carlyle's *The French Revolution* offered him most of what he needed, he also incorporated into his fiction aspects of his earlier reading and a good deal of fresh research. To assume that the novel is simply an ill-thought out joining of the sensational sacrificial story of *The Frozen Deep* with a time and a place garnered from *The French Revolution* is a crude over-simplification. The fictional relationship between Lucie and Sydney Carton holds great private meaning for Dickens and his dating of their story at the time of the Revolution places the fiction in the midst of a political, intellectual and cultural storm which held a vital significance for all mid-Victorians, notably so at a time of tension between Britain and the France of the Second Empire. In terms of the care that Dickens took with his story we are dealing with a far, far better thing than many twentieth-century commentators have allowed for.

Notes

1. See Robert Louis Brannan's detailed study, *Under the Management of Charles Dickens: His Production of 'The Frozen Deep'* (Ithaca, N.Y.: Cornell University Press, 1966).
2. See Carl R. Dolmetsch, 'Dickens and *The Dead Heart*', *The Dickensian*, 55 (September 1959) 179–87. See also Malcolm Morley, 'The Stage Story of *A Tale of Two Cities*', *The Dickensian*, 51 (December 1954) 34–40.
3. Walter Dexter (ed.), *The Letters of Charles Dickens*, Nonesuch Edition 3 vols (1938) vol. ii, 21 August 1857.
4. The manuscript of the novel is preserved in the Forster Collection at the Victoria and Albert Museum. It is bound in two volumes (Catalogue no. F47.A.36).
5. Michael Slater, *Dickens and Women* (London: Dent, 1983) pp. 47–8.
6. See Katharine M. Longley, 'The Real Ellen Ternan', *The Dickensian*, 81 (Spring 1985) 31.
7. See Fred Kaplan (ed.), *Charles Dickens' Book of Memoranda* (New York: New York Public Library, 1981) pp. 18–19.
8. See especially Dickens's comments on the Eastern Penitentiary at Philadelphia (*American Notes for General Circulation*, 2 vols (1842) vol. i, pp. 238–9).
9. Nonesuch *Letters*, vol. iii, 27 January 1858.
10. Ibid., vol. iii, 11 March 1859.
11. Ibid., vol. iii, 21 February 1859.
12. At the time of his death Dickens possessed a run of the *Annual Register* from 1748 to 1860. See J. H. S. Stonehouse (ed.), *Catalogue of the Library of Charles Dickens* (1935).
13. Dickens had a copy of the six-volume edition of Walpole's *Letters* according to the catalogue of his library at Gad's Hill. It bore the inscription 'Mrs Charles Dickens. 19 May 1847'. See *Gentleman's Magazine*, xx (1750); *The Letters of Horace Walpole, Earl of Orford*, 6 vols (1840) vol. ii, pp. 326–9.
14. Voltaire, *Relation de la Mort du Chevalier de la Barre* (1766) and *Le Cri du Sang Innocent* (1775). Dickens possessed the *Oeuvres Complètes* of Voltaire (1785–9) at the time of his stay in Italy in 1844. He took several volumes of this edition with him. Kathleen Tillotson (ed.), *The Letters of Charles Dickens*, Pilgrim Edition (Oxford: Oxford University Press, 1977) vol. iv, note to p. 174. These volumes are not recorded in the catalogue of the books at Gad's Hill.
15. According to Charles Dickens the Younger in his Introduction to the Macmillan edition of *A Tale of Two Cities* (1902) p. xx.
16. Nonesuch *Letters*, vol. iii, 24 March 1859.
17. See, for example, Michael Goldberg, *Carlyle and Dickens* (Athens, Ga.: University of Georgia Press, 1972), and William Oddie, *'Dickens and Carlyle: The Question of Influence* (University of Leicester Phd dissertation, 1972).
18. Nonesuch *Letters*, vol. ii, July 1851.
19. For Carlyle's concept of Homeric epic and the shaping of *The French Revolution* see John Clubbe, 'Carlyle as Epic Historian', in James R.

Kincaid and Albert J. Kuhn (eds), *Victorian Literature and Society: Essays Presented to Richard D. Altick* (Columbus, Ohio: Ohio State University Press, 1983) pp. 119–45.

20. For further details of Dickens's debt to *The French Revolution* see my forthcoming Companion to *A Tale of Two Cities* in the Allen & Unwin Dickens Companions Series.

21. Louis-Sébastien Mercier, *Le Nouveau Paris*, 6 vols (Paris, 1797): 'Massacres de Septembre', I.xviii. Dr John Moore, *A Journal during a Residence in France* (Dublin, 1793).

22. *The French Revolution: A History*, 2 vols (London: Chapman & Hall, 1857) III.i.4, vol. ii, p. 149. This was the edition in Dickens's library at the time of his death.

23. Mercier, *Nouveau Paris*, 'Massacres de Septembre', I.xviii.

24. John Forster, *The Life of Charles Dickens*, edited and annotated by J. W. T. Ley (1928) p. 731; Nonesuch *Letters*, iii, 5 June 1860.

25. Louis-Sébastien Mercier, *Le Tableau de Paris* (1782–88) II.clxxii.

26. 'A "Revival" under Louis the Fifteenth', *All the Year Round*, 30 (19 November 1859) 81–6.

27. See my article 'Monsieur Heretofore the Marquis: Dickens's St Evrémonde', *The Dickensian*, 81 (Autumn 1985) 148–56.

28. Ibid., 154–5. Pueckler-Muskau's letters appeared in England as *Germany, Holland, and England in the Years 1826, 1827 and 1828 . . . in a Series of Letters by a German Prince*. The letters were translated and bowdlerised by Sarah Austin and published in four volumes in 1832. It has long been held that Dickens based Count Smorltork, the 'well-whiskered individual in a foreign uniform' who appears at Mrs Leo Hunter's public breakfast in *Pickwick Papers*, on Pueckler-Muskau.

29. J.-J. Rousseau, *Confessions*, Livre 4ième, Edition Pléiade, 4 vols (1964–8), vol. i, pp. 163–4.

30. *A Tale of Two Cities*, bk iii, ch. 1. The 'Trees of Liberty' or 'Mais' were modelled on the first such tree, crowned with a red Phrygian cap, set up in the Champ de Mars in July 1790 for the Feast of Federation. See Carlyle, *FR*, vol. ii, bk 1, ch. 12; vol. ii, bk 5, ch. 12; vol. ii, bk 6, ch. 3. Mercier, *Nouveau Paris*, I.xvi, 'Arbres de Liberté'.

31. *TTC*, bk iii, ch. 4; *FR*, vol. iii, bk 4, ch. 8; Mercier, *Nouveau Paris*, iii. xcvii.

32. *TTC*, bk iii, ch. 5; *FR*, vol. iii, bk 1, ch. 1; Mercier, *Nouveau Paris*, ii. lxiv, 'Citoyen'.

33. See my 'Monsieur Heretofore the Marquis', pp. 149–51.

34. *TTC*, bk iii, ch. 8; *Mémoires sur les Prisons*, 2 vols (Paris, 1823) i.73.

35. *TTC*, bk iii, ch. 6; *Mémoires sur les Prisons*, i.158.

36. *Mémoires sur les Prisons*, i.57.

37. Dickens refers to Mme Roland as 'one of the most remarkable sufferers by the same axe' as Carton shortly before giving us Carton's own dying words. He knew from Carlyle (vol. ii, bk 5, ch. 2) that Mme Roland had asked for pen and paper to write down her thoughts before execution, but the request had been refused.

38. Sir James Fitzjames Stephen, *Saturday Review*, 8 (17 December 1859) 741–3.

39. Dickens possessed the 21 volumes of *State Trials and Proceedings for High Treason and other Crimes and Misdemeanours* (1809–14) at Gad's Hill. For his knowledge of the trial of de la Motte, see Philip K. Skottowe, 'The King against Darnay', *The Dickensian*, 27 (Summer 1931) 179–81.
40. Alexandre Dumas, *Le Comte de Monte Cristo*, ch. 16.

4

The Dickens World Revisited

K. J. FIELDING

I have often used this title for various versions of a lecture, which I now want to recast. The original version arose with two ideas or questions in mind. One was to present and re-examine some lost articles which Dickens wrote for the *Examiner* which Alec W. C. Brice and I discovered some time ago. John Forster, in his *Life* of Dickens, had obliquely referred to them; his editor J. W. T. Ley had pronounced that they were entirely irrecoverable; and then we did recover them – anonymously buried in annual volumes of 600 pages or so of double-column and small print. It was possible to draw on them confident that quotation from Dickens could be used to provide a strong script.[1]

Here is not the place to quote from them at length, nor are they now quite so unknown. But a question then raised remains, whether there is any fruitful relation to be found between Dickens's journalism and his fiction. For that journalism is not just entertaining in itself; it takes us back to the Dickens world of his time. It may help us respond to the novels as they were addressed to their first readers, not just in those particular articles for the *Examiner* but in all his journalism. It reinforces the exciting sense we can have that his novels are both immediately addressed to his readers of any period and that their point may be particularly sharpened if we can see how they were meant for their own time.

These words, then, 'the Dickens world', have often been used: by Angus Wilson, in 1970, for example, in *The World of Charles Dickens*; by Hillis Miller, in 1959, in *Charles Dickens: The World of his Novels*; and particularly by Humphry House in his book in 1941, *The Dickens World*. What do they mean?

It may be assumed that House's *The Dickens World* is familiar; it has been fairly said to have 'laid the foundations of Dickens scholarship';[2] it has received many high and direct tributes (as from

Philip Collins, for example, towards the end of his *Dickens and Education*), or indirectly, as in the baffled ferocity of references to it throughout the Leavises' *Dickens the Novelist*, especially in the chapter on *Great Expectations*. At one time my connection with House was close. But I was puzzled, not only by that remaining general question of what the relation is between fiction and the world that lies about it – the contemporary world which Dickens lived in, wrote about and for – but by the paradoxical remark with which House closed:

> It seems more likely that [Dickens] is now read and will go on being read because he made out of Victorian England a complete world, with a life and vigour and idiom of its own, quite unlike any other world there has ever been.[3]

House had begun by saying that the aim of the book was 'to show in a broad and simple way the connection between what Dickens wrote and the times in which he wrote it, between his reformism and some of the things he wanted reformed, between the attitude to life shown in his books and the society in which he lived' (p. 14). In a 'conclusion' he explained that he had 'deliberately treated' Dickens 'as if he were a journalist more than a creative artist' (p. 215), and he had made several comments of the kind throughout: but now this! It led on to the same remark being taken by Hillis Miller to open the introduction of his own very different book:

> A complete world, with a life and vigour and idiom of its own, *quite unlike any other world there has ever been* [my italics].

Perhaps I took them literally, and so found them curiously misleading. But I still do. They can't be *'quite unlike'*. It is not a matter of quoting contemporary witnesses to the contrary, of drawing parallels and showing them in notes and footnotes. A major purpose of the novels was to look outside themselves; it was partly the spirit in which they were conceived; ambiguous as Dickens's own comments and prefaces may be, they draw attention to it; it is a *part* of his technique. House's remark was meant to be paradoxically challenging, by being literally and in any sense *un*true.

I hasten to add that, of course, I see that any writer, whether journalist or novelist, may stamp his work with his peculiar vision.

That must be what those final words meant; but it is not the same thing.

It is unnecessary, now, to go through Dickens's fiction and non-fiction (even keeping to examples from the *Examiner*) to show that there is often a striking likeness between them, in expression, in insight, detail, attitude, through specific reference, and in the way he expressed the degree and kind of his commitment. There are marked differences, too. Nor perhaps is it necessary to argue that it is any more simplistic to see such correspondences than to make assumptions supposedly drawn solely from the work itself. In fact, many correspondences *are* drawn from the works themselves, and there may be no dividing line between the two worlds.

Perhaps an example will help to show what I mean. To take one of the most obvious, it was House after all, who redrew attention to the likeness between Jo the crossing-sweeper of *Bleak House* and a crossing-sweeper George Ruby, who appeared in the witness-box before Alderman Humphery of the Guildhall on 8 January 1850. House was struck by a report in Dickens's *Household Narrative*, a twopenny monthly news supplement to *Household Words*. As it was the first number to be published it was over-cautious for House to say that Dickens 'almost certainly' read it and that it was 'almost certain' that Ruby was an original for Jo; they are obviously related and there would be no point in quoting the passage if they were not:

Alderman Humphery: Well, do you know what you are about? Do you know what an oath is?   Boy: No.   Alderman: Can you read?   Boy: No.   Alderman: Do you ever say your prayers?   Boy: No, never.   Alderman: Do you know what prayers are?   Boy: No.   Alderman: Do you know what God is?   Boy: No.   Alderman: Do you know what the devil is?   Boy: I've heard of the devil, but I don't know him.   Alderman: What do you know?   Boy: I knows how to sweep the crossings.   Alderman: And that's all?   Boy: That's all. I sweeps a crossing.

The point of all this was to see whether the uneducated boy could be accepted as a witness; and (unquoted in *The Dickens World*) the report went on to say that he was rejected: 'The Alderman said that in all his experience he had never met with anything like the deplorable ignorance of the poor unfortunate child in the witness-box.'[4]

As far as Jo goes, at the Sol's Arms, before the coroner, it is not very different:

> Here he is, very muddy, very hoarse, very ragged. Now, boy! – But stop a minute. . . . This boy must be put through a few preliminary paces.
> Name, Jo. Nothing else that he knows on. Don't know that everybody has two names. Never heerd of sich a think . . . Spell it? No. *He* can't spell it. No father, no mother, no friends. Never been to school. . . . Knows a broom's a broom, and knows it's wicked to tell a lie. . . . Can't exactly say what'll be done to him arter he's dead if he tells a lie to the gentlemen here, but believes it will be something wery bad to punish him, and serve him right – and so he'll tell the truth.
> 'This won't do, gentlemen!' says the Coroner, with a melancholy shake of the head.
> 'Don't you think you can receive his evidence, sir?' asks an attentive Juryman.
> 'Out of the question', says the Coroner. 'You have heard the boy "Can't exactly say" won't do, you know. . . . It's terrible depravity. Put the boy aside.'   (ch. 11)

Now, it happens that Dickens might have read this interchange in several other places as well as his own monthly *Narrative*. In several newspapers, for instance, and in Forster's *Examiner*. In fact, it was part of a whole campaign that the *Examiner* was running against the practice of rejecting witnesses because they could not answer elementary questions from the catechism – a practice not entirely absurd, when they were required to take an oath on the Bible and in the name of God. And Dickens was not only a regular contributor, but he had joined in a series of articles in this campaign, which (for its part) was based on commonsense and related to Bentham's discussion of the nature of evidence, arguing that a decision about a witness's validity should depend on everything relevant and not on this narrow 'test'. The other articles Dickens and others wrote in the series have a particular interest and relevance to the same novel, which I resist for the sake of brevity and keeping to the issue of *likeness*.[5] Perhaps we should add, though, that Dickens's *Household Narrative* has the report of a similar case in March 1852, the month when the serialisation of *Bleak House* began, when another boy witness was rejected. It was actually given not once but twice in the same number. He knew it was 'wicked . . . to tell a lie' (using Jo's expression) and 'was aware that something would be done to wicked people who told lies, after they were dead, but he *did not know what it was'* (italics added, and exactly the same sense). So runs the report from the *Dickensian* of 1912.[6]

The likeness is not in question, though what Dickens made out of it is. Any novel, no doubt, by definition (i.e. by its kind) must to some extent be a recreation of common life. So we are – or I am – merely baffled by a doubtful expression designed to force us away from the naïve belief that it is a simple reflection. They *are* different, but they are not unlike. And, since then, we have sometimes become involved in a critical reaction against seeing novels as written for their own times. This arises not only from critical theory, but from real limitations to the 'historical' approach (its apparently finite nature), and the immense popularity of Dickens's novels as teaching texts combined with the complete impracticality of bringing into effective teaching anything which requires much additional teaching and knowledge.

Old-fashioned enthusiastic 'Dickensians' were often more leisured readers who once had the time and a wider knowledge which allowed for a closer understanding that protected them from many possible misconceptions and the wilder criticism. But even the plainest current students at once catch from the novels that Dickens was – to use that admittedly desperate cliché – a *reformer*; and, in fact, our teaching experience invariably is that they look up and ask what he 'reformed', only sometimes to be told – because it is all too complicated – that he made no measurable difference.[7] We may sympathise here with both teacher and taught.

Such readers are right to see, from the novels themselves, that their drift and observation is largely directed outwards. They do not have the epigraph that Forster advised Dickens to withdraw from *Martin Chuzzlewit*, 'Your homes the scene, yourselves the actors here' because it was removed as unnecessary. But every novel has the same message: one cannot read or teach *Pickwick* without seeing how clearly it was designed to show how Mr Pickwick's eyes are opened to the world about him; it was followed by *Oliver*, which was certainly and successfully written with a similar purpose; the illusions of *Great Expectations* are not seen merely as Pip's, and so on. Once again, there is no need to embellish with examples. As Forster plainly explained: 'Debtors' prisons, parish Bumbledoms, Yorkshire schools were vile enough, but something more

pestiferous was not the object of his satire'. And so it continued after
Chuzzlewit. It is true, in Hillis Miller's words, that with each novel
we pass *from* Dickens's experience *to* the world of his imagination,
but, in the course of this, we are always directed outwards again (by
innumerable allusions) to the social world about us.

Nor is it meant to be only in innocent benevolent Pickwickian
observation that we are to look on it, as if (in Walter Bagehot's
phrase) Dickens was really 'a special correspondent for posterity'.[8]
In the same brilliant but unperceptive paragraph Bagehot spoke of
London as being 'like a newspaper', and how this suited Dickens
because he observed everything but did not care to piece it together.
Bagehot would have been closer to the point if he had seen that,
imaginative as they are, the novels were more like the journals in
which they sometimes appeared, with a decided bias and critical
edge if not a programme; like the *Examiner* itself, in fact, or the best
of *Household Words*. This is not their only function but a vital part
which, if we are discussing Dickens, cannot be left to take care of
itself. Not to see it is to miss the kind of work that Dickens wrote,
what kind of author he was – and even though (for fear of mis-
understanding) I have to avoid emphasising it – what kind of man.[9]

All this might be more easily recognised, but for the general
discouragement at seeing such likenesses which in some ways are
only too obvious. But, as I return to consult House's *Dickens World*, I
am almost shocked by the way he could then so easily assume that in
1941 'criticism' was effortlessly becoming more sociological, and
'shifting its attention to the social and economic environment in
which particular works are introduced', typified by the example of
Dobree and Batho's recent *Introduction to English Literature*. Shocked
not at him, but at the sharpness of the way we have since seen that
shift quite altered (though for the better on the whole) and how we
have been left without any comparable study of 'Social Criticism in
Dickens', except (in their most welcome way) Philip Collins's books
and writings, and one essay with that title by Raymond Williams[10]
plus another from him on 'Dickens and Social Ideas', in Michael
Slater's *Dickens 1970*. The first essay has not been republished so far
as I know.

Williams expresses some disappointment with House, always
with respect, conscious of the advantage of writing after the passing
of more than 20 years. 'The best book on Dickens's social views and
their context', he says, 'is still Humphry House's *The Dickens World*'
(p. 214). But he is disappointed because of House's many

qualifications about Dickens's reformism, at signs of some complacency and some patronising of Dickens, and House's over-concern about the confused 'dating' of the novels. This was House's reason for noting George Ruby's appearance in court on exactly 8 January 1850, in a novel in which the railway had reached but was not running as far as Lincolnshire, Chancery was unaltered, and figures from Dickens's youth appear to people scenes from contemporary London. Williams, I think rightly, is more concerned at our seeing that such novels are not an accurate model of society at any one time, but that Dickens 'deeply and vividly dramatised' situations to bring about an imaginative 'regeneration'. Dickens may well, for example, recreate a world which is not 'quite unlike' the world about him, but which *is* a vision of society taking into account 'a writer's whole life – his childhood memories, his contemporary observation, his readings of published accounts' (p. 218).

There is much more to it than this. In particular Williams's opening declaration that to 'understand social criticism' fully is possible only for 'those who are themselves both interested and engaged in it'. This, he says, may exclude most of us – including Philip Collins, who is somewhat sharply and unfairly criticised (p. 216). But Williams was right to argue that we should see Dickens as the kind of man 'whose view of society is not available for reduction or detachment from his whole view of life', but to whom it is a matter of 'directly personal energy and commitment'.

There *are* reservations and qualifications: the way in which Dickens often withdraws in the novels from the situations he has created (as at the end of *Bleak House*, for example), the way he was often limited by his period, and some personal weaknesses – and we might not always agree about all of these. But we are persuaded that the novels are directly related to their society as well as being inspired by this imaginative vision; and, whatever the limitations or depth of our own reforming commitment, it is right to see this, if only as a matter of literary criticism.

That, so far, is an entirely rewritten version of my old lecture in which I refrained from looking at Dickens criticism in order to let Dickens speak for himself in some of his journalism, and just used passages from those articles of his to make a scrapbook of observations that illustrated the novels, and in a less focussed way made similar points, about his freshness, his insight and concern.

For they are no more than a scrapbook if we do not see a purpose in them. But, though they came out periodically, they are not isolated in themselves; for they not only show what he saw about him, and how it inspired the same kind of commitment, but the sort of novel he wrote.

We may glance at this in two ways: by the briefest selective reference to examples from this journalism and (a new topic) a look at the annotation of his novels which editors could use to illustrate this kind of writing and not just to provide miscellaneous observations for earnest students. To take the latter first as the most familiar, the notes to the Penguin editions, for example, sometimes seem disappointing, no doubt because they try to do the impossible. Within the framework of a limited number of pages, possibly with a little guidance, notes are devised because they help to sell such volumes. Sometimes there may be a connection between them and the critical introductions; at others, the star role is given to a well-known writer and annotation delegated to someone else. *Oliver Twist*, in which Peter Fairclough deals well with the difficult subject of the New Poor Law in an appendix, has it dismissed as largely irrelevant in Angus Wilson's introduction. We must not carp, because there is much that is useful. But the edition of *Hard Times*, for example, runs out of space for notes well before the last third of the book (the whole of Book III), and as a parting shot tells us the date when telegraph wires first ran alongside railways, but ineffectively uses what might be learned about the Preston strike to which the situation in the novel was related. *Bleak House* is more interesting, because Hillis Miller's introduction makes a special point about recognising the 'topicalities' of the novel and its mimetic intent (well annotated by Norman Page), and rewardingly brings out how Dickens explores the mysterious complexity of society shown with sharp local perception. Hillis Miller does what he says, and passes from the actual Dickens world to the world of the imagination, and there should be no complaint there. But we might also wish to be aware how far the novel is not only mimetic, but how almost every topicality arguably shows a critical insight into contemporary society. Nor is it just as a matter of detail, but such topicalities are a way of seeing and dramatising the general condition. Raymond Williams's own sensible explanatory procedure, in fact, usually lies rather in quoting familiar set-pieces at length:

Oh, for some good spirit who would take the housetops off. (*Dombey and Son*, ch. 47)

Shares. O mighty Shares. (*Our Mutual Friend*, Book i, ch. 10)[11]

How the world rolled on from year to year, alike careless and indifferent, and no man seeking to remedy or redress it.
(*Nicholas Nickleby*, ch. 53)

But, especially for those who do not allow for the place of such passages in the novels, they may seem over-rhetorical. We should take account of the local allusions as well – at least to be aware that they exist and affect the nature of the novel, even if not to annotate them all or try to call attention to all of them in teaching. To take a familiar example, just as Jo cannot have seemed a purely fictive character to his first readers, so the Snagsbys' servant Guster has a similar extra dimension. The novel makes the small point that she came from a pauper establishment 'at Tooting' (ch. 10) and, once again, that she was 'the orphan child of the Christian saint whose shrine was at Tooting' (ch. 25). In fact, the Penguin edition's notes, fully up to date, remind us that Dickens wrote four articles for the *Examiner* about the recent death at Tooting of over 150 children from cholera, and wrote some of them when he was desperate to start *David Copperfield*; and we see how delicate his irony is, expressed in passing, as Guster offers Jo her meagre supper.[12] An even abstruser allusion, perhaps, lies in Dickens's conception of Mr Creakle (of *David Copperfield*) who eventually heads a prison and becomes a Middlesex magistrate. Philip Collins has shown that this was an indirect allusion to a Mr Benjamin Rotch; and one of the new articles in the *Examiner* shows how Dickens caught Rotch in his sights again in a powerful essay on Temperance reform and its entire irrelevance to the real ills of society.[13]

Elsewhere in the *Examiner*'s pages, we find Dickens writing at length about public health in these years immediately before *Bleak House*; at least, I think we can, writing in collaboration with his brother-in-law Henry Austin, Secretary to the General Board of Health, before they joined in the same campaign in *Household Words* – all of which has only slowly come to light over the last 40 years, since publication of *The Dickens World*.[14]

Again, in the *Examiner*, we can read a comment (not by Dickens) on the burial ground in Portugal Street, just round the corner from John Forster's house, where you might have bought a fairly fresh human head, and where corpses were left unburied and rotting, that summer when Dickens began the novel: 'There is really no burial, as the body deposited in the earth one day is soon disturbed, dismembered, and thrown to the surface again, to make room for other corpses.' 'They lower our dear brother down a foot or two: . . . sow him in corruption, to be raised in corruption. . . . "They was obliged to stamp upon it to git it in. I could unkiver it for you with my broom, if the gate was open".'[15] It really was not a world 'quite unlike' or just a mimetic reflection of the actual one, but one with a likeness which could arouse awareness, dissatisfaction and, in spite of the novel's ending, a response. It is right, Dickens wrote in the preface, that 'the parsimonious public should know what has been doing and still is doing', and vital to the novel.

Such an argument is well-laboured, though the examples are few, of a practice which is widespread, varied, persistent, systematic, often informing whole novels, at times exceptional, easily taken for granted, and understandably of less account in our own world than Dickens's. But it still means something.

Notes

1. See *The Letters of Charles Dickens*, Pilgrim Edition, ed. Graham Storey and K. J. Fielding (Oxford: Oxford University Press, 1981) vol. v, pp. 710–11, for details of articles published in 1848–9. Republished articles referred to in this paper include 'Ignorance and its Victims', by Alex W. C. Brice, *Dickensian* (hereafter *D*), 63 (1967) 5–14; by Fielding and Brice, jointly, 'Charles Dickens and the Tooting Disaster', *Victorian Studies*, XII (1968) 227–44; 'Charles Dickens and the Exclusion of Evidence', I & II, *D*, 64 (1968) 131–40, and 65 (1969) 34–41; '*Bleak House* and the Graveyard', in *Dickens the Craftsman: Strategies of Presentation*, ed. Robert B. Partlow Jr (Carbondale, Ill.: Southern Illinois University Press, 1970) pp. 115–39.
2. *Charles Dickens: A Critical Anthology*, ed. Stephen Wall (Harmondsworth: Penguin, 1970) p. 315.
3. Humphry House, *The Dickens World* (Oxford: Oxford University Press, 1941) p. 224.
4. *Household Narrative*, January 1850, p. 7.
5. See articles cited in note 1.
6. John Suddaby, 'The Crossing Sweeper in Bleak House: Dickens and the

Original Jo', *D*, 8 (1912) 246–50 (thanks to Dr Michael Slater who
pointed it out), and *Household Narrative* (March 1852) pp. 50 and 64.
7. House, *Dickens World*, p. 223: 'In the face of these facts it is clear that the
immediate effect of Dickens's work was negligible'; A. O. J. Cockshut,
The Imagination of Charles Dickens (London: Collins, 1961) p. 55: 'It is a
strangely neglected fact that most of the social abuses castigated by
Dickens had already ceased to exist when he wrote about them.' In spite
of these alleged facts the evidence grows stronger that Dickens was an
effective advocate of reform. On Dickens's radicalism, see Graham
Storey's essay in this volume (Chapter 5).
8. *Charles Dickens*, ed. Wall, p. 127; originally 'Charles Dickens', *National
Review*, 7 (1858) 459–86.
9. The way he operated as an artist is related to the sort of man he was,
much as described by the *Examiner* ('The Spirit of the Age', 9 January
1831), in which, somewhat surprisingly, John Stuart Mill once wrote:

> A statesman . . . is supposed to have studied history . . . but is it ever
> asked . . . whether he understands his own age? Yet that also is
> history . . . and the only part which a man may know and
> understand, with absolute certainty, by using the proper means. He
> may learn in a morning's walk through London more of the history of
> England during the nineteenth century, than all the professed
> English histories in existence will tell him concerning the other
> eighteen; for, the obvious and universal facts, which every one sees
> and no one is astonished at, it seldom occurs to any one to place upon
> record; and posterity, if it learn the rule, learns it, generally, from the
> notice bestowed by contemporaries on some accidental exception.
> . . . The present alone affords a fund of materials for judging, richer
> than the whole stores of the past, and far more accessible.

Dickens had other resources as well, but, in a way different from most
novelists and akin to journalism, observation, insight and experience
were vital to him.
10. Raymond Williams, 'Social Criticism in Dickens: Some Problems of
Method and Approach', *Critical Quarterly*, 6 (1964) 214–27.
11. A similarity between the two worlds is brought out by Michael Cotsell,
The Companion to 'Our Mutual Friend' (London: Allen & Unwin, 1986),
one of a series of forthcoming volumes devoted to each novel (general
editors, Cotsell and Susan Shatto), which shows what can be done in
annotation. Here, apart from general contemporary allusion it is shown
that Dickens cannot fail to have had in mind the long series of *All the
Year Round* articles on finance, in 1864–5, by M. L. R. Laing, a fact not (I
believe) previously noticed.
12. In 'Miscarriage of Justice', *Examiner*, 30 March 1850, probably not by
Dickens, the Tooting scandal was again discussed in connection with a
trial for the murder of a pauper child-servant (Mary Parsons) which
may also have contributed something much less recognisable to the
conception of Guster. Philip Collins has called attention to this, and
another similar case, in '*Bleak House* and Dickens's *Household Narrative*',

Nineteenth-Century Fiction, 14 (1960) 345–9. In looking at such *Household Narrative* reports it is not just the 'likeness' that we can see, but that Dickens is a highly special instance of a novelist who, alongside writing fiction, chose to run a monthly magazine made up almost entirely of scissored news extracts. Other mid-Victorians (Carlyle, Arnold, Ruskin) made a point of using sharp topical references, but Dickens exploited the fascination it held for him and his public.

13. Philip Collins, 'The Middlesex Magistrate in *David Copperfield*', *Notes and Queries*, 206 (1961) 86–91; *Examiner*, 27 October 1849; K. J. Fielding and A. W. C. Brice, 'A New Article by Dickens: "Demoralisation and Total Abstinence"', *Dickens Studies Annual*, IX (1981) 1–19.

14. See Fielding and Brice, '*Bleak House* and the Graveyard'. House's book was and is a foundation work, but new information is now available. As we have it, it was rewritten (as he told me), from imperfect carbons, sitting on his army bunk, after the publishers had lost his top copy by sending it to America for safe keeping in 1940. It was to have been revised, and I was invited to help, but it was reissued without his being given the opportunity he expected.

15. 'Intramural Interment', *Examiner*, 8 September 1849; *Bleak House*, chs 11 and 16.

5

Dickens in his Letters: the Regress of the Radical

GRAHAM STOREY

Like all Dickensians, I owe a great debt of gratitude to Philip Collins for the two books which most corrected – sometimes sharply, always judiciously – an over-simplified view of Dickens: *Dickens and Crime* and *Dickens and Education;* and I am delighted to acknowledge that debt here. The approach he countered was at its most dangerously simple in T. A. Jackson's *Charles Dickens: The Progress of a Radical* (1937), an account which saw Dickens advancing to socialism, on all fronts, in virtually a straight line; it was modified – though within a Marxist context – by the distinguished Hungarian critic, Georg Lukács, who, in *The Historical Novel* (1962), criticised *Barnaby Rudge* and *A Tale of Two Cities* for not being sufficiently Marxist.[1] By giving a wealth of evidence from Dickens's journalism, speeches, letters, as well as the novels, Philip Collins gave us, in both books, a much more *real* picture of a complex, inconsistent, often obsessed and tormented mind: a 'wobbler', as he put it, in penology; increasingly authoritarian in his attitude to criminals, prisons, capital punishment, flogging; increasingly an admirer of the police – even, on one occasion, of the Austrian police – and the military; a demander for ruthless vengeance on the Indian mutineers; a strong supporter, with Kingsley and Carlyle (and against Mill and Huxley) of Governor Eyre's violent treatment of Jamaican rebels in 1864. And, in education, much more *imaginatively* involved in those parodies of schoolmasters, McChoakumchild and Bradley Headstone, than in all his speeches and articles demanding educational reform.

Dickens's letters, with which I shall be mainly concerned, undoubtedly support that more complex picture. They certainly show an increasing authoritarianism as part of it: hence my title – which no doubt goes too far – 'The *Regress* of the Radical'. But I must make two points first:

(1) Some critics have been, perhaps, too quick to assume a total distinction between Dickens the novelist and Dickens the letter-writer; between the imaginative sources of the novels and the imaginative sources of the letters. In fact, the partitions between his art and his life, as rendered in his more committed letters, are often surprisingly thin. That goes both ways. When he writes to Forster (11 September 1841) at the very moment of writing *Barnaby Rudge* – between chapters – he *relives* the novel: 'I have just burnt into Newgate, and am going in the next number to tear the prisoners out by the hair of their heads';[2] and, a week later, 'I have let all the prisoners out of Newgate, burnt down Lord Mansfield's and played the very devil. . . . I feel quite smoky when I am at work.'[3] When he writes to Miss Coutts (7 January 1853), after seeing a slum-child in the East End of London gazing at a starved old white horse feeding on oyster-shells, he *could* be writing a novel: 'The sun was going down and flaring out like an angry fire at the child – and the child, and I, and the pale horse, stared at one another in silence for some five minutes as if we were so many figures in a dismal allegory.'[4]

As the volumes of *Letters* so far published have shown, the sense of *energy* uncontained, boiling over, is their dominant impression. It is the quality in the novels that most, perhaps, worried Henry James. Comparing Dickens and Balzac, he wrote: 'they most of all resemble each other in the fact that they treated their extraordinary imaginative force as a matter of business; that they worked it as a gold-mine, violently and brutally; overworked and ravaged it.'[5] Shrewd as that is, it is obviously unfair to both. But it strongly supports my first essential point: that part of what James calls 'the overworking' of Dickens's imaginative force is carried over into his letters; they have their weight as *imaginative* evidence.

(2) My second point concerns the kind of radicalism Dickens either progressed to or regressed from. On most of the major public and political issues of at any rate the 1840s and early 1850s, his letters and actions show him standing firmly where we should expect him to stand. He had great sympathy with the Revolution in France of 1848 ('Citoyen C.D.' he signed an excited letter to Forster). He knew and sympathised strongly with Mazzini and helped to raise funds for the exiled Italians in London. He supported Kossuth; regarded Napoleon III as the most dangerous man in Europe and hated the Second French Empire. At home, he consistently loathed the legal system, the magistracy, the Established Church – and particularly the bishops. Parliament he despised throughout his life: 'That great dust-heap down at Westminster, of imbeciles and dandies, that there is no machinery for sifting', he described it in a letter to Harriet Martineau.[6] On deprived and exploited children – always for him a key symbol of oppression – he is consistently ferocious. Writing (31 January 1841) to Mrs Gore, who had just satirised a Royal-nurse type of book, *Portraits of Children of the Nobility* (1838–41), he bursts out: 'These books are the gall and bitterness of my life. I vow to God they make me wretched, and taint the freshness of every new year . . . . these aristocratic dolls do turn me sick. I only know one good those books are likely to achieve. If I were a poor labouring man and saw them in the shop windows as I went slouching home, I should think of my own children and the no-regard they had from anybody, and be a greater Radical than ever.'[7]

So far, so good. Though, for a politically progressive Radical, there are some perhaps unexpected gaps: only one less than enthusiastic comment on Robert Owen and his 'New Moral World'; no mention at all of Marx and Engels's first Working Men's International of 1864. But, in the letters at least – and I think we can see some reflection in the novels – the tone of the radicalism changes: it becomes increasingly less than pure. If I were to categorise, I would say that three things happen to it. First, it becomes *mixed*, with a strong admixture of the comic and the grotesque in it; second, it becomes increasingly authoritarian and exasperated; and third, as the probably inevitable result of both those changes in direction, it becomes more and more personal, concerned ultimately with areas of human experience far below the social and the political. In the *purer* terms that Jackson and Lukács and many others have claimed for Dickens, that resultant mixture represents, surely, a 'regression'. Let me give some examples of what I see as the changes in direction.

The mixed tone begins early. After contributing three anti-Tory rhymed squibs to the *Examiner* in August 1841 – to greet Peel's new Tory Government (the first, '"The Fine Old English Gentleman", New Version (To be said or sung at all Conservative Dinners)', beginning 'The good old laws were garnished well with gibbets, whips and chains, / With fine old English penalties, and fine old English pains') – he writes to Forster (13 August 1841): 'By Jove how radical I am getting! I wax stronger and stronger in the true principles every day.'[8] I do not for a moment deny the proclaimed radicalism there: we know how much Dickens hated the Tories. But both lampoon and letter are, of course, *a performance*. Robert Garis, I am sure, was right in claiming that this theatrical stance gave Dickens the freedom he needed for his attacks on systematised society.[9] But such play could also, obviously, become a delight in the comic and the grotesque for their own sakes. Dickens at first wanted, he told Forster, to have his rioters in *Barnaby Rudge* led not by Lord George Gordon, Barnaby and Hugh, but by three lunatics escaped from Bedlam. Forster, aghast, said 'no' – and somewhat sanctimoniously recorded in the *Life*: 'He saw the soundness of this'[10] (and Wilkie Collins, as a good sensation-novelist, scrawled in the margin of his copy: 'the more's the pity!').

But, of course, the stressing of madness here is much more than sensation-writing. Barnaby in his innocence, Hugh in his brutishness, are essentially folk-images. The introduction of this fable-like element into an account of social violence points to something *below* the social and political: to an irrational, anarchic, not fully human force, that lies behind the irrupting mob. Such perception may have its own radicalism; but, ultimately, it makes nonsense of all order, all systematised institutions, all civilisation. The Reign of Terror, the blood-lust of the Avengers, does much the same – or more so – in *A Tale of Two Cities* 18 years later. But, again, revolutionary fervour is not finally allowed to have all its own serious way. There is, first of all, that extremely interesting letter (5 June 1860) that Dickens wrote to Bulwer-Lytton, defending the strange tragi-comic death of Mme Defarge, shot by her own pistol in the struggle with the hardly tragic Miss Pross. 'And when I use Miss Pross . . . to bring about that catastrophe', writes Dickens, 'I have the positive intention of making that half-comic intervention a part of the desperate woman's failure, and of opposing that mean death – instead of a desperate one in the streets, which she wouldn't have minded – to the dignity of Carton's wrong or right; this *was* the design, and seemed to be in the fitness of things.'[11] And there are still some critics who seem to doubt that Dickens knew exactly what he was doing!

Second, there is that famous comment on the revolutionary Paris mob sharpening its swords at the Grindstone: inhuman and terrifying, they have eyes, writes Dickens, 'which any unbrutalized beholder would have given twenty years of life to petrify with a well-directed gun'. The sudden authoritarian snap there shows the other side to Dickens's fascination with violence: the deep fear of class-warfare, of the breakdown of order, that he shared with Carlyle.

Dickens had used a similar explosive image of exasperation in an earlier letter to Miss Coutts's friend Dr William Brown of 1 August 1853, threatening to 'explode at this point like a shell, on the subject of the English law in general, and [this] instance . . . of its leaving grievous delinquents alone'.[12] The time was, of course, that of *Bleak House*; the 'instance' that had so infuriated him the Court's leniency with a madman who had tried to blackmail Miss Coutts. The hatred of the 'English law in general' we expect from Dickens. It never lifted. But note that it is the law's *leniency* here that has really angered him: a significant change from sympathy for the Chancery prisoner in *Pickwick* and the more recent Chancery victims of *Bleak House*. Even the possibility of leniency, in a case that he considered cut-and-dried, drove him to fury. In August 1859, one of those celebrated poisoning cases – of which the century seems so full – ended with Chief Baron Pollock sentencing a surgeon, Dr Smethurst, to death, for poisoning his bigamous 'wife'. Dickens was delighted: no praise could be too high for Pollock. *And*, he wrote to Forster (25 August 1859), after strong public doubts about the medical evidence (in a letter described by Forster as 'too characteristic of the writer to be lost'[13]), '(though a merciful man – because a merciful man I mean), I would hang any Home Secretary (Whig, Tory, Radical, or otherwise), who should step in between that black scoundrel and the gallows. I can*not* believe – and my belief in all wrong as to public matters is enormous – that such a thing will be done'.[14] But it *was* done. Smethurst was granted a free pardon by the Queen that November, though imprisoned for bigamy. His reprieve provoked Dickens's sarcastic 'Five New Points of Criminal Law', suggesting reforms 'grounded on the profound principle that the real offender' in such trials 'is the Murdered Person'.[15]

But the Chancery prisoners were individuals; it is the institutions that can do no right. 'Radicalism' at least posits root-and-branch reform. Dickens's increasing exasperation, from the mid-1850s on, with almost every public institution and political issue – and its often authoritarian tone – mirrors instead the attitude of those whom W. O. Aydelotte has well called 'administrative nihilists':[16] as having an ultimate scepticism about any form of governing that, even if expressed in an apparently radical form, must be anathema to the true Radical.

Take the two great national issues of the mid-century: the Crimean War and the Indian Mutiny. Dickens's support of Austen Layard's Administrative Reform Committee – his only real venture into practical politics – has been seen as a boldly radical act. But his motives were in fact rather different. This is how he put them to Miss Coutts (11 May 1855):

> Take my knowledge of the state of things in this distracted land, for what it may be worth a dozen years hence. The people will not bear for any length of time what they bear now. I see it clearly written in every truthful indication that I am capable of discerning anywhere. And I want to interpose something between them and their wrath. For this reason solely, I am a Reformer [i.e. a supporter of Layard] heart and soul. I have nothing to gain – everything to lose (for public quiet is my bread) – but I am in desperate earnest, because I know it is a desperate case.[17]

Fending off the people's wrath, ensuring public quiet, were not at all the motives of the genuinely radical Layard.

If a deep fear of public disorder was one side of Dickens's attitude in this disturbed decade, fury with a Government that allowed it to happen – even if many thousand miles away – was the other. The ferocity of Dickens's response to the Indian Mutiny is still disturbing; it was hardly a radical, much less a liberal one.

His letter to Miss Coutts (4 October 1857), in which he wished he were Commander-in-Chief in India, so that he could do his utmost – I quote – 'to exterminate the Race upon whom the stain of the late cruelties rested . . . and was now proceeding, with all convenient dispatch and merciful swiftness of execution, to blot it out of mankind and raze it off the face of the Earth',[18] is sufficiently notorious. Another letter, to his Swiss friend Emile de la Rue (23 October 1857), castigates the Government ('Asses in power') for its total ignorance of 'the Hindoo character'.[19] The total lack of faith in Government – in what Carlyle called the governing class who do not govern – seems to me to go right *through* any form of accepted political and social radicalism – and to leave very little believable-in social organisation standing the other side. I am not claiming Dickens as an anarchist: he had much too much belief in discipline and order for that. But I do stress, as I said earlier, the *personal*, the concern with areas of experience far below the social and political. The pastoral endings to all four of the great novels of the 1850s and 1860s – and I include the revised ending of *Great Expectations* – may all be wish-fulfilments, vanishings into something, for most of us, rather less than mystery. But the sense of closure, of immanent, even inevitable, vindication, is strong in all of them; and it is a very personal closure. I know it is a long way back from Dickens to the mid-seventeenth century; but I think of one of the great personal closures there, *Stanza* 76 of Marvell's 'Upon Appleton House':

> How safe, methinks, and strong, behind
> These Trees have I incamp'd my Mind.

It was feminine beauty Marvell was mainly frightened of there – never, I think, an object of fear to Dickens – but the sense of the strongly encamped mind giving personal superiority over the world and all its tricks and corruptions is equally strong in both:

> And where the World no certain Shot
> Can make, or me it toucheth not.
> But I on it securely play,
> And gaul its Horsemen all the Day.

Whatever the encampment of Dickens's mind or will, there can be no doubt of his 'gauling' the world's Horsemen from it; and his letters show him doing it with increasing anger. Leaders of Church and State are, of course, the prime targets: Palmerston, characterised as the 'Twirling Weathercock' in Dickens's 'The Thousand and One Humbugs',[20] becomes, in a letter to Miss Coutts (13 August 1856), 'the emptiest impostor and the most dangerous delusion, ever known'.[21] Just as, five years earlier, during the writing of *Bleak House*, Derby had been a similar emblem of chicanery: 'Apart from any political feeling, I think the evasion, shifting and juggling, with which Lord Derby's government took office has, for many years, if not for ever, materially damaged the character and honor of public men in England.'[22] In almost his last letter to Bulwer-Lytton, four months before his death – one of his bitterest – he tells him that he has now completely lost faith in the governing of 'my blessed country'.

The bishops fare no better and are savagely attacked in the Great Frost of 1861, when they continued their hot debate on Bishop Colenso and *Essays and Reviews*, 'pitching their right reverend mud about in all directions', while the poor were freezing and starving to death.[23]

There is a well-known rhetorical device in two of the novels that carries this tone of sarcastic fury: the change from description or narrative to apostrophe. Dickens's use of it twice in *Bleak House* emphasises its effect. 'Call the death by any name Your Highness will', of Krook's Spontaneous Combustion, is echoed closely on Jo's death: 'Dead, your Majesty. Dead, my lords and gentlemen.' Though 12 years divide *Bleak House* from *Our Mutual Friend*, not only the device, but the targets, just before the death of Betty Higden, are almost identical. 'Honourable boards' are as appropriate to Betty's terror of the Parish Work-house as 'Right Reverends and Wrong Reverends of every order' are to Jo. 'My lords and gentlemen' they share. The effect of both apostrophes is, of course, deliberately to implicate every reader: an effect enhanced by the iambic pentameter that ends the apostrophe on Jo: 'And dying thus around us every day'. And that seems to me a much more *personal* 'gauling' – an insistence on grass-roots responsibility – than a purely politically or socially radical exposure of wrong: though, of course, it subsumes that too.

Little Dorrit, published while Dickens was writing his furious letters about Palmerston and the mishandling of the Crimean War, does not use the apostrophe as such. But at certain points, particularly in the second book, he uses a topsy-turvying technique, an image of society as the Ship of Fools, that, in its aboluteness, has much the same effect. I think of the procurement of a Lordship in the Circumlocution Office – through bribery, of course – for Mrs Merdle's son, the fatuous Sparkler (the in-joke for Dickens's friends was, of course, that it was one of his own names for himself): Sparkler, called to direct England's 'genius, learning, commerce, spirit, and sense'. 'The land of Shakespeare, Milton, Bacon, Newton, Watt, the land of a host of past and present abstract philosophers, natural philosophers, and subduers of Nature and Art in their myriad forms, called to Mr Sparkler to come and take care of it, lest it should perish.' That turns humanism on its head. But the final comment on Merdle, after his true 'complaint' is known, goes, in a Christian country, even further: 'he, the shining wonder, the new constellation to be followed by the wise men bringing gifts, until it stopped over a certain carrion at the bottom of a bath and disappeared – was simply the greatest Forger and the greatest Thief that ever cheated the gallows'.

The furiously sarcastic insistence on the way society turns *all* values, human and Christian, upside-down, in both those passages – the almost Shakespearean delight in the exposure – seems to me, again, to go quite beyond generally accepted radicalism; and, in its tough, scornful scepticism, a *very* long way beyond the 'sentimental radicalism' proposed for Dickens by Walter Bagehot.

I have stressed in this essay Dickens's inconsistency on many social issues: perhaps the inevitable inconsistency of the life of the imagination turned outward to public life. But let me end with an ambiguity: the famous one, made in a Presidential speech of September 1869 to the Birmingham and Midland Institute, in which he proclaimed his faith in 'the people governing' as 'on the whole infinitesimal', his faith in 'the People governed' as 'on the whole illimitable'.[24] We know how he settled it, to his own, if not to everyone else's satisfaction: a small 'p' for the first 'people'; a capital 'P' for the second. And how, when he returned to Birmingham a few months later, he capped his explanation with a good radical piece of Henry Buckle: people 'will learn that lawgivers are nearly always the obstructors of society, instead of its helpers'; on the few occasions when they are not, 'contrary to their usual custom, they have implicitly obeyed the spirit of their time, and have been, as they always should be, the mere servants of the people, to whose wishes they are bound to give a public and legal sanction'[25] (*Loud applause*).[26]

But he would not be Dickens, if he did not re-perform the speech and its consequences in a letter: this time, to his American friend and publisher, James Fields (14 January 1870): 'I hope you may have met with the little touch of Radicalism I gave them at Birmingham in the words of Buckle? With pride I observe that it makes the regular political traders, of all sorts, perfectly mad. Such was my intentions [*sic*], as a grateful acknowledgement of having been misrepresented.'[27]

That, I think, does two things. It returns us to what I called earlier the mixed, less than pure tone of some of Dickens's radicalism – the 'little touch of Radicalism' is almost in inverted commas, and the speech itself (as I have said) treated as a performance, a near-comic performance. But it also, assisted by that tone, suggests a more fundamental ambiguity. Hatred of injustice and oppression, besides inefficiency, muddle and apathy, never left Dickens: novels, letters and speeches all bear witness to that. But the writer of that letter, as of many other letters, was a man contained *within* a society: superior, and knowing it, to 'the regular political traders, of all sorts'; 'gauling' them when they became intolerable, excessive, interfering; but ultimately *accepting* his society's contours – and his own highly formidable 'encampment' within them. That does not seem to me a truly 'radical' position.

Notes

1. Georg Lukács, *The Historical Novel* (London: Merlin Press, 1962) pp. 243–4.
2. *Letters of Charles Dickens*, Pilgrim Edition, ed. Madeline House, Graham Storey and Kathleen Tillotson (Oxford: Clarendon Press, 1969) vol. II, p. 377. (Hereinafter cited as *Letters*).
3. *Letters*, vol. II, p. 385.
4. *Letters from Charles Dickens to Angela Burdett-Coutts, 1841–1865*, ed. Edgar Johnson (London: Cape, 1953) p. 219. (Hereafter cited as *Letters to Miss Coutts*.)
5. Henry James, *French Poets and Novelists* (London, 1878) p. 187.
6. *Letters*, vol. VI (1987).
7. *Letters*, vol. II, p. 201.
8. *Letters*, vol. II, p. 357 and note.
9. Robert Garis, *The Dickens Theatre* (Oxford: Clarendon Press, 1965).
10. John Forster, *The Life of Charles Dickens*, ed. J. W. T. Ley (London, 1928) p. 168. (Hereafter cited as John Forster, *Life*.)
11. *The Letters of Charles Dickens*, Nonesuch Edition, ed. Walter Dexter (London, 1938) vol. III, p. 163. (Hereafter cited as *Letters* (Nonesuch).)
12. Unpublished letter: to appear in *Letters*, vol. VII.
13. John Forster, *Life*, p. 730 note.
14. *Letters* (Nonesuch), vol. III, p. 118.
15. *All the Year Round*, I (24 September 1859) 517.
16. W. O. Aydelotte, 'The England of Marx and Mill as Reflected in Fiction', *Journal of Economic History*, Suppl. VIII (1948) 45.
17. *Letters to Miss Coutts*, p. 298.
18. *Letters to Miss Coutts*, pp. 350–1.
19. Unpublished Letter: to appear in *Letters*, vol. VIII.
20. *Household Words*, VI (21 April 1855) 265.
21. *Letters to Miss Coutts*, p. 326.
22. *Letters*, vol. VI.
23. Unpublished letter: to appear in *Letters*, vol. IX.
24. *The Speeches of Charles Dickens*, ed. K. J. Fielding (Oxford: Clarendon Press, 1960) p. 407. (Hereafter cited as *Speeches*.)
25. H. T. Buckle, *History of Civilization in England* (London, 1902) vol. III, p. 170.
26. *Speeches*, p. 411.
27. *Letters* (Nonesuch), vol. III, p. 760.

6

From Outrage to Rage: Dickens's Bruised Femininity

U. C. KNOEPFLMACHER

In his recent *Dickens and Women*, Michael Slater tries to refute the long-standing notion that Dickens's presentation of his female characters is 'false and feeble'. Citing 'Dr Leavis's discussion of Amy Dorrit or Professor Barbara Hardy's of Edith Dombey' as precedents for his own enterprise, he insists that 'modern criticism' must regard such characters as more than stereotypes and contributes to this process of revalidation by looking, in the second part of his book, at a gallery of female portraits from *Boz* to *Drood*.[1] Yet this approach is not without its shortcomings. Interestingly enough, it is in its first part, where Dr Slater assembles, and valuably interprets, Dickens's relation to the actual women in his life, that *Dickens and Women* proves to be the most helpful, since he documents there a dynamic that his consideration of the fictive 'women' as mimetic replications does not fully tap. For it seems fair to say that Dickens's most powerful responses to the feminine are far more likely to be dramatised through the actions of male self-personations such as David Copperfield and Pip than by the static 'womanly ideal' embodied in a Biddy or Agnes Wickfield.

'My father did not understand women', Kate Dickens is reported to have said,[2] and, despite Dr Slater's efforts, her testimony may after all have been valid. But what Dickens did so vividly understand, and what he consequently dramatised, is the importance of femininity as an indispensable requisite for the well-being of a fully gendered psyche. The creative imagination, whether female or male, heterosexual or homosexual, is necessarily bi-gendered, and, as such, very much like that hermaphroditic dove that, in the opening of *Paradise Lost*, hatches its own creation as it broods over the vast abyss. Feminist criticism has alerted us to the

ways in which the imagination of a female writer must struggle to
assimilate masculine components needed for internal harmony and
external accommodation. Conversely, the imagination of a male
writer struggles just as arduously to incorporate the female
components needed for its own psychic balances both within and
without.

Yet the Dickens who probably owed his dramatic talent to his own
mother enlisted that talent to depict a gender imbalance that was
rooted in the deprivation he had felt when she 'was warm' for his
being sent back to what he would render as Fagin's den or
Murdstone's and Grinby's warehouse. Though disguised, his
'resentment' and 'anger' at Elizabeth Dickens can be glimpsed in his
earliest work.[3] Elsewhere in this volume, Sylvère Monod fastens on
the figure of the Unpleasant Boy in *Sketches by Boz*. He rightly notes
that the 'viciousness of boys as a rule' not only outweighs by far that
of the few girls in the *Sketches* but is also persistently countered by
the ever-recurring figure of a fond and self-sacrificing mother.
Monod is amused to discover 'more paedophobia than paedophilia'
in the production of an author who would be noted for such ideal
(and feminised) children as Oliver Twist and Tiny Tim.[4] Yet the
paedophobia of a Boz can also be read as an avoidance or act of
deflection from the far more unsettling gynophobia that a more
mature and autobiographical Dickens would have to overcome
when he faced the growing up of boy and adolescent in *David
Copperfield* and *Great Expectations*.

This essay intends to show how residuals of psychic
disappointment can turn into anger, how an imagination
dissatisfied with its earlier representations of such disappointment
may eventually erupt into more violent representations of sadism
and rage. I shall draw on Dickens's two 'I'-novels, written a decade
apart, to illustrate this shift. My discussion remains necessarily
incomplete, for it would require a fuller look at other fictions by
Dickens as well as by the female writers whose rival fables he
inscribed in both *David Copperfield* and *Great Expectations*. These
inscriptions remain unacknowledged. Dickens denied having read
Jane Eyre before he embarked on the story of David Copperfield,
and, for all his praise of George Eliot, he would never acknowledge
his inversion, through Pip's story, of certain features of *The Mill on
the Floss*. But his insertion of a reference to still another female
fiction, *Frankenstein*, in *Great Expectations* deserves to be noted here
for its relevance to my subject.

When Dickens has Pip think of himself as a combination of both 'the imaginary student pursued by the misshapen creature he had impiously made'[5] and of the creature itself, he calls attention to his understanding of a gender-struggle that underlies his fiction as much as Mary Shelley's own. Pip cannot bear the thought that the coarse and 'savage' Magwitch he has been observing is more of a nurturer than the patroness of Satis House. Before he can alight on the images of a 'ghost' and a Frankenstein Monster, Pip tries to convey his repugnance by noting the effect of Magwitch's use of cosmetic 'powder' to hide his identity: 'I can compare the effect of it, when on, to nothing but the probable effect of rouge upon the dead, so awful was the manner in which everything in him that it was most desirable to repress started through that thin layer of pretence' (p. 362). Cosmetics, a female veneer, no longer can conceal a sadistic energy that has been persistently denied by a Pip who needed to cling to binary opposites by separating country from city, child-self from adult-self, low-life from gentility, creature from creator, and, finally, the masculine from the feminine. Such segregation is no longer possible. Neither Pip, nor Dickens behind him, can continue to rely on thin layers of pretence. The monstrosity of anger is about to erupt.

And that monstrosity, as Dickens now recognises through his allusion to Mary Shelley's story, stems from what I have called a gender imbalance that harks back to childhood loss. Just as the Frankenstein Monster mirrors the incompleteness both of its fictive male creator, Victor Frankenstein, and of its real-life female creator, Mary Wollstonecraft Shelley, so does Magwitch mirror the incompleteness of both Pip and Dickens. In *Frankenstein*, Victor tries to compensate for femininity lost by appropriating his dead mother's life-giving role; yet Mary Shelley confronts her own incomplete identity by replicating herself as a motherless, masculine creature who obsessively seeks the female component it lacks for its own completion. Only when denied a mate, does the Monster fully unleash its anger.

Yet just as Dickens attacked the figure of the unpleasant boy in the *Sketches*, his first work, so does the Monster make a male child the first victim of its own, unpremeditated rage. For the unthinking fury that leads the Monster to throttle Little William is a form of self-rage, akin to that self-directed anger that will ultimately lead to its suicide. Shelley has her Monster wrest from the boy's corpse the portrait of a lovely, and loving, mother. As it hungrily feeds on the maternal eyes, lashes and lips, the creature's sense of its own incompleteness returns and, with it, a renewal of its anger: 'presently,' the Monster explains, 'my rage returned: I remembered that I was forever deprived of the delights that such beautiful creatures could bestow, and that she whose resemblance I contemplated would, in regarding me, have changed that air of divine benignity to one expressive of disgust and affright'.[6]

Thought not a literal orphan, Charles Dickens, too, continued to regard himself as similarly 'deprived'. And rage returned for him as much as for the Monster after he had vainly tried to recover the female components lost by a childhood self. In *David Copperfield*, Dickens launched a full-scale attempt to feminise a male psyche he tried to shield from the sadistic expressions of anger of a Frankenstein Monster. In his second male 'I' novel, written after he had tried to balance a female 'I' with a male voice in *Bleak House*, Dickens activated a passive sense of outrage into more overt and self-conscious manifestations of anger. He was ready to exorcise that long-smouldering anger. For, in his bitter fable of one-sided parental malformations and false expectations of completeness, Dickens at last faced the monster of his own rage. And he now directed that rage at his own gender-incompleteness as much as at the monster-women and monster-men he had created as its agents.

I

Both *David Copperfield* and *Great Expectations* are autobiographical fables of identity. And in both works a remembering male 'I' becomes pre-eminently defined by his relation to women. Yet these definitions are markedly different. David Copperfield seeks to replace the fragile mother whom a male rival, Murdstone, has wrested away from him. In the process of that search, the boy who could show his anger by biting Murdstone becomes an increasingly passive and effeminate bourgeois young man. In *Great Expectations*, however, a Pip unfairly denounced as 'Naterally wicious', wants to find a replacement for the harsh and masculine sister who usurped a maternal role by raising him 'by hand' after their mother's death. When Mr Wopsle proclaims that what is detestable in a pig is more detestable in a boy, Mr Hubble ventures to add, 'Or girl', only to be rebuked: '"Of course, or girl, Mr Hubble," assented Mr Wopsle rather irritably, "'but there is no girl present"'" (ch. 4, p. 34). Indeed, the only feminine presence in the Gargery household is provided by a Joe who has so internalised the beatings received by his mother that he refuses to return the blows his wife's Tickler hammers on Pip's back as well as his own. Yet when Pip seeks the girl who has been absent in his own home, he prefers Estella to Biddy. Although the refined femininity he hopes to find at Satis House proves to be far more damaging tham the physical and psychological abuse he suffered from his sister, Pip almost welcomes its cruelty. Only gradually can he shed the female stereotypes that David Copperfield so gratefully and blindly embraced. Miss Havisham is not at all the kindly and eccentric benefactress that David had found in that other maternal surrogate, his Aunt Betsey. And nor does Estella, even when purged of her haughtiness by the beatings of Bartle Drummle, in the least resemble the meek and saintly Agnes Wickfield on whom David can rely for his total support at the end of the first novel.

After burying his mother and the male infant she had borne Murdstone, David Copperfield comments: 'The mother who lay in the grave, was the mother of my infancy; the little creature in her arms, was myself, as I had once been, hushed forever on her bosom.'[7] Yet even though David tries to displace his living self unto the dead infant forever pressed against his mother's breast, he remains eager to find other replacements for that lost symbiosis. In the chapter that follows his mother's death, he therefore reactivates his fantasies of oneness with Little Em'ly, the child his fancy had already 'etherealized' into an 'angel' (ch. 3, p. 34). There is a new urgency to his return to the fantasy about a little girl as angel-mate. Clara Peggotty, his mother's namesake, has just married. And to forestall the impact of this new desertion, the boy now imagines himself married as well, but to Little Em'ly: 'Ah, how I loved her! What happiness (I thought) if we were married, and were going away anywhere to live among the trees and in the fields, never growing older, never growing wiser, rambling hand in hand through sunshine and flowery meadows, laying down our head on moss at night' (ch. 10, p. 136).

David's desexualised yearning belongs to the realm of the Victorian fairy-tale. His vision of an Eden shared by a pre-pubescent female Other can, of course, be no more sustained than the Frankenstein Monster's similar desire to share a child-world with Little William after it, too, has suffered the trauma of parental rejection. Disappointment is inevitable. David's sentimental vision of an arrested child-Eve must be cruelly shattered as soon as Little Em'ly turns into Emily, the 'I' in her name no longer elided, an alluring, fully sexual young woman promptly seduced by the much-admired Steerforth.

Despite its rejection of childhood make-believe, Dickens's novel attempts to find an outlet for David's nostalgic need for compensation. Anger at the sexual mother who yields to Murdstone and anger at an Emily who now yields to Steerforth are emotions that Dickens refuses his male protagonist to express. Nor can the adult David who, as a boy, fiercely bit Murdstone, be allowed to hate the aristocratic Steerforth he so admires. For David has himself been seduced by Steerforth, who called him a 'girl' and continues to feminise him by calling him 'Daisy'. Only Uriah Heep, the parvenu who lusts after Agnes Wickfield, can draw from David some of that anger which he had instinctively managed to loosen on Murdstone. When Uriah claims that he loves 'the ground my Agnes walks on', a shocked David finds himself harbouring a sadistic fantasy he cannot repress: 'I believe I had a delirious idea of seizing the red-hot poker out of the fire, and running him through with it. It went from me with a shock, like a ball fired from a rifle: but the image of Agnes, outraged by so much as a thought of this red-headed animal's remained in my mind . . ., and made me giddy. He seemed to swell and grow before my eyes' (ch. 25, p. 350). David abhors this phallic rival for tarnishing the angelic female stereotype he so desperately needs to uphold. He can fend off his resentment of Steerforth's seduction of a child-angel because he manages to convert her into a lower-class fallen woman, an object of pity but no longer of desire. But the lower-class Uriah's presumption in forcing the genteel Agnes to think of him as a suitor is, for David, an outrage to the feminine 'image' he so assiduously wishes to preserve. David cannot permit himself to tamper with that image, and image which, in *Great Expectations*, will be ruthlessly shattered when Pip (who eyes the sexually threatening Orlick much in the way that David abhors Heep) discovers that the refined Estella of his dreams is the daughter of a convict and a murderess. For David any such tampering would force him to acknowledge his resentment of another genteel angel of the house, his delicate mother who had inflicted so much pain.

David Copperfield thus prefers to displace on Uriah both his hatred of others and of himself. Yet even his anger at Uriah must be repressed as much as possible, only fitfully admitted as a temporary and aberrant fantasy. David thus stands by almost as passively as Agnes herself in the violent scene in which Uriah is exposed by Micawber, later in the novel. For his part, Uriah now reveals his own concealed hatred. He lashes out at David and contends that this arch-enemy is, in fact, his double: 'Copperfield, I have always hated you. You've always been an upstart, and you've always been against me' (ch. 52, p. 704). Uriah is incensed by David's aloofness, his unwillingness to be drawn into the frenzy: 'Has that Copperfield no tongue?' he sneers (p. 703). To aid him against his perceived enemy, Uriah calls for an ally, the only relation on whom he can still count: 'Where's mother?'; yet he soon turns 'angrily' on her when Mrs Heep advises him to fall back on his mask of meekness (pp. 692, 700). But David will not admit his own hatred for the unmasked double whom Micawber calls a 'monster in the garb of man' (p. 701). He prefers to allow that ineffectual father-figure and two other feminised males, Traddles and Mr Dick, to attack this rival, potent mother's son. Like the self-effacing Agnes who silently witnesses the scene, David refuses to be drawn into masculine explosions of anger.

The text of David's life thus involves the suppression of an anger that Dickens cannot allow his male protagonist to express. That anger can at best surface indirectly in a novel which must insist on feminising the male. As the story progresses, the David who has been reared by Aunt Betsey increasingly comes to resemble an Agnes to whom he will eventually confide: 'You have not taught me quite in vain. There is no alloy of self in what I feel for you' (ch. 62, p. 799). Shaped by the passive femininity he so desires, David's self gradually erodes. He is, after all, not 'the hero of my own life' (ch. 1, p. 1). His own 'I' becomes increasingly elided.[8]

Thus, when, near the end of his narrative, David professes to find in the quiet Agnes 'the source of every worthy aspiration I ever had; the centre of myself' (ch. 62, p. 802), Dickens indirectly calls attention, not just to David's persistent lack of such a centre ever since his mother's death, but also to his lack of a self. David has not grown. For he merely adores Agnes in the selfsame childish fashion in which he had formerly worshipped first his mother, then Little Em'ly, and then Dora, his child-bride. As a long-suffering, self-suppressing angel in the house, Agnes has merely become the sum-total of all the women in David's life, a replacement both for the women who failed him and for those who, like Peggotty and Aunt

Betsey, have nursed and supported him. She epitomises a type of femininity he has both coveted and himself displayed by adopting the role of a victim incapable of anger. As a budding novelist, David identifies with the stereotypes the patriarchy has foisted on females in his culture. And he admires Steerforth as much as he hates himself in Uriah Heep because that Byronic patrician can dominate the women to whom David prefers to submit. Like Boz, David the novelist may well begin his career by writing books about boys as repulsive as Uriah or about bachelors whose practical world becomes threatened by a mother and her unpleasant male child. In embracing the feminine ideal represented by Agnes, however, both David and Dickens seem to have forgotten the furious act of self-assertion that led him to bite the hand of Murdstone and leave it forever scarred. Yet a scarred Dickens would remember that anger in the story of Pip, the boy raised – and hurt – by a female hand.

II

If anger is the sub-text of David's life, it becomes the full text of Pip's life in *Great Expectations*. David accepts the account of his birth as passively as he accepts the female sobriquets given to him by others: Daisy, Doady, Scheherezade, Trot.[9] Pip, on the other hand, both births and names himself through the double contraction of Philip Pirrip. David was told that the maternal placenta or caul that clung to his head at birth would act as a safeguard against all disasters in his later life. But Pip the self-namer is immediately pitched 'head over heels' at the very spot where he gains his first impression of the 'identity of things' (ch. 1, pp. 9, 10). In the churchyard where his two parents and five little brothers lie buried, 'a fearful man' bolts up 'from among the graves' and seizes the boy. Magwitch at once resurrects the male anger that had remained buried throughout *David Copperfield*.

Near the end of *David Copperfield*, a mysterious old man who 'looked like a farmer' was announced at the household of David and Agnes. Their children, especially the oldest, 'little Agnes' with her 'little heap of golden curls', are frightened by this intruder. For they remember the 'beginning of a favourite story Agnes used to tell them, introductory to the arrival of a wicked old Fairy in a cloak who hated everybody' (*DC*, ch. 63, p. 803). But the cloaked stranger turns out to be no malicious goblin, much to the little girl's relief. Instead, he is none other than the kindly uncle of Emily. Mr Peggotty, who has returned from Australia still 'vigorous and robust', now rounds out his avuncular role by joining the children by the hearth. The scene recapitulates the visit by Aunt Betsey Trotwood in the book's first chapter. Disappointed on discovering the male gender of her godchild, she had walked out, in David's mother's account, 'vanishing like a discontented fairy' who 'never came back' (ch. 1, p. 11). But like Emily's protector, Aunt Betsey will not renege when called upon to assume a dead mother's nurturant role.

Dickens carefully reread his own *David Copperfield* before re-inscribing these scenes into the bitterly ironic framework of *Great Expectations*. Pip fears the dreadful male ogre who threatens to eat him unless fed with ordinary 'wittles'.[10] Magwitch expects Pip to bring this sustenance from a mother. '"Now lookee here!" said the man. "Where's your mother?" "There, sir!" said I.' When he realises that Pip is pointing at a tombstone, Magwitch overcomes his fear at being surprised by a living mother. He begins to recognise the child as a fellow outcast, a potential Little William Frankenstein. He asks cautiously: 'Who do you live with – supposin' ye're kindly let to live, which I hadn't made up my mind about?' In his answer, the boy gives precedence to the more powerful of the two adults with whom he lives: 'My sister, sir – Mrs Joe Gargery – wife of Joe Gargery, the blacksmith, sir' (*GE*, ch. 1, p. 11). Pip does not realise that the food he is about to steal from his non-nurturant sister will transform this angry stranger from the monster he now seems into a nurturing male mother or female child-man, much like Mr Peggotty or Joe Gargery. Instead, Pip wishes to forget this figure altogether. He hopes that the recaptured convict might never again reappear.

When Magwitch does reappear from Australia, however, Pip will be forced to reassess his false expectations not only about class but also about gender. He has tried to shed his own coarseness in order to be worthy of an Estella he idealised far more drastically than David ever idealised Little Em'ly or Agnes. He must now recognise that both the fierce convict and the mild-mannered Joe have, in effect, been more maternal and providing than the masculine women who so selfishly deform their nurslings in this novel: the termagant Mrs Joe who deforms Pip and the man-hating Miss Havisham who deforms Estella and Pip. And in the process of making this discovery Pip must learn an even more difficult lesson. Only by fully facing his resentment of female betrayal can he come to terms with the femininity that he, like David Copperfield, so obsessively desires for his self-completion. His very anger, paradoxically enough, will lead him to the therapeutical selving that David Copperfield continued to avoid.

It is Pip's anger at Mrs Joe that proves the most difficult for him to acknowledge. He resents Joe's unwillingness to stand up to a shrewish wife who hits this powerful man as freely as she hits her little brother. Joe tries to explain the reasons for his refusal to return his wife's anger. As the son of a wife-beater who 'hammered away at my mother most unmerciful', Joe refuses to follow his father's example: 'I'm afeerd of going wrong in the way of not doing what's right by a woman, and I'd fur rather of the two go wrong the t'other way, and be a little ill-conwenienced myself. I wish it was only me that got put out, Pip; I wish there warn't no Tickler for you, old chap; I wish I could take it all on myself' (ch. 7, pp. 55, 59). Joe's message is clear. He allows himself to be abused by Mrs Joe as long as he can himself nurture 'the poor little child' she brought with her (p. 57). In *David Copperfield* Dickens had still idealised the strong Mr Peggotty for offering his home to outcast children and for suffering the abuse of the querulous Mrs Gummidge. In *Great Expectations*, however, Dickens looks far more sceptically at Mr Peggotty's counterpart. For all his endearing loving-kindness, Joe cannot really shield Pip's fragile psyche from the woman who hurls Pip at him 'as a connubial missile' (ch. 2, p. 15). The blacksmith who doggedly insists that Mrs Joe is 'a fine figure of a woman' is an impotent bystander to her abuses of power. Though he can pummel an Orlick, he does so because incited by his wife. His passivity thus resembles that of a David Copperfield. For he, too, must falsify experience by remaining an unprotesting child-man. Only at the end of the novel, when tutored by Biddy, will he assume a more mature masculine role.

The young Pip thus welcomes a transfer to the more genteel forms of femininity he expects to find at Miss Havisham's Satis House. But he refuses to see that he has been merely transported from one incomplete mother-surrogate to another who is just as deficient. It is Mrs Joe, after all, who induces the boy to go to Satis House. When he and Joe wonder who the 'she' is to whose house Pip is to be conducted, Mrs Joe sarcastically replies: 'And she is a she, I suppose? . . . Unless you call Miss Havisham a he. And I doubt if even you'll go so far as that' (ch. 7, p. 60). But in *Great Expectations*, where the male 'he' of a Magwitch or Joe can harbour qualities traditionally associated with the female, 'she'-characters, such as Miss Havisham and Mrs Joe herself, adopt the mode of an angry 'he'. It is female anger, more than male anger, that Pip must confront before he can be brought to exorcise his own deepest anger at the 'she' both outside and inside his own psyche.

III

I should like to devote the last two sections of this essay to an analysis of four closely related scenes. Although the first of these scenes, examined in the ensuing paragraphs, takes place in *David Copperfield* while the other three, examined in the next section, occur in *Great Expectations*, they fit into a sequence that illustrates Dickens's orchestration of male and female anger. All four scenes are highly melodramatic. But whereas the first one uses melodrama to veil masculine anger by displacing it onto the female, the three scenes in *Great Expectations* brilliantly intermingle the two in order to unveil rage as a mode of self-recognition. Let us first look at *David Copperfield*.

David's passivity is most radically manifest in chapter 50, deceptively entitled 'Mr Peggotty's Dream Comes True'. For there, in what is surely the most brutal scene in the book, David stands by, conveniently screened by a 'back-door', as he watches one woman savagely demolish another. The attacker is Rosa Dartle, the fierce gentlewoman, whose power and face, disfigured by the scar she received from a Steerforth she continues to desire, had once attracted and then repelled David. Rosa has flushed out Emily's hiding place a bare moment before David, accompanied by the prostitute Martha,[11] can reach the outcast. Ascending the stairs, David observes 'in the distinct light the skirts of a female figure going up before us' (*DC*, ch. 50, p. 663). Those female skirts dominate the scene which the hidden David will now observe with an intensely voyeuristic fascination.

Rosa's verbal battering of the guilt-ridden Emily is painful to read. And David professes to wallow in the pain that Rosa causes. But he is mesmerised by the sadism he recreates in all its agonising detail as he renders the 'resolute hatred of her tone, its cold stern sharpness, and its mastered rage' (p. 663). Michael Slater considers this scene as Dickens's dramatising of 'what he saw as something horribly unnatural, the rejection of sisterhood'.[12] But Dickens is clearly as fascinated as David by the unnaturalness of a rejection he can impute to an agent of the same female gender. Rosa's total power is established from the start. She threatens Emily physically: 'If you will try to evade *me*, I'll stop you, if it's by the hair' (p. 664); she would 'have this girl whipped to death' (p. 666). But it is Rosa's verbal 'mockery' that proves more expressive 'than her undisguised rage' (p. 666). She contemptuously dismisses Emily's protestations of guilt. She does not care about the pain caused to Mr Peggotty's home, that 'low place'. It is a genteel home that Emily has presumably polluted: 'I speak of *his* home', Rosa insists, alluding to Steerforth. And, 'looking down upon the prostrate girl', she sarcastically denigrates her: 'Here . . . is a worthy cause of division between lady-mother and gentleman-son' (pp. 665–6).

The last words indicate that more than a sisterly struggle is being dramatised. Rosa Dartle's attempts to convert Steerforth's victim into the victimiser of a 'gentleman-son' do not seem to strike David as perversely incongruous. For the recriminations that Rosa hurls at Emily clearly express the feelings of 'division' that another gentleman-son has long harboured against his own 'lady-mother'. On first yielding to the allurement of Murdstone, Clara Copperfield had called herself a 'poor girl' (ch. 2, p. 18), just as Emily now protests that she, 'a weak, vain girl', could not have been expected to withstand Steerforth's 'power' (ch. 50, p. 666). The young David abased himself before the girlish mother; unable to reproach her for having borne Murdstone a rival child, he pathetically tried to 'embrace her' and 'once more' feel 'her beautiful hair drooping over' him (ch. 8, p. 103). Now it is Emily, 'her hair streaming about her', who kneels before Rosa and tries to 'clasp' this avenger (ch. 50, p. 665). The tables have been turned. No wonder David refuses to stir.

Instead, David continues to allow Rosa to berate, in Steerforth's name but really in his own service, an Emily who has betrayed his idealisation of her. Rosa's physical restraint of her fury keeps this hidden voyeur spell-bound: 'Her lips were tightly compressed as if she knew that she must keep a strong constraint upon herself – I write what I sincerely believe – or she would have been tempted to strike the beautiful form with her foot. I saw her, distinctly, and the whole power of her face and character seemed forced into that expression. Would he never come?' (p. 665). The rescuing 'he' whom the impotent David so abjectly invokes is, of course, Emily's uncle, Mr Peggotty, who had, in the original draft of the chapter, been David's passive fellow-observer. Again and again, in the final version of the scene, Dickens has David melodramatically interject: 'Would he never, never come? How long was I to bear this? How long could I bear it?' (p. 667). In rereading the first version, Dickens was undoubtedly struck by the unlikeliness that Mr Peggotty, though more directly wronged by Emily than David, would remain as passive a by-stander to the humiliation of his niece. Joe Gargery, as noted above, at least is given a sound motive for his similar refusal to intervene against Mrs Joe. The notion that Mr Peggotty has to wait until Rosa is gone, 'as if his duty were too sacred to be discharged in such a presence', must have seemed too thin a veneer of pretence to the novelist himself.[13]

Yet even the revised version retains a measure of incongruity. It never occurs to David that he could easily have stopped this scene of unmitigated fury by simply bursting into the room, as Mr Peggotty finally will do in both versions – though only after Rosa has exited. David prefers to linger on this act of aggression against a helpless female, just as his creator compulsively returned, in his dramatic readings, to the blows that another fallen woman, Nancy, receives from a male agent whose sadism required no genteel veneers. Like Bill Sikes, Rosa invites her victim to die: 'There are doorways and dust-heaps for such deaths, and such despair – find one, and take your flight to Heaven!' (p. 668). David hears Rosa's parting threat: she will expose Emily unless the girl goes away or does herself agree 'to drop your pretty mask' (p. 668).[14] Set into motion at last, David enters the room just in time to see Mr Peggotty lift the 'motionless and unconscious' Emily, kiss her, and tenderly place a handkerchief over her face. But the David who has consciously identified himself with this 'insensible' female figure still seems to deny his identification with her tormentor. He cannot afford to drop his own 'pretty mask'. He thus remains as silent as before, and as detached, as he allows Mr Peggotty to remove the fallen female form, 'with the veiled face lying on his bosom', as if Emily were dead rather than merely in a swoon (p. 668).

By abusing one of her own gender Rosa Dartle becomes a safe instrument of David's veiled anger against women. She does not only confirm the unconscious presence of that anger in David's psyche, as did Uriah Heep, but also acts as his unacknowledged agent in directing it towards female betrayal. It is Rosa's masochistic infatuation with Steerforth that leads her to berate Emily. She can thus express David's own tortured bonding to the same masterful male. For David's allegiance, like her own, is to Steerforth. He finds himself siding with this master and humiliator of women rather than with Steerforth's victims, Emily, Ham and Mr Peggotty. A former victim himself of Murdstone, David, like Rosa Dartle, cannot resist his attraction to the male oppressor both he and Rosa would like to, but cannot, become.

Significantly enough, Rosa continues to act out David's rage when, after Uriah's 'explosion' and Steerforth's death, she will cruelly turn on still another female, the dead man's 'lady-mother'. Rosa nurses her anger even as she nurses Mrs Steerforth, who is now reduced to a 'fretful wandering of the mind' (p. 812), the same imbecility that Dickens would visit on Mrs Joe in *Great Expectations*. David professes pity for this 'bent lady' in whom he detects 'some traces of old pride and beauty'. But the husband of Agnes Wickfield clearly remains far more fascinated by the spectacle of the 'sharp, dark, withered woman, with a white scar on her lip' (p. 812), who acts as Mrs Steerforth's tender nurse and hateful nemesis. For Rosa's scarred lip can freely continue to utter what David, the child wounded by a mother's neglect, must never permit himself to express.

IV

The anger that is so intricately deflected in *David Copperfield* moves into the forefront of *Great Expectations*. Dickens, for whom the separation from his wife Catherine had revived 'his own childhood loss of mother-love',[15] was ready to examine old psychic patterns with a clarity that seems to stem from deepened self-understanding. In *David Copperfield*, where a figure like Micawber becomes wonderfully independent from the convolutions of the plot, Dickens and David, as Philip Collins has suggested, must avoid psychological penetration to retain their own protective inviolability; 'analysis' is neither Dickens's nor David's prime vehicle for 'presenting and exploring character'.[16] *Great Expectations*, however, a novel begun after Dickens had read those fictions by George Eliot which Collins rightly opposes to a work like *David Copperfield*, is sharply analytical, though not in the Eliot manner. The mechanisms of repression through which David could successfully conceal his deep resentment of the female will now be relentlessly ironised. Whereas David could hide behind the skirts of both Agnes Wickfield and Rosa Dartle, Pip must not only be brought to face his anger at women but also be brought to see that the abuses inflicted on Miss Havisham, Estella, and Mrs Joe are similar to those he has himself suffered. In *The Mill on Floss*, George Eliot tried to overcome a gender-division by making brother and sister into fellow-victims of an adult reality; she was disturbed to discover that her readers felt that she had been much harder on Tom than on Maggie. *Great Expectations* tries to repair a similar imbalance. But the recognition forced on Pip is more powerfully sustained than that which George Eliot imposes on Tom Tulliver just before he and his sister are engulfed by the river. Dickens's own river-child faces a harder task than a Tom whose resentment of Maggie was unjustified and disproportionate. For Pip must admit his identity with Miss Havisham, Estella, and, hardest of all, with the sister who replaced his mother, the entombed presence he only knows as 'Also Georgiana Wife of the Above'. Only by recognising that his scars and their scars are the same, can Pip go beyond anger at these man-haters and try to repair the bruised femininity that he, like David, requires for a restoration of his psychic wholeness.

To forgive Miss Havisham is easier for Pip than it is for him to come to terms with the damage done by his sister. Herself deserted by Estella, the self-betrayed Miss Havisham evokes in Pip a compassion that is far more genuine than David Copperfield's pseudo-pity for the childless Mrs Steerforth. Indeed, just as Pip replaces Estella for a Magwitch who can project on him a thwarted paternal love, so does he, when he last meets Miss Havisham, become an object of her own quasi-maternal affection. Stung by his sharp recriminations, Miss Havisham suddenly displays 'an earnest womanly compassion in her new affection' for the young man she can now call, 'Pip – my dear' (ch. 49, p. 429). Their reconciliation is convincing. Chapter 49, which ends with Pip's touching 'her lips with mine' just as the dying woman calls for his absolution, tries to exorcise the anger that both characters have so deeply felt. The unfulfilled longing for – and betrayal by – the opposite sex has created a bond between them. The fire that leads the two to fall 'on the ground struggling like desperate enemies' burns off that thwarted desire as well as the 'faded bridal dress' (p. 431). Described as becoming 'insensible' after her ordeal, just as Emily had been, Miss Havisham is not carried off by a third party. David had watched the transfer of Emily from Rosa Dartle to Mr Peggotty's strong arms; Pip, 'afraid to have her moved, or even touched' by any one but himself, is astonished to find that both the hands he had used to hold Miss Havisham 'forcibly down' have been badly burnt. The 'disturbed beetles and spiders running away' from the conflagration are the castoffs of passions that can at last be purged.

But Pip finds it far more difficult to exorcise his anger at the mother-figure who had preceded Miss Havisham: Mrs Joe. Thus it is that after being maimed by the fire that consumed Miss Havisham, an impaired Pip must still confront the man who maimed Mrs Joe, Orlick the journeyman. Earlier in the book, when Pip had come upon the battered body of Mrs Joe, he found himself 'at first disposed to believe that *I* must have had some hand in the attack on my sister', but soon, 'in the clearer sight of next morning', began to 'reconsider the matter', considering himself to be almost as innocent as 'poor Joe', whom the police at first 'suspected' of the crime, 'though he never knew it' (ch. 16, pp. 135, 138). Still, Pip was uneasily aware of his own implication in the attack. The manacle which had maimed Mrs Joe's 'head and spine' was, he decided, 'my convict's iron'. And the attacker wielding the weapon, he concluded, must either have been the envoy through whom Magwitch sent Pip some money, or, more likely, the resentful Orlick, who had earlier in the day quarrelled with Mrs Joe.

Pip kept these inferences to himself until some vague future day when, as he tells himself, he might find a 'chance of helping in the discovery of the assailant' (ch. 16, p. 137). He persistently regards Orlick with the same discomfort with which David regarded Uriah Heep; he is disturbed to find this crude double in the proximity of both Biddy and Estella. Yet Dickens ironically suggests that Pip needs to deny the identification that would mark *him*, and not just a male Other, as his sister's assailant. For Orlick's anger at Mrs Joe is Pip's very own. And, as the carefully crafted events that lead up to her maiming ironically show, Pip was Mrs Joe's attacker in more than a purely symbolic sense. Orlick's explosion of anger at Pip's sister was, after all, caused by Pip. When Pip requested that he be allowed a half-holiday to get a glimpse of Estella at Satis House, Orlick had demanded the same privilege ('Two can go up town. Tain't only one wot can go up town'), causing Mrs Joe to berate both her husband and the journeyman. Unlike the passive Joe or the equally passive Pip, Orlick savagely returned Mrs Joe's abuse:

'You're a foul shrew, Mother Gargery', he growled. 'I'd hold you, if you was my wife. I'd hold you under the pump, and choke it out of you' (ch. 15, pp. 128–9). 'In a perfect fury', the screaming Mrs Joe demanded that her husband avenge this slight. Although the two huge male combatants soon become reconciled to each other, Orlick's anger at the female continued to smoulder. And so, of course, did Pip's own anger. His disappointment was exacerbated by the visit to Satis House, where he not only failed to find Estella but also had to meet the cruel taunts of a Miss Havisham, who, with 'malignant enjoyment' asked him: 'Do you feel that you have lost her?' (p. 131).

Through an elaborately worked out time-table, Dickens makes clear that if the despondent Pip, cheated of the genteel feminine presence he had hoped to find at Satis House, had not sauntered in the village, he could have prevented the physical attack on his sister.[17] But if Pip denied his complicity in the event, he also refused to acknowledge his pleasure over its outcome. Just as the verbal hammering of Emily by Rosa Dartle makes the runaway tractable again and submissive to Mr Peggotty, so does the literal battering Mrs Joe has received convert a termagant into a placid idiot child, whose temper has become 'miraculously improved' (ch. 16, p. 138). The fire that shreds Miss Havisham's bridal garments frees her from an arrested adolescence; the beating administered to Mrs Joe has the effect of returning the adult woman to a childhood far more placid than that which she had soiled for Pip. Her invalidism brings a more nurturant female, Biddy, and a 'greater quiet' into Joe's life, although not into that of a Pip still yearning for the absent Estella. The dying Miss Havisham holds up a pencil to induce Pip to record his forgiveness. When the mute Mrs Joe signifies her desire to see Orlick by scrawling a picture of what Pip first assumed to be a crutch yet turned out to be a hammer, Pip expects her at last indignantly to 'denounce' her assailant. Instead, to his surprise, she shows 'every possible desire to conciliate' Orlick. The woman who failed to nourish the bottle-fed Pip, now indicates that she wants Orlick 'given something to drink' (p. 139). Orlick's sadistic rage thus has effected a reversal not unlike that produced by Pip's measured recriminations before the fire had its full effect on Miss Havisham. But it is a reversal that neither Pip nor the feminised Joe could have brought out in this much harsher, 'all-powerful sister, who repulsed me at every turn' (ch. 2, p. 21). Sadism alone could overcome her resistance: 'there was an air of humble propitiation in all she did, such as I have seen pervade the bearing of a child towards a hard master' (p. 139).

When, after being burned in the fire that killed Miss Havisham, Pip confronts Orlick, he must face the same 'hard master' to undergo an internal change that becomes as radical as that undergone by his sister. Pip's encounter with Orlick not only echoes the journeyman's attack on the woman he had berated as 'a foul shrew, Mother Gargery' (ch. 15, p. 129) or Pip's fiery embrace of the mother-surrogate who will demand a filial kiss of forgiveness, but it also reworks the attack on Emily that had so fascinated the son of a 'lady-mother' in *David Copperfield*. Indeed, Pip's confrontation with his double begins where the scene in the earlier novel had ended. The fainted Emily was pressed against the strong breast of the masculine Mr Peggotty who veiled her face. The impotent Pip is now pressed against the strong breast of the masculine figure who will unveil the sadistic anger David managed to conceal.

It is hardly accidental that Orlick's attack on Pip should be described as nothing less than a rape:

> 'Now,' said a suppressed voice with an oath, 'I've got you!'
> 'What is this?' I cried, struggling. 'Who is it? Help, help, help!'
> Not only were my arms pulled close to my sides, but the pressure on my bad arm caused me exquisite pain. Sometimes a strong man's hand, sometimes a strong man's breast, was set against my mouth to deaden my cries, and with a hot breath always close to me, I struggled ineffectually in the dark, while I fastened tight to the wall.   (ch. 53, pp. 455–6)

The scene that follows superbly recasts that in which David Copperfield had so passively observed Rosa's attack on Emily. Not only has Rosa now turned into a male attacker who forces himself on Pip, but another metamorphosis has taken place as well: David and Emily have at last become conflated. For Pip, whose burned 'bad arm' prevents him from fighting off this more powerful male attacker, has assumed the form of the defenceless female whom David (and Dickens) could profess to pity only from a safe distance. David silently asked a 'he' to rescue Emily from her degradation. Pip, however, screams out in terror and in pain, as he faces his own imminent destruction. No single Mr Peggotty, but the combined efforts of three male figures – Pip's friends Herbert and Startop, led by Trabb's boy, Pip's old double, now turned into 'an overgrown young man' (p. 463) – rescue Pip from certain death, while Orlick slinks 'into the night', like the disappearing Frankenstein Monster (p. 462). After her ordeal, the fainted Emily had to be carted off by Mr Peggotty. The shaken Pip, however, can walk away under his own power, though his 'throbbing arm' is 'violently swollen and inflamed' (p. 463). His psychic impairment is about to end: femininity lost, replaced by a femininity within, better far, can yield to masculinity regained.

For Pip has faced more than his potential self-destruction in the lime-kiln. He must also see himself in a new light, as Orlick flares a candle 'so close at me that I turned my face aside' (p. 461).[18] The creature whom Orlick taunts as 'the burnt child' who 'dreads the fire' must be brutally violated before he can confront his own murderous desire: 'Old Orlick's a-going to tell your somethink. It was you as did for your shrew sister.' Pip's denial is prompt: 'It was you, villain.' But Orlick remains unrelenting: 'I tell you it was your doing – I tell you, it was done through you', he retorts. 'It warn't Old Orlick as did it; it was you. You was favoured, and he was bullied and beat. . . . Now you pays for it. You done it; now you pays for it' (p. 459). Pip's long-repressed double has cast himself as the unfavoured outsider, a fellow-victim, a monster denied of its female complement. The analogies are there: like Pip, Orlick has been dismissed from Satis House and kept away from Estella by Miss Havisham; like Pip, he has been unable to obtain Biddy; like Pip, he has been denigrated by Mrs Joe.[19]

In the very act of recognising himself as Orlick, however, Pip must also recognise himself as Mrs Joe. As he finds himself overpowered, he suddenly notes 'the force of the pictures that rushed by me instead of thoughts' (p. 462). By returning to the pictorial, non-verbal imagination of childhood, Pip can be stripped of the defences which prevented David the novelist from confronting the primal female in his life. Miss Havisham had given Pip a pencil on her death-bed. But the woman battered by Orlick had herself resorted to a picture on regressing to childhood. The object Pip mistook for a crutch was a drawing of a hammer. It is a 'stone-hammer with a long heavy handle' that Orlick now wields to bash in Pip's head before throwing the body into the blazing kiln. Orlick admits that on that other murderous night, 'I left her for dead, and if there had been a limekiln as nigh her as there is now nigh you, she shouldn't have come to life again' (p. 459). Mrs Joe's shrieks went unheard by a Pip who lingered in the village while impersonating George Barnwell. But now, as he is forced to re-enact his sister's own moment of agony, Pip shatters the silence that both he and David Copperfield had maintained. He shouts out 'with all my might', and in that shout resuscitates her own cry. The rescue he denied her is now allowed him. For in this struggle to live and into that shout, Pip has put, as he says, 'all the force, until then unknown, that was within me' (p. 462). That 'force' is the same life-instinct preserved by the hardy woman who brought him up by 'hand'. His scream brings her own hardiness back 'to life again' – and his own.

Early in the book, Joe had tried to explain how an identification with his battered mother had led him to suppress all anger at Mrs Joe and had thus resulted in his own feminisation. Pip's anger, however, could not be as easily expunged as Joe's. It was a harsh mother-surrogate rather than a brutal father whom Pip has had to contend with. Unlike, Joe, therefore, Pip must actually assume the condition of a battered female before he can bring to a halt the gender-conflict within. Pip's feminisation, if one even can call it that, is hence perforce a far more violent process. Pip the self-namer has to be reborn, to scream once more that first scream he has for so long stifled. But the end-result is identical, none the less. Pip can forgive both Magwitch and Estella now, and in the process, can finally forgive himself. As in *Frankenstein*, so in this pessimistic novel, there can be no victors, but only chastened victims in an intense, and hard-fought, intra-psychic struggle.

Notes

1, Michael Slater, *Dickens and Women* (Stanford, Calif.: Stanford University Press, 1983) p. xii.
2. Gladys Storey, *Dickens and Daughter* (London: Frederick Muller, 1939) p. 100.
3. Slater, *Dickens and Women*, p. 11.
4. Sylvère Monod, 'Revisiting *Sketches by Boz*', this volume, ch. 2.
5. *Great Expectations*, with an Afterword by Angus Wilson (New York: New American Library, 1980) ch. 40, p. 363. All future references given in the text will be to this edition.
6. Mary Wollstonecraft Shelley, *Frankenstein, or, The Modern Prometheus: The 1818 Text*, ed. James Rieger (Chicago and London: University of Chicago Press, 1982) p. 139.
7. *David Copperfield* (New York: Bantam Books, 1981) ch. 9, p. 123. All future references given in the text will be to this edition.

8. Whereas the titles of the early chapters in *David Copperfield* still feature an active 'I' – 'I Am Born', 'I Observe', 'I Begin Life', 'I Make Another Beginning' – the later chapter-titles omit the first personal pronoun. In these later titles, when the pronoun returns at all, it appears in a strangely subordinate position: 'My Aunt Astonishes Me', 'I Assist at an Explosion', 'A Light Shines on My Way'. The lonely child, it would seem, possesses a far more forceful self than the socialised young man he will become.

9. For a discussion of the last of these names and its relation both to the nursery rhyme character of Dame Trot and to the 'ambivalent sexuality' of the Harlequinade figure whom Aunt Betsey Trotwood resembles, see Edwin M. Eigner, '*David Copperfield* and the Benevolent Spirit', *Dickens Studies Annual*, xiv (1985), 1–15.

10. When, in a remarkably similar scene, the Frankenstein Monster seizes on 'the boy as he passed, and drew him towards me', Little William shrieks, 'monster, ugly wretch! you wish to eat me, and tear me to pieces – You are an ogre – Let me go, or I will tell my papa' (*Frankenstein*, ed. Rieger, p. 139). If the Monster is confused by the identity of the boy's 'papa', Magwitch is confused by Pip's response about his 'mother'.

11. In the original version of chapter 50, Martha is accompanied by both David and Mr Peggotty.

12. Slater, *Dickens and Women*, p. 370.

13. *David Copperfield*, ed. Nina Burgis (Oxford: Clarendon Press, 1981) p. 618, n. 4. When David claims that he was so appalled by Rosa's 'malignity' that he 'had almost thrown himself between them', he is restrained, in the initial version, by 'Mr Peggotty's strong grasp of my shoulder' (p. 615, n. 10).

14. In the original version, Dickens has Rosa add, 'and show your own vile face' (*David Copperfield*, ed. Burgis, p. 613, n. 3.).

15. Slater, *Dickens and Women*, p. 147. Dr Slater's 'suggested reason for Dickens's insistence that Catherine was a bad mother' strikes me as extremely plausible, in light of the 'emotional history' he charts in the first half of *Dickens and Women*; his insight, however, is not translated into his reading of *Great Expectations*.

16. Philip Collins, *Charles Dickens: David Copperfield* (London: Edward Arnold, 1977) p. 57.

17. At the village, Pip is detained by the theatrical Mr Wopsle who promptly casts him as George Barnwell, the apprentice who murdered a relative in order to win the favours of the aloof Mistress Millwood. The sole spectator at this performance is none other than the insiduous Uncle Pumblechook, the one male whom Mrs Joe respects. Confusing fact and, fiction, Pumblechook stares at Pip, 'saying, "Take warning, boy, take warning!"', as if' – Pip interprets – 'it were a well-known fact that I contemplated murdering a near relation' (ch. 15, p. 132). The ironies are complicated by the literary allusion. George Barnwell, after all, does not murder a female, but rather his male benefactor. Pumblechook's 'warning' thus recoils on him, the avowed benefactor of Pip. But given Mrs Joe's identification with the male relative she has

appropriated and Pumblechook's role as an intermediary between Miss Havisham and Pip, the threat to a 'near relation' also has a female target. Indeed, in Victorian Christmas pantomimes such as *Harlequin and George Barnwell* (London: W. Kenneth, 1836), Mistress Millwood seems to have been played by male actors with exaggerated make-up ('Her face was rouged up to the eyes, / Which made her look prouder and prouder'). Given Barnwell's first name, she was cast as 'that dragon'; George's own anger at her is Orlick-like: 'If Millwood were here, dash my wigs, / Quoth he, I would pummel and lam her well' (pp. 5, 6). It seems significant that towards the end of Dickens's novel, Orlick, whom Pip finds materialising after his impersonation of the murderous apprentice, should rob Pumblechook's shop, just as Barnwell robs the shops of Thoroughgood. Orlick who slouches at Pip's side 'with his hands in his pockets' (ch. 15, p. 133) is a Barnwell who uses his hands to act out an aggression that David Copperfield and a Pip who will have to get his hands burned are prevented from committing.

18. Many of the film versions of *Frankenstein* enlist this scene from *Great Expectations*, when a figure cast either as 'Igor' or a jailor (neither of whom are in Shelley's novel) thrusts a flaming torch in the face of a shackled and fire-fearing Monster. The borrowing confirms the connections between the novels that Dickens recognised and which I have tried to enlist in this essay. For connections between *Frankenstein* and the fiction of George Eliot, readers may wish to turn to my 'On Exile and Fiction: the Leweses and the Shelleys', in *Mothering the Mind*, ed. Ruth Perry and Martine W. Bromley (New York and London: Holmes & Meier, 1984) pp. 102–21; for a more widespread discussion of the brother–sister trope to repair gender-division, see 'Genre and the Integration of Gender: from Wordsworth to George Eliot to Virginia Woolf', in *Victorian Literature and Society*, ed. James R. Kincaid and Albert J. Kuhn (Columbus, Ohio: Ohio State University Press, 1984) pp. 94–118.

19. For the fullest discussion of Orlick's enactment of Pip's repressed wishes, see Julian Moynahan, 'The Hero's Guilt: the Case of *Great Expectations*', *Essays in Criticism*, x (1960) pp. 60–79.

7

Chips off the Block: Dickens's Serialising Imitators

JOHN SUTHERLAND

My subject is serialisation; that is, the division of narrative into separately issued instalments, usually for commercial convenience but occasionally for art. Specifically, I am concerned with that mode of serialisation pioneered by Dickens in April 1836 with his first novel, and which he was still triumphantly practising in September 1870, the month of his death. A majority (nine) of his novels came out this way. The features of Dickensian serialisation can be given Bitzer-style as: 'The new novel in twenty monthly, self-contained, illustrated parts, each 32 pages long, selling at one shilling, wrapped in an uniformly illustrated paper cover and accompanied by an advertiser.'

Extended discussions of Dickens invariably become meditations on his uniqueness. Although my announced subject is imitators and imitations the conclusion I shall arrive at is the usual one: that Dickens was the great inimitable. The novel in monthly parts proved a bow of Ulysses which apparently only one man could consistently draw and fire on target. Dickens himself called it 'a very unusual form'[1] and for most writers that is what it remained. Only three major novelists used Dickensian serialisation for the bulk of their novels: Dickens (obviously), Thackeray and Lever. And of the three, Thackeray and Lever ultimately gave it up as unworkable. The yellow cover and the pink finally gave way to the all-conquering duck-egg green. In sum, the number of Victorian novels brought out in monthly numbers is tiny. Over the period 1837–70 an estimated 8–9,000 works of fiction were produced in England. At the beginning of this period (its boom time) there were at maximum some 15 part-issued shilling serials a year. The number settled down by the 1840s to around five. By the end of the 1860s, it had

97

dwindled to one or two. And by September 1870, there was only one.

Why, for everyone but Dickens, the novel in shilling monthly numbers should have proved so intractable is a question I shall try to answer here. The other main question addressed is why, against the tide of publishing progress, Dickens remained so happily wedded to the novel in numbers for 35 years (about ten years longer than he was happily married to his wife, Catherine).

The straight answer, of course, is that Dickens could make the novel in numbers pay handsomely, as others evidently couldn't. But the fact is that Dickens could have made any form of publication pay. If he had inscribed his novels on marble tablets, Victorians would have fought each other to buy. More than any other novelist Dickens had a choice. This was a privilege of his pre-eminence. And for 35 years, his choice was curiously repetitive and apparently unimaginative. No other first-rank novelist of the mid-nineteenth century was as faithful to one mode of publication as Dickens. Where they weren't forced into change or new fashion, they sought it; often as middle-aged people do, to escape their own sense of impending superannuation. Why didn't Dickens? Why was a man otherwise so restless in literary and personal matters so automatic in his publishing practice?

I'll leave these prefatory questions hanging. The central part of this essay will be a survey of the rise and fall of the novel in monthly numbers.

ORIGINS

The innovation of the Dickensian novel in numbers in April 1836 is wonderfully sudden. The *Pickwick Papers* emerged, fully formed, apparently from nowhere. Chapman & Hall (perhaps prodded by Robert Seymour, perhaps inspired by Jorrocks) had the idea in February. By the last day of March, the first serial part was on the bookstands. After a little tinkering with length and number of illustrations, by midsummer *Pickwick* had found the form that was to remain standard for the next 35 years.

Conventionally, the genesis of *Pickwick* has been seen as a kind of book-trade miracle, 'phenomenon' or, as Robert Patten puts it, an 'accident'.[2] But one can demystify its birth a little by uncovering precedents and possible inspirations. There was, of course, nothing new about the part issue of books. The practice (particularly with non-fiction and less than new works) goes back to the seventeeth century. Dickens himself remembered from his boyhood, 'certain interminable novels in [serial] form which used . . . to be carried about the country by pedlars'.[3] And there was a more chic nineteenth-century precursor in Pierce Egan's *Life in London* (see Plate 1). Carrying 36 illustrations by Robert, Isaac and George Cruikshank, this 'Original Work' came out in 12, 32-page monthly numbers, costing three shillings each, October 1820–July 1821 (published by Sherwood, Neeley and Jones). Egan's ramble through the metropolis was a hit with the reading public. But its form of issue doesn't seem to have been much imitated in its own day, and the revival by Chapman & Hall of *Life in London*'s style of serialisation after 15 years of disuse is surprising.

There were other possible precursors which merit a little digression. Harriet Martineau's *Illustrations of Political Economy* had appeared, 1832–4, in 25 numbers. The *Illustrations* were essentially 25 improving tracts (around 125 small octavo pages each) bundled into a series, rather than a serial novel. But there are interesting connections with *Pickwick*. Having failed to interest the SDUK and other publishers in the venture, Martineau was prevailed on by Charles Fox to coat her two dozen instructive pills with fiction and to issue them monthly (in which form they cost one shilling and sixpence). 1,000 was the maximum sale hoped for. In fact, ten times that number were snapped up.

In Martineau's case, monthly serialisation originated in the desire to spread purchasing cost, and to ease the effort of reading for readers of a distinctly lower class than the author. The *Illustrations* breathe a condescension typical of Victorian philanthropy doing its duty to the poor. The essence of the Dickensian novel in numbers is quite different. It addresses the reader in a spirit of manly equality; a sentiment confirmed in the author's habitual prefatory addresses to his reader.

With their *Pickwick* innovation of April 1836, it is more likely that the partners were inspired by the recent striking use which John Macrone had made of George Cruikshank in collaboration with Harrison Ainsworth and later 'Boz'.[4] This teaming must have revived recollections of Cruikshank's earlier liaison with Egan. There is also an interesting connection to be found with the ubiquitous publishing rogue, Henry Colburn. In late 1835–early

1836, the Prince of Puffers was down on his luck. His disastrous break up with Bentley in 1833 left him short of both capital and literary property. To raise cash, he ingeniously worked the copyrights which remained his (principally those of Bulwer-Lytton). In January 1836, Colburn was offering *Pelham* and *The Disowned* for sale in six, one-shilling, weekly parts. (Effectively, these were Standard Novels, broken up and paper wrapped for faster sale, and to expand the look of Colburn's list.) In the same month, the first instalment of Marryat's *Frank Mildmay* was also on offer in what was grandly called 'The Novelist's Library'.

Colburn's wheeze created some stir in the book trade, at the exact period when Chapman & Hall were sorting out their problems with Dickens and Seymour as how best to proceed with *Pickwick*. The *Literary Gazette*, for instance, called the Novelist's Library: 'A truly popular undertaking. The series so got up and embellished, and so cheap, must extend the fame even of the Author of *Pelham*'.[5] (This was four months before the publication of *Pickwick*.) In 14 May 1836, in allusion to Colburn, the *Athenaeum* wrote: 'It is a new feature of the literary character of the age, that publishers can find a remunerating sale when they offer works of imagination and established character in shilling numbers.' (At this period. although the *Athenaeum* was apparently unaware of its existence, *Pickwick* was languishing in an extremely unremunerative condition.)

Colburn's bright idea was latched on to by his competitors. In March 1836, Baldwin & Cradock brought out a 'fourth edition' of *Traits and Stories of The Irish Peasantry* by William Carleton, in 25 one-shilling parts, at fortnightly intervals (the work was ultimately designed to be bound up in five volumes). In February 1836, Saunders & Otley issued Bulwer-Lytton's *Pilgrims of the Rhine* in half-crown monthly parts, illustrated by Maclise, among others. This work is harshly dismissed by Michael Sadleir as 'fondant fiction at its worst'. But it was newish if not brand new fiction (the work was first published in 1834), and it was part issued.

None of these can claim unchallenged precedence over *Pickwick Papers*. But they conform that the idea of novels in numbers, illustrated and costing one shilling a part was in the air in April 1836.

THE POST-*PICKWICK* FRENZY

After its deadly slow start (sinking as low as 400 monthly sales) *Pickwick* took off meteorically, soaring past Martineau's mark to some 40,000 a number. And with hindsight one can plausibly reconstruct why the serial succeeded as it did in drumming up what was effectively a whole new reading public. The devastating slump of the early 1830s had stripped out the English bookselling network, particularly its softest sectors, the outlying distribution and retailing agencies. The novel in numbers, by using the railroad routes opened (by W. H. Smith notably) for newspapers and magazines enjoyed countrywide distribution. In numbers, the novel could sell independently of the bookshops like the newspaper, at a time when newspapers were becoming a national medium. This extension of supply across England is evident if one looks at the self-advertising in, for instance, the second number of the Mayhews' *The Greatest Plague of Life* (February 1847). The advertiser carries eulogies on the current serial from: the Bedford *Mercury*, the Berkshire *Chronicle*, the Brighton *Herald*, the Bristol *Gazette*, the Cheltenham *Examiner*, the Hull *Advertiser*, the Leeds *Intelligencer*, the Liverpool *Mail*, the Macclesfield *Chronicle*, the Nottingham *Journal*, the Northampton *Mercury*, the Plymouth *Herald*, the Somerset County *Gazette*, the Bath *Chronicle*, the Kent *Herald* and the Sheffield *Iris*.

It would have been difficult to get three-volume editions of the new novel into the bookshops and circulating libraries of all these provincial towns. And to have supplied reorders while the demand whipped up by good notices was still warm would have been frankly impossible. How to cater adequately from London for the reader in Macclesfield or Sheffield is, it may be noted, a problem which the British booktrade has still not satisfactorily solved.

Dickens followed *Pickwick* with *Oliver Twist* in *Bentley's Miscellany* and in 1839 produced *Nicholas Nickleby*, whose sales soared to 50,000 a monthly part.[6] These figures were unprecedented. Never too proud to share in somebody else's good thing, the British book trade was quick to jump on the Dickens bandwagon. Charles Lever, for instance, whose *Harry Lorrequer* had been quite serenely and haphazardly running in the *Dublin University Magazine* since February 1837 had the work reissued by his publisher (Curry) in 11 monthly parts, with illustrations by Phiz, a bright idea which was fatally damaging to what little structure the narrative possesses. Ainsworth's *Jack Sheppard*, running in *Bentley's Miscellany* from

January 1839, was simultaneously issued in weekly parts: an experiment in tandem publication that does not seem to have suited anyone.

There being no copyright in ideas (or much else in the 1830s), there was a rather desperate attempt to crack the formula and identify the active ingredients in Boz's appeal. The result over the period 1839–40 was a shambling parade of novels in numbers, most marked by some particular emphasis which was hoped to be the key to Dickensian success. Mrs Trollope and Colburn, for instance, thought the Boz secret to be the display of social conscience in fiction. Although neither had any love of numbers (women, incidentally, used the form very seldom) they together concocted a topical bleeding heart tale for monthly issue: *Michael Armstrong, the Factory Boy* (1839–40). This homage to *Oliver Twist* was promptly answered in numbers by Frederic Montagu's *Mrs Trollope Refuted: Mary Ashley or Facts Upon Factories* (published by a Manchester bookseller, the work was planned in ten monthly parts from August 1839, but collapsed after its second instalment). Frederick Marryat also played the *Oliver Twist* card in his *Poor Jack* (1840). This tale of Jack Saunders, a Thameside waif was published by another unlikely firm, Longman. They were clearly uncomfortable with the vulgar associations of monthly serialisation and produced a cover (and internal illustrations by Clarkson Stanfield) of remarkable stuffiness (see Plate 2). Even less likely a Dickensian-style serialist than Marryat was the historical romancer, G. P. R. James. He brought out his sole experiment in the form with *The Commissioner* (1841–2), published racily enough (but without any great success) by Lever's Irish publisher, William Curry with Lever's normal illustrator, Phiz (see Plate 3).

Other would-be Dickenses assumed that the spluttering consonantal alliteration in the titles of *Pickwick Papers* and *Nicholas Nickleby* were the easy way to public favour. So, in March 1839, the consumer could have chosen among: *Valentine Vox, the Ventriloquist; Will's Whim, Consisting of Characteristic Curiosities; Charley Chalk; David Dreamy* (illustrated by 'Peter Pallette') and *Paul Periwinkle or the Pressgang*.

This last was illustrated by Phiz (i.e. Hablôt K. Browne). Phiz himself was thought by many to hold the secret and he was showered with more commissions than he could conscientiously fulfil. He, like Boz, had the sincere flattery of imitation in such serials as *Heads of the People* (1838–9), where J. Kenny Meadows pseudonymised himself as 'Quizzfizzz'. ('Heads' serials – of characters in *Nicholas Nickleby*, for example – were an established line of trade at this period, and witness to a pervasive desire to visualise popular fiction. As J. R. Harvey has surmised, the ravenous appetite for visual stimulation probably explains at least part of the mania fuelling novels in numbers in the late 1830s.[7] Meadows's serial, published by Tyas, was the most popular work he ever produced.)

A main interest in the cascade of 1839–40 serials and their clumsy attempts to reconstitute Dickens's recipe is the unconscious evidence they supply on how the contemporary book trade construed the Boz phenomenon. Take, for instance, the barrage of pseudo-Dickensian elements in the following offering: *The Rector's Progress, or the Veritable amusing and interesting history of the Family Connexions, characters, doings and delinquencies of Dr Daniel Tithegripe, by Clericus*. (The tale was illustrated by the ubiquitous Phiz, and issued from 1 November 1839 by the obscure publishers Grattan & Gilbert. How many instalments it achieved before expiring I don't know.) Still others, such as G. W. M. Reynolds with *Pickwick Abroad* (1838–9, published by Sherwood, illustrated by A. Crowquill) banked on unvarnished plagiarism to suborn the Dickens public. Probably, he succeeded better than most.

Altogether, in 1839–40, the addict could have spent 15 shillings to a pound a month on novels in parts. This was far more than the market could bear. More so as the publishers of most of these serials embarked with unrealistically high hopes. The prospective advertisers of *Effingham Hazard* (1839) were informed by the publisher (Edward Ravenscroft) that the serial was 'an entirely original Work the same size as *Nicholas Nickleby* and similarly illustrated [and] A Circulation of 20,000 is guaranteed for the first part'. In fact, it sank without trace. For Marryat's *Poor Jack*, Longman's demanded 10,000 bills from prospective advertisers. What it sold I don't know. But the serial run was cut back from an announced 20 to 12. And Longman took care not to publish Marryat in this form again. The author's next foray into the novel in numbers (in 1847, with Hurst) didn't make it past the first instalment.

Alas, soundalike names and lookalike plots were easier to simulate than Boz and Phiz's sales figures. Most of the imitative serials slumped badly and a number went bust. *Paul Periwinkle*, for instance, fell into the hands of the ruthless remainderer, Tegg, after its fifth number and the insolvency of its original publisher. *The*

Comic Novel, or Downing Street in the Days of Victoria by 'Lynx'
(published by Bailliere, 'with illustrations in many styles') was
promised in 20 monthly parts, but collapsed after four in May 1840.
Will's Whim collapsed after three.

It was not entirely a lottery in which Dickens alone held the
winning tickets. Cockton's *Valentine Vox* (published by H. Lea,
illustrated by T. Onwhyn) prospered and made its author
temporarily a rich man. But he promptly lost his windfall
speculating in the East Anglian barley trade. His subsequent five
exercises in serialised fiction were as ill-fated as his business
speculations.

DEPARTURES FROM THE DICKENSIAN NORM (1): *PUNCH*

After the free-for-all of 1839–40 (resembling nothing so much as the
contemporary railway manias), the business of novels in numbers
was prosecuted with more sobriety. The smaller publishers learned
the hard way that (for the middle-class, shilling-paying public, at
least) this kind of serialisation was a rich man's game. For success it
required an expensive 'name' author working in liaison with an
expensive 'name' illustrator; lavish advertising; heavy and
awkwardly recurrent production costs (up to £600 a month for a
Dickens serial); and efficient kingdom-wide agency and co-
publishing relations.[8] Most publishers of new fiction were safer
staying with the three-decker with its low capital cost and direct,
secured line of supply to the library. As a regular thing, the novel in
numbers was left as the near-exclusive preserve of the new giants of
the trade, Bradbury & Evans and Chapman & Hall.

Originally partners (Bradbury & Evans were Chapman & Hall's
printers for *Pickwick*), by the mid-1840s the two firms had become
rivals. In a sense, Bradbury & Evans had greatness thrust upon
them when Dickens defected from Chapman & Hall in 1846, on the
grounds that: 'A printer is better than a bookseller'.[9] By 'better' he
meant 'more ductile'. But as printers (very reluctantly) turned
publishers, Bradbury & Evans had other valuable qualifications.
They were particularly expert in illustration, pioneering among
other things colour reproduction of plates in England. As a firm
based in Fleet Street, they suffered none of Paternoster Row's
traditional inhibitions about dabbling with newspapers. Thus, in

1842 Bradbury & Evans acquired *Punch*. Under the convivial management of Mark Lemon this weekly paper had made itself by 1846 a national institution, the official comic organ of the English middle classes.

For Dickens (who evidently disliked *Punch*'s 'eternal guffaw'), Bradbury & Evans retained the form of serial issue devised in 1836 by Chapman & Hall. But for the gifted coterie of writers and illustrators from their *Punch* stable, they allowed a significantly modified style of part issue to evolve. Its characteristics were an easy ironic address, a loose-knit essayistic format, a central stress on illustration in the currently modish pictorial style (including colour plates) and plentiful use of the incidental woodcuts *Punch* specialised in. (Dickensian serialisation rationed itself to two full-plate etchings, placed separately at the head of the text as a detachable unit.)

The first serial in shilling monthly numbers published 'at the *Punch* Office, 65 Fleet Street'[10] was the *Table Book*, edited by G. A. A'Beckett. This work was published in 12 monthly parts, January–December 1845, with 12 steel etchings and 116 woodcuts, all by George Cruikshank. It was followed by Cruikshank's *Our Own Times*. This monthly serial began on 1 April 1846, but petered out in July after four numbers. Why is not clear, but since Cruikshank transferred his (highly profitable) business to Bogue at this time he probably fell out with Bradbury & Evans as he usually fell out with everyone eventually. *Our Own Times* was followed on 1 July by Gilbert A'Beckett's Macaulayan spoof, *The Comic History of England* which had better fortunes. Advertisements promised that this serial would run 'from twelve to twenty' one-shilling monthly parts. Each part contained one large coloured etching and up to a dozen interspersed woodcuts by John Leech. The trade were informed that the *Comic History* 'will appear regularly with the monthly magazines' and copies were presumably bundled up on magazine day (the last of the month) with *Douglas Jerrold's Shilling Magazine* and the two-shilling parts of *Punch*.

A'Beckett's serial evidently caught on. In October 1847, it was announced that it would, after all, run to the maximum 20 numbers. The *Comic History* also served as pilot for another *Punch* writer's 'Pen and Pencil Sketches of English Society'. This story later retitled itself as 'Novel without a Hero', and finally emerged as *Vanity Fair*. Thackeray's great work began publication inauspiciously in January 1847, having been held back a year. The number to which it was to run was not initially specified by Bradbury & Evans, either in the contract or the advertisement. And, as is legendary, *Vanity Fair* did not immediately succeed with the reading public. There was a serious danger that it might terminate after particularly disappointing sales for the third instalment in March 1847, and as late as the fourteenth, Bradbury & Evans were advertising the work as running to 'eighteen or twenty numbers'.[11]

A number of reasons can be advanced for the precarious start of *Vanity Fair*. Thackeray (who had written for ten years under a pseudonym) was unknown. The opening chapters of the work (which was originally intended for another publisher) were probably something of a surprise for the *Punch* subscribers. Thackeray was technically inferior to Leech, currently the fashionable serial illustrator. There was a sharp trade depression in early 1847 which hit all periodical publications hard.

But the most plausible explanation for *Vanity Fair*'s initial inability to catch on was the state of the market. Despite being considerably thinned from five years earlier, it was still overcrowded with monthly serials. In January 1847, for example, the bookstands carried the thirteenth number of Lever's *Knight of Gwynne* (Plate 4). This was Chapman & Hall's lead title. Heavily advertised and illustrated by Phiz it was devised to fill the gap left by Dickens. There was intramural competition from the seventh number of A'Beckett's *Comic History* with its attractive Leech designs. Leech also illustrated Albert Smith's *The Struggles and Adventures of Christopher Tadpole* (see Plate 5). In January this was in its fifth number out of a promised 12. But Bentley was pleased with the work (which had a definite *Punch*ified air to it), and persuaded the author (who was as new to serialisation as Thackeray) to extend to 16 numbers. At a somewhat lower level a new series of Reynolds's *Mysteries of London* in monthly sixpenny parts had begun another of its interminable issues in September 1846 (published by G. Vickers). G. Herbert Rodwell's *Woman's Love* had opened in monthly parts on 1 February 1846, illustrated by Alfred Crowquill. According to its publisher's (W. R. Sams) schedule it should have been in its last double number in January 1847. *Rowland Bradshaw, or the Way to Fame* ('by the author of Raby Rattler', published by Sherwood, Gilbert and Piper) began on 1 November 1846, illustrated (unmemorably) by S. P. Fletcher. A month later, on 1 December 1846 there was launched *The Miser's Will*, by Percy B. St John, promised by its publisher (Hurst) in 20 monthly one-shilling numbers. And in mid-January 1847 there was announced *The Greatest Plague of Life*, in six numbers, illustrated by George Cruikshank (see Plate 6). Subtitled 'The adventures of Lady in search of a good servant' this was another *Punch*-inspired venture (authored by the brothers Mayhew and published by Bogue), drawing on the paper's standing jokes about 'servantgalism'.

A field of half-a-dozen strong runners and as many stragglers was bound to produce also-rans. *Woman's Love* ended up in 1847 the property of another publisher, and almost certainly did not get through its monthly run. St John's *The Miser's Will* immediately dropped out of sight, reappearing as a serial in the *Mirror*, in January 1848. It too seems unlikely to have made it beyond a couple of numbers. *The Greatest Plague of Life* was held back two months, until March (although dated February). *The Knight of Gwynne* had slumped disastrously and was proving a loss to Chapman & Hall by January 1847. They none the less kept it going (although Lever's reputation was irreparably damaged). Hurst, publisher of Marryat's *The Children of the New Forest* had no such compunctions. The first monthly issue appeared in April 1847 and was promptly killed. (The work appeared in complete volume form in October 1847. In the long run it went on to be Marryat's most reprinted work.)

Amid this carnage *Dombey* was enjoying the usual Dickens triumph. And trailing by five months, Thackeray had ground to make up, if he was not to close down or limp ingloriously to a dozen or less instalments. But, famously, *Vanity Fair* came from behind to contest (as Thackeray fondly thought) the leadership with Dickens. *Vanity Fair* was also a triumph for the *Punch* enclave with Bradbury & Evans. They followed up with an immediate contract for *Pendennis*, which hiked Thackeray's monthly stipend from £60 to £100. A major departure was the extension of the run, during the novel's publication, to 24 numbers. It would seem that although Thackeray's appeal was not massive (just over 9,000 copies of *Pendennis* were sold in parts and first book edition), he none the less had an extraordinarily faithful public, who would stick with him forever, apparently.

The *Punch* office put out another successful, but much less ambitious novel in numbers at this period. In October 1848 there appeared the first number of a monthly serial by Douglas Jerrold, *A Man Made of Money* (see Plate 7). The work (handsomely illustrated by Leech) ran to six parts, until March 1849, by which time it was completely overshadowed by the early numbers of *Pendennis*. The story remains Jerrold's best effort in fiction (which was never, of course, his first interest in writing).[12]

After *Pendennis*, Thackeray broke with *Punch*, rarely contributing again to the paper. He also broke with Bradbury & Evans, transferring his services to George Smith, for *Henry Esmond* (three volumes, 1852). But Thackeray had helped find a successor to himself before leaving his friends in Bouverie Street. In May 1849, Robert Smith Surtees had approached him to illustrate the reissue of *Mr Sponge's Sporting Tour*, then running as a serial in Ainsworth's *New Monthly Magazine*. The suggestion was highly presumptuous. Surtees was at this stage far from famous, and Thackeray was now the second greatest author in England. More to the point, as he tactfully pointed out, Thackeray was incapable of drawing horses. He courteously referred Surtees to his *Punch* confrère Leech, who *could* draw horses; none better. Leech was very enthusiastic about Mr Sponge, and in turn suggested Bradbury & Evans as publishers for the novel in volume form. Evans on his part liked the work. And he eventually suggested that it might be reissued in a dozen monthly numbers, with coloured plates and woodcuts by Leech. In this form, he was 'sure we shall have a hit'.[13] So, in 1852, they did. And the partnership between Leech and Surtees went on to become one of the glories of the mid-Victorian serial novel (see Plate 8).

Thackeray came back to his 'old friends' with *The Newcomes* (1853–5). Although he no longer wrote for the magazine, a definite *Punch* link was formed by recruiting Richard Doyle as his assistant illustrator. *The Newcomes* was followed by *The Virginians* (1857–9) which (to their cost) Bradbury & Evans also serialised in the now standard 24 numbers. The venture was a costly failure, and Thackeray recoiled to George Smith again. Thereafter, Bradbury & Evans largely restricted their interest in fiction to Dickens (whom they had until the mid-1860s) and to their lavishly illustrated magazine *Once a Week*. But on losing Dickens, they tried a novel in numbers with another *Punch* stalwart, Shirley Brooks. *Sooner or Later*, ran for 14 monthly issues from November 1866. The work was not much of a hit, but it remains attractive for its 17 fine illustrations by George Du Maurier.

The *Punch* variant on the novel in numbers has various achievements to its credit. It loosened up the tight authorial dominance of the Dickensian style, allowing a free interchange between pen and pencil. Its form was more elastic, moving easily from six to 24 numbers. Like everything to do with the magazine, the *Punch*ified novel in numbers was democratic, good natured, and tolerantly ironic of the foibles of life. More significantly, it introduced a far wider range of unfettered pictorial talent into the genre than Dickens would ever have permitted.

DEPARTURES FROM THE DICKENSIAN NORM (2): CRUIKSHANK

George Cruikshank's influence is everywhere encountered in the origins and progress of the Victorian part-issued novel. As a junior illustrator on *Life in London*, he embodied a direct link with *Pickwick*'s closest ancestor. And in so far as the novel in numbers meant a new liaison between narrative and pictorial art, Cruikshank was scarcely less important than Dickens in its development.

Cruikshank's first extended work with English fiction was as illustrator for the eighteenth-century texts in Roscoe's 'Novelist's Library', 1831–3. The Library was published by James Cochrane, who later went into partnership with the brilliant but ill-fated John Macrone. After the partnership broke up in 1834, Macrone had the inspiration to use Cruikshank to embellish the fiction of a living novelist. The resulting illustrated fourth edition of *Rookwood* (whose copyright Macrone had acquired from Bentley) was a brilliant success. Momentously, Macrone also teamed Cruikshank with the young Dickens for the first series of *Sketches by Boz* (1836). And in November 1836, Macrone planned a monthly serial in one-shilling numbers, *The Lions of London*: the text to be provided by Ainsworth, the illustrations by Leech and Cruikshank.[14]

Macrone's chronic financial crisis sank *The Lions of London* venture (although Cruikshank's title-page survives). Cruikshank was promptly snapped up by the better-heeled Bentley to illustrate *Oliver Twist*, which began its run with the *Miscellany* in January 1837. This was followed in the magazine by *Jack Sheppard*, in which Cruikshank was again partnered with Ainsworth, this time on a new novel. Ainsworth's Newgate romance was sensationally popular, and Bentley published a concurrent issue in numbers. And this in turn was successful enough to warrant a new, and lavishly produced independent, work in numbers, *The Tower of London* (1840).

The Tower of London was the most luxurious novel in numbers yet produced. It was beautifully printed (Bentley's speciality). It carried three full-plate designs on steel in each instalment, and a total of 58 topographic woodcuts. In fact, the work is so heavily illustrated that Ainsworth's story has trouble trickling through Cruikshank's pictorial undergrowth. But the venture was much to the public taste. Bentley paid Ainsworth handsomely (£2,000?), and the work was launched with a party at which all the literary luminaries of London attended.

As an illustrator, Cruikshank had the advantage of his pre-eminent name and reputation. But he did not come cheap. Whereas illustrators like Phiz or Leech made do with as little as £6 per etching, Cruikshank demanded a share commensurate with his name. Thus, for *The Tower of London*, he was paid as an equal partner in the profits with Ainsworth and Bentley (an agreement which yielded him £517).[15]

In addition to a fair share of the revenue, Cruikshank also demanded an equal hand in composition. His egalitarian method of working with Ainsworth is recorded by the author: 'I used to spend a day with the artist at the beginning of the month in the Tower itself; and since every facility was afforded to us by the authorities, we left no part of the old fortress unexplored.'[16] Notoriously, in old age, Cruikshank exaggerated his contributions (unusual as they were) claiming, for instance, that 'The original idea of [*The Tower of London*] was suggested by me . . . in this work Mr Ainsworth and I were *partners*, holding equal shares'.[17] Cruikshank's claim to have invented Ainsworth's novels (and *Oliver Twist* to boot) was stoutly denied. But undeniable was the aesthetic dominance of his illustrations. As Thackeray put it (in his *Essay on the Genius of George Cruikshank*, 1840), think of Ainsworth's fiction, and what do you remember? 'George Cruikshank's pictures, always George Cruikshank's pictures'.[18] A writer as strong minded as Dickens simply could not pull in harness with Cruikshank over a long period. And it is a tribute to Ainsworth, that he managed to wring so much good work out of the artist in their tempestuous collaboration on six novels (most of them published in the novelist's *Ainsworth's Magazine*).

During his intermittent spats and after his final break with Ainsworth (in 1844) Cruikshank devoted himself to his *Omnibus* and *Comic Almanacks*, published in monthly serial form by David Bogue (successor to Tilt and Bogue). And it was Bogue who also published a dried-out Cruikshank's Hogarthian serial, *The Bottle* (1847) and *The Drunkard's Children* (1848). Everything with Cruikshank's name on it was popular, particularly *The Bottle* which on publication sold 100,000 copies at a shilling for the eight-picture set.

With this kind of tribute to his independent genius, Cruikshank may well have felt collaboration with mere novelists unnecessary. None the less, he made a number of subsequent, highly characteristic contributions to novels in numbers. Of these, his longest relationship was with the Mayhew brothers, Augustus and Henry. With them he brought out *The Greatest Plague of Life* (published by Bogue, 1847). The six-part work is a *Punch*ian burlesque, supposedly written by a lady at her wit's end, on the difficulties of finding a good servant. The cover design is remarkable for the prominence given to Cruikshank's name, and the invisibility of the authors of the 48 pages of text contained therein (see Plate 6).

This initial venture was followed by the similarly conceived *Whom to Marry and How to get Married* (Bogue, six parts, 1847-8). The finest fruit of the collaboration, however, was *The World's Show: 1851, or, The Adventures of Mr and Mrs Sandboys and family, who came up to London to 'enjoy themselves' and to see the Great Exhibition* (Bogue, eight parts, February–October 1851) (see Plate 9). No less than Dickens, Cruikshank was excited by a crowd. And the milling hordes of tourists in London in the Exhibition festive year fairly set his imagination ablaze. For Mayhew's mild comedy he supplied a series of double-paged panoramic illustrations, culminating in 'All the World Going to See the Great Exhibition of 1851'. Reaching for the modern term 'logo', the *Athenaeum* (8 February 1851) called this picture 'The sign of the show . . . the popular record to be painted on crockery and printed on calico'. Although Henry Mayhew now gets a small billing on the cover, the work clearly demonstrates Cruikshank's autocratic habit of reducing his fellow writer to a mere provider of letterpress for his designs.[19]

For Bogue, Cruikshank also illustrated Angus Reach's promising *Clement Lorimer, or the Book with Iron Clasps* (six parts, 1848-9). Possibly he might have done more with Reach had the unlucky young author lived longer. More probably, he would have crushed him into a poor second place, as he did the Mayhews. Otherwise, Cruikshank did a handful of other novels in numbers, apparently as random acts of personal friendship or to pick up a little easy income. Least interesting are the plates (shared with his brother) for the 12 monthly parts of M. H. Barker's ultra-nautical *The Old Sailor's Jolly*

Boat Laden with Tales, Yarns, Scraps, Fragments, etc. (published by W. Strange, 1843). Even less successful was Cruikshank's collaboration with another sailor, Francis Higginson RN's *The Brighton Lodging House* (published by J. How). This monthly serial lapsed in 1849 after only two numbers.

More substantial was Cruikshank's collaboration with Frank Smedley. The two were brought together professionally on *Sharpe's Magazine*, which Smedley edited and where the early (and by far the best) chapters of his tale, *Frank Fairlegh,* were published. The story, as expanded, was very popular. And since its school and college chapters chimed nicely with *Pendennis* and *Copperfield,* Hall & Virtue (publishers of *Sharpe's Magazine*) brought out an issue in 15 numbers from January 1849 (see Plate 10). The publisher specialised in illustrated books, and their treatment of Smedley's text was barbarous. The pre-existing volume edition was simply chopped into 32-page sections, the first six numbers breaking halfway between sentences. But the work was none the less a bestseller, largely due to Cruikshank's vigorous illustrations. His name alone appears on the cover. On the strength of Cruikshank's contribution, *Frank Fairlegh* went on to become one of the most reprinted of Victorian illustrated novels. Future collaboration seemed likely when the two men at last met and evidently hit it off. Smedly took up the post of editor on *George Cruikshank's Magazine* in January 1854. But the venture only last two issues. Smedley's subsequent two novels in numbers were illustrated by Phiz, and failed lamentably.

These novelists (the Mayhews, Reach, Smedley, Barker) have one thing in common. They are unredeemably second rate. As Dickens's artistic sovereignty seems to have led him to select the less than best illustrator for his serials, so Cruikshank's *amour propre* seems to have led him to work with (not for) writers far inferior to himself in ability. Dickens progressively suppressed his illustrators (as evident from the billing Phiz received over 25 years). In the same spirit, Cruikshank actually obliterated his collaborators from the title page. One of the great might-have-beens of Victorian fiction is what would have happened, had these two majestic egos been able to continue the relationship so profitably begun in 1836.

No. I.

OF

AN ORIGINAL WORK,

ENTITLED

Life in London;

OR, THE

DAY AND NIGHT SCENES

OF

JERRY HAWTHORN, ESQ.

AND HIS ELEGANT FRIEND,

CORINTHIAN TOM,

IN

Their Rambles and Sprees

THROUGH THE

METROPOLIS.

BY PIERCE EGAN,

Author of "a Sporting Anecdotes," &c.

London:

PRINTED FOR SHERWOOD, NEELY, AND JONES,

PATERNOSTER-ROW.

Price 3s.

1 The wrapper of the opening number of *Life in London* (October 1820).

POOR JACK.

BY

CAPTAIN MARRYAT, C.B.

WITH

ILLUSTRATIONS

BY CLARKSON STANFIELD, R.A.

LONDON:

LONGMAN, ORME, BROWN, GREEN, AND LONGMANS,

PATERNOSTER-ROW.

1840.

2 Longman's conservative cover for the part-issue of *Poor Jack* (January 1840).

4. The last double number of *The Knight of Gwynne* (July

3. Cruy's cover design for the part issue of G.D.R.

6 The cover design for *The Greatest Plague of Life* (February 1847). Notice that the authors' names (Henry and Augustus Mayhew) have been suppressed in order to highlight Cruikshank's.

5 Leech's cover for *Christopher Tadpole* (September 1846). Bentley chose an unusual printer (Schulze). Presumably he was expert in reproducing illustrations.

Cruikshank's cover for *1851* (February 1851).

11. The first number of the illustrated *The Gordian Knot*

10. The first number of *Frank Fairlegh* (January 1849)

LONDON: CHAPMAN AND HALL, 193, PICCADILLY.

MENZIES, EDINBURGH; MURRAY & SON, GLASGOW; McGLASHAN & GILL, DUBLIN.

The right of Translation is reserved.

12 The last double number of Lever's last novel in numbers (February 1865).

LONDON: CHAPMAN & HALL, PICCADILLY.

13 Luard's crude design was used prominently in the advertising campaign for *The Headless Horseman* (1865–6).

PART I.   APRIL.   ONE SHILLING.

SUNRISE

A Story of These Times

by

WILLIAM BLACK

Author of "A Daughter of Heth"
&c. &c.

LONDON

SAMPSON LOW · MARSTON · SEARLE · & · RIVINGTON

1880

DICKENS TRIUMPHANT

In the late 1850s and 1860s there emerged a new generation of publishers (George Bentley, John Maxwell, William Tinsley, Hurst and Blackett) and novelists (Meredith, Reade, Collins, Ouida, Braddon) for whom serialisation in monthly numbers was as antediluvian as the powdered wig or the buckled shoe. Generally speaking it remained a viable option only for a nucleus of male authors born in the same decade as Dickens and swept along, willy-nilly, in the turbulence of his success. From these sub-Dickensian authors' attempts at fiction in numbers one can assemble an impressive catalogue of 1850s failure. One of the more spectacular was Shirley Brooks's *The Gordian Knot* (published by Bentley, illustrated by Tenniel). This serial began in January 1858, suspended publication for almost a year, and limped to an ignominious conclusion in December 1859 (see Plate 11). Ainsworth's *Mervyn Clitheroe* (published by Chapman & Hall, illustrated by Phiz) collapsed after four numbers out of a scheduled 20, in March 1852. (Extraordinarily, the serial was completed in 12 numbers by Routledge, 1857–8.) Lever, who published more novels in numbers than any of his contemporaries (16), finally gave the form up in 1865 as a non-paying proposition with *Luttrell of Arran* (published by Chapman & Hall, illustrated by Phiz) (see Plate 12). Thackeray dropped out in 1859 with *The Virginians* (published by Bradbury & Evans, illustrated by the author), a serial on which the publishers made a loss of over £3,000. Bradbury & Evans also lost heavily on Surtees's and Leech's *Handley Cross* which finished an interrupted run of 17 numbers in October 1854.

It was not so much the case that occasional success could not be achieved by the novel in numbers, but that this success could not be consistently maintained. Thus Frank Smedley had a huge hit in 1849–50 with *Frank Fairlegh* (published by Hall & Virtue, illustrated by Cruikshank). But its successors *Lewis Arundel* (1850–2) and *Harry Coverdale's Courtship* (1854–6) flopped. Captain Mayne Reid seemed to have found a winning new formula with *The Headless Horseman* (published by Chapman & Hall, illustrated by L. Huard) in March 1865. This novel came out in sixpenny as opposed to shilling numbers and, aided by a high-pressure advertising campaign, became a famous bestseller (see Plate 13). But when Trollope latched on to the sixpenny instalment with *The Last Chronicle of Barset* (published by Smith Elder, illustrated by G. H. Thomas) 'the enterprise was not altogether successful'.[20] And when Trollope induced James Virtue to repeat the sixpenny experiment in 1868–9 with *He Knew He Was Right* (published by Virtue, illustrated by M. Stone), the publisher promptly slid into insolvency.

Logically the mid-1860s should have seen the end of the novel in numbers. It was an idea whose time had gone. The form had served a valuable transitional function in mobilising a nation-wide reading public before the full evolution of the fiction-carrying periodical. But now its natural span was over. There was nothing it could do that the novel in magazines could not do better and cheaper.

Dickens must have read the signs as clearly as anyone. After *Little Dorrit* finished in July 1857 he turned his novelistic energy to setting up *All the Year Round*. *A Tale of Two Cities* boosted the early numbers of that twopenny journal to unprecedented figures of 100,000 or more. But a concurrent issue of the novel in eight monthly numbers (by Chapman & Hall) slumped disappointingly, finishing on a mere 5,000 sales a month – disgraceful by Dickens's standards. His next novel, *Great Expectations*, was his first full-length novel for 20 years not to be published in monthly numbers. It was run through *All the Year Round* and reprinted as a hugely successful three-decker. (This was the sequence pioneered by Dickens's most gifted protegé, Wilkie Collins.)

Then, for mysterious reasons, Dickens chose to ignore the clear signs of the times. He wrote to Frederic Chapman proposing 'a new work in twenty monthly numbers, as of old'.[21] It is quite clear that Dickens made the necessary publishing decision about what was to be *Our Mutual Friend*'s form of issue. And equally clear that it was in the circumstances a somewhat obstinate decision to have made.

Dickens's exercise in nostalgia justified itself. Although it sold around 5,000 copies less a month than *Little Dorrit*, *Our Mutual Friend* was highly profitable for all parties. And five years later, *The Mystery of Edwin Drood* (scheduled for a curtailed 12-issue run) notched up record sales, stimulated for the first three numbers by the excitement of a new Dickens novel, and for the next three by the morbid attraction of the work now being posthumous; Dickens writing from the grave. And the last three numbers of *Edwin Drood* find Dickens eerily by himself in the field. After the ignominious petering out of Trollope's *The Vicar of Bullhampton* in May 1870,[22] there was no further competition in monthly numbers. The mêlée of 1839–40 had finally dwindled to one victorious survivor.

AFTER THE END

As a memorial to Dickens, the novel in numbers enjoyed an odd afterlife. Despite her nervousness about serialisation, George Eliot allowed *Middlemarch* to be published in parts from December 1871 to December 1872. The form she, Lewes and John Blackwood chose was strategically modified from the Dickensian norm. The novel was issued as eight five-shilling 'books', appearing at first bi-monthly, then monthly. Each book was the equivalent of four Dickensian numbers, but unillustrated. Something under 6,000 copies were sold in this form; a figure which was respectable but nothing wonderful. And at a 40% author's royalty, there was not much profit for Blackwoods. Nevertheless *Daniel Deronda* was published on the same pattern and with much the same initial sales, January–September 1876. Apart from these two experiments (together with a half-hearted stab by Trollope with *The Prime Minister*), there was no general interest in the novel in oversize numbers. It yielded too little for the publisher. When they made their stocktaking in 1879, Blackwood's reckoned Eliot's copyrights to be valueless to them, the novels having cost so much to produce.

Ever hopeful, Trollope returned to the novel in 20 numbers with *The Way we Live Now* (1874–5). He was at this stage of his career on the board of Chapman & Hall, and presumably dictated the choice of form. Why he returned to the novel in numbers is not clear. Perhaps since *The Way we Live Now* was an old man's satire on modern ways he felt an old-fashioned style of publication was fitting. But the experiment failed. Having paid the author a large sum (£3,000), Frederic Chapman economised on the artist and the work is execrably illustrated. *The Way we Live Now* was not well received, apparently did not sell well and the copyright was sold off at a tenth of what Chapman had given to Andrew Chatto, even before the end of the serial run. The contract for Trollope's next novel (drawn up in April, 1874) indicates that he originally expected this too might come out in monthly numbers. But after their experience with *The Way we Live Now*, Chapman and Trollope decided to try *The Prime Minister* in eight of George Eliot's (unillustrated) five-shilling parts. These duly appeared monthly, November 1875–June 1876 and signally failed to interest the reading public. Trollope published no more novels in numbers during the five writing years that remained to him.

In 1877–9 Blackwood's attempted yet another revival with the so-called 'Cheveley' novels by Valentine Durrant. Durrant is an obscure author.[23] The impecunious son of a Brighton baker, he worked on boys' periodicals in the early 1870s. Little else is known about Durrant. His proletarian origins may have led Blackwood's into thinking him another Dickens. If so, they were sadly mistaken. The first of the Cheveley series, *A Modern Minister*, appeared in 12 parts, from June 1877. It was followed in June 1878 by a second Cheveley novel, *Saul Weir*, designed for a similar 12-month run (which it seems not to have completed). Durrant was an appallingly bad novelist and the serials attracted reviews of bloodcurdling severity. According to the *Athenaeum* (15 May 1878): 'Durrant's style, when not a ridiculous reproduction of Dickens's worst is very ponderous. His humour is clumsy in the extreme; his incidents are melodramatic; his characters caricatures drawn with an unintelligent hand. It is sincerely to be hoped that the series may not be prolonged.' Nor was it. Why Blackwood should have perpetrated this aberration is mysterious.

The latest true novel in monthly numbers that I have seen is William Black's *Sunrise* (see Plate 14). This work was brought out by Sampson Low in 15 one-shilling 64-page parts from April 1880 to June 1881. It was printed in large type, as for a three-decker, whose tripartite pagination it in fact followed. (A case for binding the parts up in three volumes was offered at three shillings and sixpence extra). The serial was unillustrated, but carried a stunning wrapper design of the sun rising over the ocean. (Vividly described seascapes were a prized feature in Black's fiction.)

The serialisation of *Sunrise* was evidently not a success. The book edition of the work appeared prematurely in February 1881, which presumably killed any subsequent sale in parts. But otherwise the novel was warmly received. Subtitled 'A Story of These Times', the plot involves secret society adventures, and was found exciting. Critics generally thought *Sunrise* refreshingly different from Black's earlier novels. ('No yachting, no highland lochs' as the *Athenaeum* reviewer noted in some surprise.) In volume form it was something of a bestseller, running to at least six editions in the first multi-volume form.

CONCLUSION

Sunrise brings one to the setting of the novel in numbers. That it lasted 40 years is a striking tribute to the force of the Dickens mystique; a mystique that induced in imitators a blind willingness to flog away at what was for them often an extremely dead horse.

What is more interesting, perhaps, is why Dickens himself continued to use what as early as September 1841 he called 'the old form'.[24] He was not temperamentally conservative and no novelist had greater freedom to choose how his books appeared. The standard explanation is that the novel in monthly numbers gave him a sense of intimate contact with his public. This is undoubtedly true. But there were probably more material factors determining his preference. As an economic strategy, the novel in numbers spread payment at all levels of production and consumption, allowing a larger investment in time and money by the involved parties. Over 18 months, the reader could afford by hire purchase a total outlay of a pound – a huge sum for a single novel. And on his side, the publisher was allowed to pay his serialist on a stipendiary basis, month by month. Since these stipends could come out of monthly receipts (from readers and advertisers), it allowed ever higher scales of remuneration. Thackeray, Trollope, Ainsworth and Lever had the greatest rewards of their writing lives from their novels in numbers.

Like the bidding in a poker game, the novel in numbers tended to force out players as the stakes got higher. Ainsworth dropped out of the big game at around £2,000 (with *The Tower of London*) and Lever at £2,400 (with *The Knight of Gwynne*). Trollope dropped out at £3,200 (with *He Knew He Was Right*), Thackeray at £6,000 (with *The Virginians*). And this thinning of ranks finally left Dickens as the only player, earning £10,000 a novel.

Dickens evidently liked vast payments as much as the next novelist. But as important, I suspect, was the proven fact that only he could handle the novel in numbers to its full potential. The failure of others certified his success. It seems, on the face of it another example of Dickens's will to uniqueness, his burning need to be among, yet finally transcend the crowd.[25]

Notes

1. From the author's preface to the cheap edition of *The Pickwick Papers* (1847). It is quoted in John Butt and Kathleen Tillotson, *Dickens at Work* (London: Methuen, 1957) p. 13.
2. R. L. Patten, *Dickens and his Publishers* (Oxford: Oxford University Press, 1978) p. 46.
3. From the author's preface to the cheap edition of *The Pickwick Papers* (1847).
4. I have examined Macrone's seminal publishing activities in 'John Macrone, Victorian Publisher', *Dickens Studies Annual*, XIII (1984) 243–59.
5. I have not traced this quotation, which is complacently reprinted in Colburn's advertisements. He was, of course, the erstwhile proprietor of the *Literary Gazette*.
6. In general, I have taken facts about Dickens's publishing history from Patten's invaluable *Dickens and his Publishers*.
7. See J. R. Harvey, *Victorian Novelists and their Illustrators* (London: Sidgwick & Jackson, 1970) pp. 7–18.
8. Usually with Menzies in Edinburgh, Murray in Glasgow, Cumming in Dublin and a host of provincial booksellers and stationers.
9. *The Letters of Charles Dickens*, Pilgrim Edition, ed. Madeline House, Graham Storey and Kathleen Tillotson (Oxford: Oxford University Press, 1974) vol. III, p. 517. The letter in question is dated 28 June 1843.
10. Dickens's *Dombey and Son* was identified as published from 'Bradbury and Evans, Whitefriars'. Presumably technical problems in handling woodcut illustrations in the text (together with Dickens's reluctance to have a *Punch* label) was one reason for the different addresses.
11. As Robert Patten and Peter Shillingsburg have pointed out, *Vanity Fair*'s sales even after it caught on were not spectacular and do not justify Thackeray's boast that he was at the 'top of the tree' battling it out with Dickens. *Vanity Fair* (as Shillingsburg calculates) sold 10,500 in its first parts and made up edition form – about a third of what *Dombey* sold. And Dickens's reprint sales were immensely more. See Peter L. Shillingsburg, ''Twixt *Punch* and *Cornhill*: Thackeray and the Firm of Bradbury and Evans', *Victorian Studies Association Newsletter*, 11 (March 1973) 1–14.
12. The smaller format of the 48-page parts of Jerrold's serial suggest that it may have been devised for *Douglas Jerrold's Shilling Magazine*, which Bradbury and Evans killed in June 1848. The publication of *A Man Made of Money* is often misdated.
13. E. D. Cuming, *Robert Smith Surtees* (Edinburgh: Blackwood, 1924) pp. 252–3.
14. See S. M. Ellis, *William Harrison Ainsworth and his Friends* (London: John Lane, 1911) vol. I, pp. 308–17.
15. See Harvey, *Victorian Novelists*, p. 188.
16. Ibid., p. 38.
17. Ibid., p. 38.

18. Thackeray may have been motivated at this date by jealousy of Ainsworth. But his observation was an early Victorian commonplace.
19. One regrets that Cruikshank did not illustrate the Mayhews's *Paved with Gold*. This was done in a more extensive 13 numbers by Chapman & Hall, 1857–8, with plates by Phiz at his darkest. The novel (which seems to have been finished by Augustus) is an interesting adaptation of *London Labour and the Poor*.
20. A. Trollope, *An Autobiography*, ed. F. Page (London: Oxford University Press, 1950) p. 274.
21. The letter is dated 28 September 1863, and is quoted in J. A. Sutherland, *Victorian Novelists and Publishers* (London: Athlone Press, 1976) p. 79.
22. Trollope originally expected Bradbury and Evans to serialise *The Vicar of Bullhampton* in their upmarket *Once a Week*. They proposed instead bringing it out in the humbler *Gentleman's Magazine*. As a compromise, it was brought out in a dozen monthly numbers, illustrated by H. Woods, July 1869–May 1870.
23. Robert Lee Wolff (wrongly) supposes the name to be a pseudonym. See *Nineteenth-Century Fiction*, vol. II D–K (New York: Garland, 1982) pp. 41–2.
24. See Butt and Tillotson, *Dickens at Work*, p. 89.
25. In comments after this essay was written, Philip Collins made the point (insufficiently stressed by me) that Dickens remained remarkably uncombative, and good-natured about his would-be competitors. This, I think, is very true.

NOTE: The illustrations accompanying this essay are published by permission of the Huntington Library.

Part Two

Part Two

8

Re-reading Victorian Poetry

ISOBEL ARMSTRONG

The habit of thinking of literary periods as segments creates the same kind of history that produces it. The Victorian period has always been regarded as isolated between two periods, Romanticism and modernism. Thus Victorian poetry is seen in terms of transition. It is on the way somewhere. It is either on the way from Romantic poetry, or on the way to modernism. It is situated between two kinds of excitement, in which it appears not to participate. What has been called the 'genetic' history of continuous development through phases and periods, a form of history which the Victorians themselves both helped to create and to question, sees Victorian poetry as a gap in that development.[1] Modernism, in spite of its desire to see itself in terms of a break with history, actually endorses that continuity, for a radical break must break with something. And correspondingly it endorses the gap which Victorian poetry is seen to inhabit. The anxieties of modernism, trying to do without history, repress whatever relations the Victorians may seem to bear to twentieth-century writing. Thus Joyce's frivolous 'Lawn Tennyson, gentleman poet' appears dressed for tennis in *Ulysses*. Virginia Woolf dissociates herself from the Victorians in her unscrupulously brilliant impressionistic account of them in *Orlando*.[2] There ivy covers buildings and large families come into being with almost equally magical suddenness. She intuitively registers the drive to produce in Victorian society, whether it is children or industrial goods, and the need to muffle. The eroticisms and the euphemisms of bourgeois capitalism and its ideology, its inordinate excesses and concealments, are embodied for her in the voluptuous taxidermy of the stuffed sofa.

So the major critical and theoretical movements of the twentieth century have been silent about Victorian poetry. As the stranded remnants of high bourgeois liberalism, the poets have been

123

consigned to sepia. New criticism, encouraged by T. S. Eliot, who said that Tennyson and Browning merely 'ruminated', considered Victorian poetry to lie outside its categories.[3] When Raymond Williams began to theorise the cultural criticism which has been so fruitful in *Culture and Society*, he concentrated on the nineteenth-century novel.[4] Feminism likewise made its claims through a critique primarily of the novel.[5] Deconstruction concentrated on Romantic poetry, blatantly periodising in a way which goes against its theoretical preconceptions.[6] No major European critics have seen Victorian poetry as relevant to their purpose. It is symbolism and imagism which have proved attractive when the novel was displaced as a centre of interest. Walter Benjamin wrote wonderfully on Baudelaire, but Lukács or Bakhtin on Tennyson would be unthinkable.[7] Oddly, biography in this area *has* flourished. The worse the poets seem to be, the more avidly their lives are recuperated. We 'covet' biography, as Browning once brilliantly said.[8] And biographers have dominated in literary scholarship of the Victorian period, even though Browning turns out to be a brash opportunist and Tennyson a surly and duplicitous snob.[9] An honourably uncovetous study is Lionel Trilling's classic biography of Matthew Arnold.[10]

What, then, can be the motive for writing about Victorian poetry? Is it worth it? The enterprise cannot be justified in terms of the genetic history which would simply fill in the gap, recreate continuity and restore the forgotten. Some principles must govern this reclaiming process beyond the notion of even continuity and positivist accounts of development.

A way of beginning to rediscover the importance of Victorian poetry is to consider the heavy silence surrounding it in the twentieth century as a striking cultural phenomenon in itself. We have to see that silence historically. T. S. Eliot's dismissive account of Tennyson deflects attention from the Tennysonian echoes in *The Waste Land* and *Four Quartets*. Yeats, virtually quoting Shelley in 'The Second Coming', silently appropriates Tennyson's 'The Kraken' as the governing motive of his poem.[11] We have learned to understand that to constitute something as a gap is a strategy for concealing anxiety. What kind of anxieties could the Victorians have created for the twentieth century and why are they still culturally significant? To clarify these anxieties it is necessary to see what the Victorian poets were worried about themselves.

They were worried about being 'modern'. 'Modern', in spite of its long history, has a resurgence as a Victorian term – the 'modern' element in literature (Arnold), 'modern' love (Meredith), a 'modern' landlord (William Allingham).[12] To see yourself as modern is actually to define the contemporary self-consciously and this is simultaneously an act which historicises the modern. Victorian modernism sees itself as new but it does not, like twentieth-century modernism, conceive itself in terms of a radical break with a past. A 'modern' Victorian poet was post-revolutionary, existing with the constant possibility of mass political upheaval and fundamental change in the structure of society, which meant that the nature of society had to be redefined. Victorian poetry was post-industrial and post-technological, existing with and theorising the changed relationships and new forms of alienated labour which capitalism was consolidating, and conscious of the predatory search for new areas of exploitation which was creating a new colonial 'outside' to British society. It was post-teleological and scientific, conceiving beliefs, including those of Christianity, anthropologically in terms of belief *systems* and representations through myth.

Lastly, the supreme condition of posthumousness, it was post-Kantian. This meant, in the first place, that the category of art (and for the Victorians this was almost always poetry) was becoming 'pure'. Art occupied its own area, a self-sufficing aesthetic realm over and against practical experience. It was *outside* the economy of instrumental energies (for in Kant art and technology spring into being simultaneously as necessary opposites). And yet it was at once apart and central, for it had a mediating function, representing and interpreting life. These contradictions were compounded by post-Kantian accounts of representation, which adapted Kant to make both the status and the mode of art problematical by seeing representations as the constructs of consciousness which is always at a remove from what it represents. Thus the possibility of a process of endless redefinition and an ungrounded, unstable series of representations was opened out. So the Victorian poets were the first group of writers to feel that what they were doing was simply unnecessary and redundant. For the very category of art itself created this redundancy.

A history genuinely appropriate to the rereading of Victorian poetry – one which would enable an adequate criticism of it to emerge – would look at the ways in which the radical and reactionary critiques of Victorian society converge. It would consider both Carlyle and Marx. It would consider their analyses of

alienated labour; it would consider the connection of this with the
technologising of the sign and a new account of alienated language
emerging in the phenomenon of what Carlyle called 'movable
type';[13] it would consider the politics and epistemology of new
accounts of representation, including the significance of Carlyle's
'new mythos', or the imaginative representations of a culture.

It is not possible to do more than point to this here in a very
abbreviated way. But what such a history would undoubtedly
discover is that Victorian culture and literature generate the same
problems we find addressed by modernism – the status of the
experiencing subject, the problems of representation, fiction and
language. A new history would discover, perhaps to its surprise,
that sexual politics is at the heart of Victorian poetry. And perhaps
through discovering this content it would be possible to discover the
great difference between Victorian poetry and modernist works; it is
that the Victorians struggle to give abstract epistemological and
political questions a content, whereas modernism is happy to
abstract and aestheticise. This has to be left as a flagrant
generalisation in this essay but I write in the belief that it can be
supported. The modernists are haunted by the Victorians because
they are haunted by a plenitude of content which eludes them. Thus
they present the Victorians, who actually produced the most
sophisticated poetry to be written in the last 200 years, as lumpenly
ethical or theological. The task of rereading Victorian poetry is to
return a content to it for the twentieth-century reader. And this is
also to show how the Victorian poem struggles with language.

Interestingly, the nature of language in Victorian poetry is largely
ignored by recent critics of it, Marxists, Feminists and
Deconstructionists. Alan Sinfield's *Alfred Tennyson* is an impressive
Marxist intervention which quite properly shakes up accounts of
Victorian poetry.[14] He reads Tennyson as a cultural materialist and
inevitably sees him, as he was, as a conservative poet. Sinfield's
hindsight enables him to argue that Tennyson's aesthetic solutions
to political problems were either timid or straightforwardly
reactionary. Two difficulties emerge in the necessity to establish an
unequivocally reactionary Tennyson. First, in order to pin
Tennyson to political and religious positions, Sinfield has to
eliminate the possibility of ambiguity in poetic language. Or, when
confronted with two contending meanings he has to opt for one as
being 'really' the intended meaning. Similarly, in order to argue
Tennyson's political bad faith he has to argue that Tennyson's 'real'

interests as a sympathiser with the landed gentry and as a supporter of nationalism and imperialistic interests must give a poem a particular historical meaning even when it appears to be struggling against it. Thus he virtually makes Tennyson personally responsible for the colonialist ravaging of Tahiti as a result of *The Lotos Eaters*. He excludes the element of struggle with the element of ambiguity.

Eve Sedgwick's brilliant feminist reading of *The Princess* in *Between Men* adopts rather the same strategy.[15] She argues that far from being a para-feminist poem, as the stated project of *The Princess* insists, Tennyson's poem actually or 'really' deals with the patriarchal homosocial bonding which makes a woman an object of exchange between men. She makes an impressive analysis of the structure of the poem in order to demonstrate the case. However, rather like Sinfield, she makes her argument stick by first excluding ambiguity, or staying with those elements of ambiguity which corroborate the case. Second, the deconstruction of the poem has to take place by the introduction of a very narrow form of intentionality. Tennyson 'meant' to write a poem in celebration of women but the manifest intention of the text is subverted by its latent homosocial desires. This distinction between what is meant and what happens assumes that the text has a manifest and a latent content, a conscious and unconscious desire. The difficulty about this is that everything that is observed is all there in the text anyway, and it is a strangely arbitrary decision which makes some elements of the text manifest and some latent, some conscious and some unconscious, since all elements of the text are actually manifest. A process of selection has gone on, in which the critic has decided to select an intentional and an unintentional project. To simplify a text's projects and then to invoke the complexities of the text itself to undermine the simple project is an odd procedure. A text is not quite like a patient in analysis and actually anticipates these strategies of deconstruction by enabling them to take place.

The problem of deciding what are 'really' a poet's interests politically or what is 'really' intentional as against unconscious can be circumvented by a more open understanding of the text as struggle. A text is endless struggle and contention, struggle with a changing project, struggle with the play of ambiguity and contradiction. This is a way of reading which gives equal weight to a text's project and the polysemic and possibly wayward meanings it generates. The *Lotos Eaters* for instance, can be read as a struggle with an impossible ideology of consciousness, labour and consumption which lays bare the poverty of accounts of social relationships underlying these conceptions in a language which libidinously orchestrates the deranged perceptions and desires of the subject who is either consumed by work or destroyed by cessation from it. Rather than longing for retreat, the poem struggles with what constitutes the self as divided between labour and the cessation of labour. Its exploration is nearer to Marx's understanding of the estranged labour which converts all energy expended outside work into sub-human or animal experience than to an account of the text as a simple desire for escape and a wanton exploitation of resources. The desire for escape is involved, of course, in the struggle with the nature of work. But it is not the primary 'intentional' project of the poem.

To see the text as a complex entity defining and participating in an area of struggle and contention is to make intentionality a much wider and more complex affair and to include the contradictions and uncontrolled nature of language within the text's project. For the escape of language from univocal order becomes one of the text's areas of contention and not part of its latent unconscious. Perhaps this encounters the danger of accepting complexity to the extent that we can map deconstructive processes on to the text and, as it were, leave the text alone with its intricacies and to its ludic activities. To do this, however, would be to attribute to it a composure with its difficulties which few texts have. It is precisely not to engage in that understanding of the unsettled nature of the text which deconstruction has elicited. And it ignores the ideological struggles of the text. Post-Derridean criticism, however, tends to ignore the aspect of active struggle in a text. Volosinov, taking up a different form of the Hegelian tradition than the one from which deconstruction stems, puts the struggle with language at the centre of a text, and such a concentration on language should help in the rereading of Victorian poetry.[16]

A clever critic of Browning, Herbert Tucker, has noticed the linguistic intricacy of Victorian poetry and uses the strategies of deconstruction to elicit Browning's complexities, but he tends to stay with them rather than to probe what is problematical and conflicting.[17] To concentrate on the ludic energies of language rather than its conflicts is to miss its underlying element of struggle in poetry of this period. What is linguistically and formally complex in Victorian poetry seems to me to arise from stress. To understand what is stressful and why it is important it is necessary to link linguistic and formal contradictions to the substantive issues at stake in the poems – issues of politics, gender and epistemology, the problem of relationship and the continual attempts to reinvest the content of self and other. An earlier generation of writers attempted to understand the form of Victorian poetry as the function of a complex of social and psycho-social problems. E. D. H. Johnson, in *The Alien Vision of Victorian Poetry*, explored the terms of Victorian poetry in relation to an increasingly severe lesion between the poet and society.[18] Robert Langbaum, in *The Poetry of Experience*, studied the dramatic monologue as an attempted solution to a cultural crisis in which the conceptualisation of the self and its relations acknowledged a split between insight and judgement, empathy and detachment.[19] Though Johnson tends to remain too narrowly with existential subjectivity and Langbaum's readings return a trifle rapidly to the ethical, these books are important in their attempts to read Victorian poetry in a sophisticated way in terms of a cultural analysis, attempts which, along with Morse Peckham's readings of Victorian poetry, seem to have terminated the valuable project they began.[20]

Perhaps what was lacking in these studies was an account of the language of Victorian poetry in relation to both formal and cultural problems, an attempt to see these things as inseparable from one another. The link between cultural complexities and the complexities of language is indirect but can be perceived. We might start with the nature of language in Victorian poetry, for to read a Victorian poem is to be made acutely aware of the fact that it is made of language. Whether it is the strange, arcane artifice of Tennyson's early poems or the splutter of speech in Browning, the limpid economy of Christina Rossetti, Swinburne's swamping rhythms, Hopkins's muscle-bound syntax, the sheer verbalness of poetry is foregrounded. It is as if the poet's secondariness takes a stand on the self-conscious assertion of the unique discourse of poetry. This is connected with the over-determination of ambiguity. The open nerve of exposed feeling in Tennyson is registered in a language fraught with ambiguity. Christina Rossetti's distilled exactitude analyses into an equally precise ambiguity. Signification in Browning shifts and lurches almost vertiginously. The structural ambiguities of Romantic syntax have intensified to an extent that coalescing syntax and semantic openness is the norm. In an age of 'movable type' and mechanical reproduction in which signification moves beyond the immediate control of the writer, it is as if the writer can only resort to an openness in advance of the reader, testing out the possibilities of systematic misprision. Such language draws attention to the nature of words as a medium of representation.

Hopkins saw the openness of his contemporaries as anarchy and flux and desperately tried to arrest it, reintroducing an agonised, sundered language of ambiguity in spite of himself.[21] Arnold saw it as the product of disorganised subjectivity, 'the dialogue of the mind with itself', and attempted to freeze poetry back into classical form.[22] Neither, however, saw that this was a systematic and organised ambiguity. The doubleness of language is not local but structural. It must be read closely, not loosely. It is not the disorganised expression of subjectivity but a way of exploring and interrogating the grounds of its representation. What the Victorian poet achieved was often quite literally two concurrent poems in the same words.

Schopenhauer wrote of the lyric poet as uttering between two poles of feeling, between the pure undivided condition of unified selfhood and the needy, fracturing self-awareness of the interrogating consciousness.[23] The Victorian poet does not swing between these two forms of utterance but dramatises and objectifies their simultaneous existence. There is a kind of duplicity involved here, for the poet often invites the simple reading by presenting a poem as lyric expression as the perceiving subject speaks. Mariana's lament or Fra Lippo Lippi's apologetics are expressions, indeed, composed in an expressive form. But in a feat of recomposition and externalisation the poem turns its expressive utterance around so that it becomes the opposite of itself, not only the *subject's* utterance but the *object* of analysis and critique.

It is, as it were, reclassified as drama in the act of being literal lyric expression. To reorder lyric expression as drama is to give it a new content and to introduce the possibility of interrogation and critique. Mariana's torture in isolation, for instance, is the utterance of a subjective psychological condition, but that psychological expression is reversed into being the object of analysis and restructured as a symptomatic form by the act of narration, which draws attention to the reiterated refrain of the poem as Mariana's speech, speech which attempts to arrest temporality while time moves on in the narrator's commentary. The poignant *expression* of exclusion to which Mariana's state gives rise, and which is reiterated in the marking of barriers – the moat itself, the gate with clinking latch, the curtained casement, the hinged doors – is simultaneously an *analysis* of the hypersensitive hysteria induced by the coercion of sexual taboo. These are hymenal taboos, which Mariana is induced, by a cultural consensus which is hidden from her, to experience as her own condition. Hidden from her, but not from the poem, the barriers are man-made, cunningly constructed through the material fabric of the house she inhabits, the enclosed spaces in which she is confined. It is the narrative voice which describes these spaces, not Mariana as speaker.

The dramatic nature of Victorian poetry was understood by its earliest critics, by W. J. Fox and Arthur Hallam in particular, but seems to have been lost to later readers.[24] Twentieth-century readers have been right to see the dramatic monologue as the primary Victorian genre, even though they have too often codified it in terms of technical features. Other devices, such as the framed narrative or the dream dialogue or parody are related to it. All enable double forms to emerge. Rather than to elicit its technical features, it is preferable to see what this dramatic form enabled the poet to explore. By seeing utterance such as subject and as object, it was possible for the poet to explore expressive psychological forms simultaneously as psychological conditions *and* as constructs, the phenomenology of a culture, projections which indicate the structure of relationships. I have called this objectification of consciousness a phenomenological form. Phenomenology seeks to describe and analyse the manifestations of consciousness rather than its internal condition. Thus such a reading relates consciousness to the external forms of the culture in which it exists. The gap between subjective and objective readings often initiates a debate between a subject-centred or expressive and a phenomenological or analytical reading, but above all it draws attention to the space between two readings. In doing so, it draws attention to the act of representation, the act of relationship and the mediations of language, different in a psychological and in a phenomenological world. It is a deeply sceptical form. It draws attention to the epistemology which governs the construction of the self and its relationships and to the cultural conditions in which those relationships are made. It is an expressive model and an epistemological model simultaneously. Epistemological and hermeneutic problems are built into its very form, for interpretation, and what the act of interpretation involves, are questioned in the very existence of the double model. It must expose relationships of power, for the epistemological reading will explore things of which the expressive reading is unaware and go beyond the experience of the lyric speaker. It is inveterately political not only because it opens up an exploration of the unstable entities of self and world and the simultaneous problems of representation and interpretation, but because it is founded on debate and contest. It has to give the entities of self and world a provisional content in order to dramatise the debate. The Victorian dramatic poem is not the dialogue of the mind with itself so much as the dialogue of the poem with itself, using the dialogue of the mind, the labour of the self on the world, as its lyric entry into the phenomenological world which is a labour on that labour. If the poet knows that the act of representation is fraught with problems, and if it is not clear to what misprisions the poem might be appropriated, then a structure which analyses precisely that uncertainty and which makes that uncertainty belong to struggle and debate, a structure which fills that uncertainty with content, is the surest way to establish poetic form. The surest way to answer uncertainty is creative agnosticism.

The struggle between two kinds of reading is highly complex. It is not a question of a simple dialogue or dialectic form in which the opposition between two terms is fixed and settled. Such an opposition too often is what the dialogic has come to mean.[25] We have only to look at 'Mariana' to see that the cultural or phenomenological reading which changes the status of Mariana's utterance as lyric expression is subject to unsettling pressures in its turn. In the phenomenological reading, Mariana's anguish becomes no longer something for which she is psychologically responsible. When under the scrutiny of phenomenological critique the terrible privacy of her obsessional condition, her inability to gaze on the external world except at night, become the function of a death wish to which she has been induced without fully realising that she has been driven to it. On the other hand, this suicidal condition asks questions of the cultural reading. Is not the phenomenological reading too ready to concede that this is a situation 'without hope of change', too ready to metaphorise Mariana's emotions in terms of projections on to the external world ('blackest moss', 'blacken'd water'), which becomes an extension of her condition even though the landscape operates quite independently of her? The external world becomes both her psychic environment and an existence from which she is irretrievably estranged. The phenomenological reading seems uncertain of these relations. Is it not too ready to narrow the grounds of feminine sexuality as the passive object of experience (notice the 'wooing wind')? Thus it arrives at a self-fulfilling reading of estrangement in which Mariana *must* be alienated. And so the status of the phenomenological reading is changed. It cannot be metacommentary entirely in charge of the grounds of debate. And this reflects back on to Mariana as subject. Her loathing of the day and the derangement of her perception is a rebellious act in this context and questions have to be asked about her autonomy and the extent of her passivity. It might well be that the fragmented self she becomes is both cause and effect of a particular way of conceiving of feminine subjectivity. And it is difficult to say whether Mariana's condition is a violent protest or a passive response to such conceptions of the feminine.

What is here is nothing so straightforward as a simple opposition but a dynamic text in which lyric description and analysis are repeatedly redefining the terms of a question and contending for its ground. To probe the status of one form of utterance is to call forth an analysis of the status of *that* interpretation, and so on. If this is a dialogue or a dialectical form it is so in all the antagonistic complexity of the Hegelian master/slave dialectic in which the mediations between different positions are so rapid and subtle, so continually changing places in the relationship of authority, that the play of difference can hardly be resolved. Bakhtin's dialogism is clearly derived from this, indeed, just as Volosinov's to me preferable linguistic model is, but it is worth going back to Hegel to restate the complexity of the case. For the status of the hermeneutic act is continually re-investigated in the double poem at the same time as the terms of the struggle are invested with a new content.

True to its status as a transitional form Victorian poetry has been used either to confirm a general critical theory, as in the readings of Bloom, or seen simply as an instance of a particular historical case, for which a particular critical reading is necessary, as in the readings of Johnson or Langbaum. What I have done is to develop the political implications of Johnson's work and the epistemological implications of Langbaum. Langbaum is also concerned with the double reading, though his way of seeing the judgemental reading as a *control* on the empathetic reading seems to me to state the problem too rigidly in moral rather than analytical terms. It is without that sense of a new content which evolves when the

subjective reading reverses into critique and so back and forth
between critique and expressive form. 'Mariana' is an exemplary
case of this process.

When the full importance of Victorian poetry is recognised,
however, it becomes apparent that it need not be discussed either
as illustrative material for theory or as a particular case. It surely
marks an extraordinarily self-conscious and sophisticated moment
of awareness in history. Victorian history produces the double
poem, two poems in one. The double poem, with its system-
atically ambiguous language, out of which expressive and
phenomenological readings emerge, is a structure commensurate
with the 'movable type' which Carlyle saw as both the repercussion
and the cause of shifts in nineteenth-century culture. The double
poem belongs to a post-teleological, post-revolutionary, post-
industrial and post-Kantian world and its interrelated
manifestations. The double poem signifies a godless, non-
teleological world because as soon as two readings become possible
and necessary, the permanent and universal categories of the 'type'
dissolve. For the 'type' is, of course, an ancient theological word,
meaning those fixed categories of thought and language ordained by
God which governed relationships, before it becomes associated
with print. The double reading inevitably dissolves such fixity, just
as it means a shift from ontology to epistemology, a shift from
investigating the grounds of being to a sceptical interrogation of the
grounds of knowledge, which becomes phenomenology, not belief.
In a post-revolutionary world in which power is supposedly vested
in many rather than a privileged class, the double poem dramatises
relationships of power. In the twofold reading struggle is structurally
necessary and becomes the organising principle as critique
successively challenges and redefines critique. Movable type,
where technology mobilises the logos, makes the process of
signification a political matter as it opens up a struggle for the
meaning of words which is part of the relations of power explored
through the structures of the poem. Hence the poets' systematic
exploration of ambiguity. This reveals not only the confounding
complexities of language and the anxieties this generates but boldly
establishes that play of possibility in which meaning can be decided.
It draws attention to the fact that meaning *is* decided by cultural
consensus even while its ambiguity offers the possibility of
challenging that consensus through the double reading. The poem
of the post-industrial world recognises the displacement of

relationships in its structure as well as in its language. The formal ploy in which the uttering subject becomes object and the poem reverses relationships not once but many times indicates that epistemological uneasiness in which subject and object, self and world, no longer in lucid relation with one another, are alienated and have to be perpetually redefined. The structure of the double poem emerges from the condition in which self-creation in the world is no longer straightforward but indirect. Finally, the double structure inevitably draws attention to the act of interpretation, since one reading encounters another and moves to a new content in the process. Hermeneutic self-consciousness leads in its turn to concentration on the nature of representation, for if interpretation is in question as a construct, so also are the categories of thought it deals with. In a post-Kantian world the double poem becomes a representation of representation, not only secondary historically but a second order activity in itself. Mariana's poignant utterance is framed as the solipsistic construction of her world and this reflects back on the complexity of the framing process which presents that self-enclosed utterance. It, too, cannot be exempted from the second order status. If one utterance is a representation, so is the other. Both are ideological and both confront one another.

Committed to going through the processes of 'movable type', the double poem confronts the scepticism of the deconstructive moment and challenges it. Victorian poems are sceptical and affirmative simultaneously for they compel a strenuous reading and assume an active reader who will participate in the struggle of the lyric voice, a reader with choices to make, choices which are created by the terms of the poem itself. The active reader is compelled to be internal to the poem's contradictions and recomposes the poem's processes in the act of comprehending them as ideological struggle. There is no end to struggle because there is no end to the creative constructs and the renewal of content which its energy brings forth.

Rereading Victorian poetry, then, involves a reconsideration of the way we conceptualise history and culture, and the way we see the politics of poetry. It also involves rethinking some of the major criticism of this century, Marxist and feminist criticism and deconstruction, and considering how the language and form of Victorian poetry question the theories they have developed. Putting the stuffing back into the Victorian sofa then becomes a process of reconstruction which asks living questions.

Throughout this introduction I have used Tennyson's 'Mariana' as a running commentary on the arguments I have put forward about the double poem and its significance. As a tail-piece I include a brief discussion of Browning's 'Love Among the Ruins' to indicate how the general principles discussed above might work.

The risk-taking, ambiguous forms of the double lyric are present in the first poem in *Men and Women*, 'Love Among the Ruins'. Why was this poem, an ostensibly affirmative statement of subjective values, 'Love is Best', given primacy in the two volumes, and how is its title to be interpreted – *Love* Among the Ruins, Love Among the *Ruins*? Are these teleological as well as material ruins? Both present and past reject an ordered universe, one by depending on private subjectivity and the other by depending on violence. The different emphases on 'Love' and 'Ruins' enunciate contending terms, the certainties of private passion over and against a communal but now fragmented history and culture which has become simply archaeology. Perhaps Volney's *Ruins of Empire* (1791) is behind the title of the poem.[26] A lover anticipates a meeting with a girl on the site of an unnamed, obliterated city – Babylon, Rome, anywhere. The poem looks like a simple antithesis between the consummation of intense passion and the wasteful aggression, violence and cupidity of a vanished society – a primitive will to power through war and gold. It is arranged as a series of flowing lines which alternate with curt, abrupt, single anapaests and are puncuated by them like a drum beat. (Browning rearranged the stanzas after 1855 but this does not affect the essential form of the poem.) The short lines mockingly disrupt the easy, homogeneous flow of the long lines but – and a conviction of the strangeness of *this* poem grows – the long lines make perfect sense without them. The short lines can be repressed. Except for the fifth and the last stanza and for the completion of each stanza, they are inessential. It is as if another more critical language is refusing to be excluded and threatening private feeling with a mocking analysis of its limitations. This is movable type, or removable type, in action. There are two poems here. One is a simple celebration of private feeling, which attempts to exclude everything but the moment of union. The other is an assent to, or at least a recognition of, the subversive and dangerous energies of an alien culture, the aggression and power of its predominantly male hierarchy.

Where the quiet-coloured end of evening smiles,
   Miles and miles
On the solitary pastures where our sheep
   Half-asleep,
Tinkle homeward thro' the twilight, stray or stop
   As they crop –
Was the site once of a city great and gay,
   (So they say) . . .   (I)

All the mountains topped with temples, all the glades'
   Colonnades,
All the causeys, bridges, aqueducts, – and then,
   All the men!
When I do come, she will speak not, she will stand . . .   (VI)

In the first stanza the short lines impart a suspect tedium and torpor
to the pastoral, a tedium which is absent without them. The
plenitude of the city and above all its populace is repressed in the
sixth stanza without the short lines to insist upon them. 'Where the
quiet-coloured end of evening smiles, / On the solitary pastures
where our sheep / Tinkle homeward thro' the twilight . . .'. 'All the
causeys, bridges, aqueducts, – and then, / When I do come, she will
speak not, . . .'. 'Shut them in', the lover says of the competitive
violences of the past, but with inadvertent ambiguity. The long lines
attempt to shut the mocking pressure of the half lines away, but they
are shut *into* the poem, for the lovers' privacy is defined against
them. 'Love is Best' is defensively defined against the ironies and
energies the short lines represent. The relationship between the
long and short lines, each a critique of the other, is what enables the
poem to be both actor and spectator of itself. Browning knew about
the hubris of lovers, and gives assent to passionate feeling, but
subjective experience becomes its opposite, the object of
investigation. It shuts out history, culture, here. The lovers exist in
'undistinguished grey' (V) extra-historical, extra-cultural,
contextless, not redeeming, but perpetuating 'the Ruins' about
them. In Stanza V history converges on them as the violent figures of
the past, 'breathless, dumb', are allowed to share the same syntax
with the girl who is also, the structure allows, 'breathless, dumb'.
The will to see passion as self-sufficing is as aggressive and exclusive
as the desires of the dead society for triumph and empire. All history
waits 'Till *I* come', one form of the syntax hubristically proposes.

Revelation in history is reserved for the puny lover. There is a
struggle between two interpretations of the same syntax here and
this culminates the series of reversals in which the priorities of the
language of feeling and its values and the language of history
change places as first one then another achieves dominance. The
pressures of power explored in the structure of the post-
revolutionary double poem are apparent here.

   'Love among the Ruins', written the day after 'Childe Roland to
the Dark Tower Came' and sharing with it the landscape of ruin and
tower, initiates *Men and Women* because it enacts and subverts a
contemporary *mythos* inherited from Romantic values, a myth about
the all-sufficing energies of mutual passion and the setting up of
private enclaves of feeling against the crude values of a threatening
culture. But the structure of the poem makes it clear that this myth is
a construct and entails and depends upon another more seductive
but equally vitiating myth. The values of private passion necessarily
entail a structuring of social and cultural relationships in terms of
fracture, the splitting off of individuals from an alien culture. The
lesions and breakages which come into being in the arrangement of
the long and short lines are inherent in the account of isolated
human nature, the myth of estrangement, the fall from a unified
culture.

> It was civilisation itself which inflicted this wound upon modern
> man. Once the increase of empirical knowledge, and more exact
> modes of thought, made sharper divisions between the sciences
> inevitable, and once the increasingly complex machinery of State
> necessitated a more rigorous separation of ranks and operations,
> then the inner unity of human nature was severed too, and a
> disastrous conflict set its harmonious powers at variance.[27]

This is Schiller defining the fractures of modern scientific culture.
'Love Among the Ruins', more savagely controlled and ironical,
points to the fallaciousness of the account of original unity as well as
analysing in its form the structure of estrangement. Browning is
likely to have found this kind of cultural diagnosis in Carlyle as well
as directly from the German writing which was frequently Carlyle's
source. In *Sartor Resartus* Carlyle asked for a new *mythos* and new
symbols to emerge from the ruins of the old. The 'Genius of
Mechanism' smothers the soul, and the poet, a phoenix out of the
fire (one is reminded of the fiery landscape at the end of 'Childe

Roland'), 'Prometheus-like can shape new symbols', a Shelleyan task, 'and bring new Fire from Heaven to fix it there'. Symbols emerge out of silence, and 'Fantasy', the Promethean imagination, 'plays into the small prose domain of sense'.[28] 'Love Among the Ruins' is about the exhaustion of symbol and the emergence of a new and impoverished mythos. The new symbol creates a silence in which the poet's Promethean task can, perhaps, begin again. The girl, 'breathless, dumb', 'will speak not'. Perhaps when she *does* speak, instead of being the addressee of a lover haunted by the male culture of the past, the present can be changed. After all, Elizabeth Barrett Browning's *Aurora Leigh* (1856) was being composed when Browning wrote his poem.

But the poem carries with it the possibility that the cry for mythos may itself be a symptom of exhaustion. The last cry of secondariness. It stands at the head of *Men and Women* because it implicitly questions the possibility of creating a Promethean symbol in a culture which defines itself as fragmented. It knows itself as a sceptical representation of the mythos and understands its second order status. Lawrence intuitively and perhaps unconsciously grasps something of the meaning of 'Love Among the Ruins' when he makes Birkin quote it as he approaches London with Gerald in *Women In Love* (ch. v). Browning's poem is uncannily prescient: it sees just how long the myths about myth and cultural exhaustion and fragmentation might last. It is a step ahead of Lawrence, however, because it refuses the romantic account of the feminine with which Birkin struggles.

The regressing ironies of this poem mean that it refuses to privilege the statement 'Love is Best'. But this *is* a double poem, and sceptical and affirmative readings struggle actively with one another to gain the ascendent in a strenuous effort to reorder the processes of the poem's movable type. The deficiencies and impoverishment of the subjectivist confessional are declared through the critique mounted by the energy of past society. The violence of that society, however, establishes the need for love and negatively enables the statement 'Love is Best' to be given a new content. The reordering is always provisional, always dependent on the evolution of new possibilities from the particulars of the poem, but it is necessarily a continuous process of construction and reconstruction.

In my last book I developed Hegelian categories for a reading of the language of nineteenth-century poetry. What is described here is a generalisation of these principles to a strong-Hegelian reading which recognises the antagonistic struggle of dialectic rather than its resolutions or its free play. It assumes that an active ideological creativity is constitutively at work in the poems' structure and language and is thus necessarily a political and cultural way of reading. Such a criticism is particularly appropriate to Victorian poetry, perhaps, but it is relevant to all nineteenth- and twentieth-century poetry. Since Victorian poetry is the most sophisticated poetic form to arise in the last 200 years it is proper that Victorian poems should generate principles for reading the poetry of the last 200 years.

Notes

1. Michel Foucault makes a critique of continuous 'genetic' history in his foreword to the English edition of *The Order of Things: An Archaeology of the Human Sciences* (London: Tavistock Publications, 1974): 'It was not my intention, on the basis of a particular type of knowledge or body of ideas, to draw up a picture of a period, or to reconstitute the spirit of a century' (p. x). Such a history ignores 'the implicit philosophies . . . the unformulated thematics . . . the rules of formation' of knowledge which were not always consciously understood by those who were living at the time (p. xi). 'Archaeology' abandons the notion of 'genesis' and 'progress' and adopts instead a procedure for looking at 'unformulated thematics' which considers 'widely different theories and objects of study' (p. xi).
2. The Tennyson joke is given to Stephen Daedelus in the 'Proteus' section of *Ulysses* (1922) and Tennyson reappears in 'Circe'. Virginia Woolf's *Orlando: A Biography* (1933) describes the onset of Victorianism as a morbid condition in ch. v.
3. T. S. Eliot, 'The Metaphysical Poets', *Selected Essays*, 3rd edn, (London: Faber and Faber, 1951) p. 288.
4. Raymond Williams, *Culture and Society, 1780–1950* (London: Chatto and Windus, 1958).
5. The new wave of influential feminist writing on the nineteenth-century novel in the late 1970s is represented by Elaine Showalter, *A Literature of Their Own: British Women Novelists from Brontë to Lessing* (Princeton, N.J.: Princeton University Press, 1977).
6. Illustrative of the preoccupation with Romantic poetry among Deconstructionist critics is the collection of essays by Harold Bloom, Paul de Man, Jacques Derrida, Geoffrey Hartman and J. Hillis Miller, *Deconstruction and Criticism* (London: Routledge and Kegan Paul, 1979). Derrida's major literary text beyond Rousseau is Mallarmé.
7. See Walter Benjamin, 'On Some Motifs in Baudelaire', *Illuminations* (London: Fontana, 1973) pp. 157–67.

8. Robert Browning, in his essay on Shelley (1832), *Robert Browning: The Poems*, ed. John Pettigrew and Thomas J. Collins (New Haven, Conn., and London: Yale University Press, 1981) 999–1013; see esp. p. 1001.

9. Substantial biographical work has appeared on Tennyson and Browning in particular. See, for instance, Robert Bernard Martin, *Tennyson: The Unquiet Heart* (Oxford: Clarendon Press, 1980); William Irvine and Park Honan, *The Book, the Ring, and the Poet* (London: Bodley Head, 1974); John Maynard, *Browning's Youth* (Cambridge, Mass.: Harvard University Press, 1977).

10. Lionel Trilling, *Matthew Arnold* (New York: W. W. Norton, 1939).

11. Fifteen years after his disparaging comments on Tennyson, T. S. Eliot came to consider *In Memoriam* as a great poem. He described it as a spiritual diary, a description which is also appropriate to *Four Quartets* and its preoccupation with time (T. S. Eliot, 'The Metaphysical Poets', p. 334). Tennysonian echoes in both *The Waste Land* and *Four Quartets* are numerous but it is the poems of nightmare and madness which seem to press closely on Eliot's work. See, for instance, *The Waste Land*, ll. 377–84 and section LXX of *In Memoriam* and *Four Quartets*, 'Burnt Norton', II, ll. 1–15 and *Maud*, ll. 102–7, 571–98. The allusion to Shelley's *Prometheus Unbound* in Yeats's 'The Second Coming' is familiar (see *Prometheus Unbound*, Act I, ll. 625–8). Less frequently remarked is the inversion of the ending of Tennyson's 'The Kraken' in 'The Second Coming'. Tennyson's barely sentient monster dies a violent death on the surface of the sea in apocalyptic unheaval. Yeats's 'rough beast' stumbles towards a violent, apocalyptic birth at the end of his poem.

12. Matthew Arnold's inaugural lecture as Professor of Poetry at Oxford was entitled 'On the Modern Element in Literature' and published in *Macmillan's Magazine* (1869). George Meredith's *Modern Love* was published in 1862, two years before William Allingham's *Laurence Bloomfield in Ireland: A Modern Poem* (1864), reissued in 1869 and subtitled *Or, the New Landlord*.

13. Thomas Carlyle, *Sartor Resartus: The Life and Opinions of Herr Teufelsdröckh*, Centenary edn (London, 1896) vol. I, p. 31.

14. Alan Sinfield, *Alfred Tennyson*, Rereading Literature Series (Oxford: Blackwell, 1986).

15. Eve Kosofsky Sedgwick, *Between Men: English Literature and Male Homosocial Desire* (New York: Columbia University Press, 1985).

16. V. N. Volosinov, *Marxism and the Philosophy of Language*, trans. L. Matejka and I. R. Titunik (London: Seminar Press, 1973). Volosinov's contention that both written and spoken language participates in a struggle for the sign long precedes, of course, the work of deconstruction but the possibilities of his work, even though he excluded poetry from the activity of struggle, are only recently being discovered. In saying that both Volosinov's work and that of Derrida stem from Hegel I am over-simplifying both. Volosinov is a Marxist in contention with linguistics, but his concept of struggle goes back to Hegel's master/slave dialectic. Derrida develops and transforms the premises of Saussurian linguistics, as Volosinov does not, and he dissents from the master/slave dialectic and develops the alternative

concept of 'differance'. Arguably, however, 'differance' as the constant re-positioning of relationship arrests a stage of Hegelian thought. The strength of Volosinov is that he finds a way of conceptualising linguistic struggle.

17. Herbert F. Tucker Jr, *Browning's Beginnings: The Art of Disclosure* (Minneapolis, Minn.: University of Minnesota Press, 1980).

18. E. D. H. Johnson, *The Alien Vision of Victorian Poetry: Sources of the Poetic Imagination in Tennyson, Browning and Arnold* (Princeton, N.J.: Princeton University Press, 1952).

19. Robert Langbaum, *The Poetry of Experience: the Dramatic Monologue in Modern Literary Tradition* (London: Chatto and Windus, 1957).

20. There is much valuable uncollected work by Morse Peckham: for example, his centenary essay on Browning's *The Ring and the Book*, 'Historiography and *The Ring and the Book*', *Victorian Poetry*, 6 (1968) 243–57.

21. G. M. Hopkins believed that the looseness of the language of nineteenth-century poetry reflected the lax relativism of the age, which he describes in some of his earliest writing. See 'The Probable Future of Metaphysics', *The Journals and Papers of Gerard Manley Hopkins*, ed. Humphry House and Graham Storey (London: Oxford University Press, 1959) pp. 118–21.

22. Arnold's brilliant but limited diagnosis of modernity and its problems appears in the Preface to his *Poems* of 1853, in which he explained his reasons for withdrawing that modern poem, *Empedocles on Etna* (1852) from his volume: 'the dialogue of the mind with itself has commenced; Modern problems have presented themselves' (*The Poems of Matthew Arnold*, ed. Kenneth Allott (London: Dent, 1965) p. 591).

23. Nietzsche quotes Schopenhauer's account of lyric critically in *The Birth of Tragedy*: 'It is the subject of the will, i.e. his own volition, which fills the consciousness of the singer, often as a released and satisfied desire (joy), but still oftener as an inhibited desire (grief), always as an affect, a passion, a moved state of mind . . . the stress of desire, which is always restricted and always needy' (*The Birth of Tragedy*, trans. Walter Kaufmann (New York: Vintage Books, 1967) p. 51).

24. Both W. J. Fox and A. H. Hallam conducted sophisticated analyses of Tennyson's early poems in terms of drama. See *Victorian Scrutinies: Reviews of Poetry 1830–1870*, ed. Isobel Armstrong (London: Athlone Press, 1972), pp. 75–9, 99–101.

25. Mikhail Bakhtin, *The Dialogic Imagination: Four Essays*, ed. Michael Holquist, trans. Caryl Emerson and Michael Holquist (Austin, Tx.: University of Texas Press, 1981). Bakhtin's dialogic form is not quite the same thing as Volosinov's struggle for the sign and I prefer to keep the two names separate rather than viewing them as two names for the same person. Bakhtin writes of the literary text, whereas Volosinov's interest is in challenging post-Saussurian linguistics. Bakhtin's dialogic form is oppositional and depends on the reversal of fixed positions, whereas Volosinov's struggle for the sign is a dynamic ongoing process in which contending ideologies constantly redefine the content of the sign. Neither believed that poetry could generate dialogic structures or

that poetic texts could participate in struggle. Manifestly, however, the Victorian double poem generates the drama of contending principles. I prefer the model of linguistic struggle rather than dialogism because the nature of language is crucial to Volosinov's thought (whereas it is not to Bakhtin) and his model seems particularly appropriate to *poetic* forms, where the complexity of language is foregrounded. Moreover, the model of struggle leads to perpetual redefinition in a way which the dialogic form does not. Volosinov's ideas, however, require far more rigorous development than they can be given in a book of this kind. That is why I have placed this discussion of Victorian poetry in a general post-Hegelian tradition, to which, of course, both Marx and Volosinov belong.

26. The Comte de Volney's *The Ruins; or, A Survey of the Revolutions of Empires* was known as *Ruins of Empire* and was translated in 1795.

27. Friedrich Schiller, *On the Aesthetic Education of Man in a Series of Letters*, trans. Elizabeth M. Wilkinson and L. A. Willoughby (Oxford: Clarendon Press, 1967) sixth letter, paras 3, 6, 33.

28. Carlyle, *Sartor Resartus*, p. 173.

9

The Gaskells as Unitarians

R. K. WEBB

The 33 years from the marriage of William and Elizabeth Gaskell in 1832 to her death in 1865 coincided almost exactly with a generation-long crisis in English Unitarianism, a crisis that turned on the validity and relevance of the teachings of Joseph Priestley. In his zeal to extirpate what he saw as 'the corruptions of Christianity', Priestley had drawn on an extraordinary range of intellectual weaponry – from natural philosophy to biblical criticism to history – and on an imposing set of forebears – Locke and Newton, the heterodox Anglican Samuel Clarke, Philip Doddridge, Nathaniel Lardner, David Hume (as a caution against improper reasoning from Lockean postulates), and, above all, David Hartley, whose *Observations on Man* of 1748 gave Priestley the psychological and theological bases for the determinism that set English Unitarians apart from all other Unitarians for two or three generations. That determinism, which Priestley called 'necessarianism', along with affirmation of the sole divinity of God the Father, materialism and universal restoration, were the chief doctrines of matured Priestleyanism, as he bequeathed it to his followers. Priestley insisted that no one need follow him in all of them, but James Martineau saw them as so tightly linked that an attack on any one would bring the whole system crashing down.[1]

To make Christians of everyone in the world, as Priestley and his disciples wanted, demanded elimination of the mysteries, historical errors, and trickery that had allowed superstition (and so Catholicism) to flourish. But two other extinctions were even more urgent. One was his ancestral Calvinism. Priestley's God differed from Calvin's in being infinitely benevolent, a judge who issued only interlocutory decress. No divine fiat predestined a few to salvation and many to damnation, and in time Priestley came to believe that all men would be saved. But his God was also an all-encompassing, all-seeing legislator, who laid down the laws by which the universe and society worked and whose foreknowledge extended to all the actions of His agents on earth. Only a closed, deterministic system, rigorously causal and enforced by the very constitution of the human mind, could be consistent with that foreknowledge or with the moral responsibility on which ultimate judgement would be based. Evil, therefore, proceeded as much from God as did good, though earthbound mortals could not perceive its exact place in the divine economy. But ignorance and wilfulness could be overcome, sin – really error, a violation of God's law – could be vanquished, and evil would thus disappear. Mankind was, one might say, involved in a vast process of learning, a divinely ordained means by which men could work out their own salvation and help others to do so, to promote the ultimate, predetermined happiness of the human race.

Priestley had abandoned his inherited Calvinism at Daventry Academy in the early 1750s; by the late 1760s, he had given up the Arianism that, for him as for many, had served as a means of escape from orthodoxy without abandoning belief in some sort of secondary divinity for Christ. Priestley's materialism gave him a powerful weapon against the notion of a soul apart from the body and so against the idea of pre-existence, but the case against Arianism could be argued from morality as well as from science. What became of individual responsibility if Christ took upon Himself, in His death on the Cross, the sins of men, original or particular? A truly moral man could not thus abdicate his salvation. Nor was a God useful as an example to humanity. Jesus's mission was unquestionably divine, but His person was not: when He judged, He knew what it was to sin; if He had learned to be perfect, so everyone could learn to be perfect. More than any other of their tenets, the denial of the divinity of Christ allowed orthodox enemies to insist that Unitarians were not Christians. But beyond admiration for Jesus as a man, Priestley's radical Christology retained two indispensable biblical elements to buttress the Unitarian claim to be Christian: the historical evidence of miracles (or such as withstood critical tests) as testimony to the divinity of Christ's mission, and the similarly attested fact of His resurrection, which carried with it the promise of our own resurrection, though we could not know the means by which an individual, immortal soul, dying with the body, would put on immortality.

This grand synthesis proved peculiarly persuasive to young men in the Dissenting academies in the 1780s, stirred as they were by the brilliant controversial works Priestley had published in the preceding decade and by his equally brilliant advocacy of radical politics. Through the influence of these students as they entered pulpits, and through the parallel (and sometimes antecedent) enthusiasm of able and convinced laymen, the transition to Unitarianism within English Presbyterianism (and the remnant of the Old Connexion of the General Baptists) began in earnest, to be substantially completed by the 1820s, though at great cost in numbers of both congregations and adherents and in political persecution and social ostracism during the wars against the French Revolution and Napoleon. Faced with these evils, persuaded Unitarians were bolstered in their confidence by Priestley's own example in his martyrdom in the Birmingham Riots of 1791 and his subsequent exile, and by his assurance that, however dark the passage and however great the suffering, in the end they would triumph. The defence and further systemisation of Unitarian doctrine fell in the first instance to the Rev. Thomas Belsham, followed by a host of lesser divines; while a cohort of recruits from the orthodox Baptists – and to some extent from less socially elevated circles than those from which Unitarian leaders had traditionally come – began an aggressive campaign to found new congregations, to defend the Unitarian position from attack, and to carry their war into the centres of orthodoxy from the pulpit and through the new engine of journalism.[2]

James Martineau was the most prominent, devious and difficult of the leaders of the 'new school' of Unitarians that emerged in the 1830s to supplant Priestleyanism with their grounding of religion in internal promptings rather than external evidences, the substitution of free will for necessity and a different perception of conscience. Martineau's own theological evolution was tentative and gradual, but he masked his gradualism in extreme statements and with, it often seems, deliberate attempts to provoke, outrage and wound; thus he battled steadily, harshly and unfeelingly to eradicate the Unitarian name, warning those who had fought so hard to support Unitarian claims against the orthodox that they were fighting for a mere sect as against the Church he wanted. But time was on the side of the new school, inspired by Martineau, his colleague at Manchester College J. J. Tayler, and the great Liverpool preacher J. H. Thom. Younger ministers responded warmly to their eloquence and soon outstripped them in theological radicalism or, as many saw it, nihilism. Congregations, too, came round to admiration. And, inevitably, some in the old school overreached themselves. In

1865, Samuel Bache, Martineau's brother-in-law and minister of the Church of the Messiah in Birmingham (the successor to Priestley's New Meeting), organised a demand that the British and Foreign Unitarian Association adopt some form of statement of belief to turn back antisupernaturalism. Bache's failure, in the year of Mrs Gaskell's death, marks a turning point in Unitarian history. But a rearguard action went on until the end of the century and beyond, and so Unitarianism remained a contentious, fragmented grouping at just the point at which other denominations (or parts of them) were turning to the liberalism to which the Unitarians had for so long been the lonely witnesses.

Two currents of thought in mid-century Unitarianism cut across the warring camps. One was the influence of the American minister William Ellery Channing, whose warm eloquence appealed to a generation no longer satisfied with the style of eighteenth-century preaching and devotion, while his courageous denunciation of slavery gave a new example of the commanding conscience. The other cross-current was the domestic mission movement, inspired by the work of Channing's friend Joseph Tuckerman, as minister to the poor in Boston. Dedicated to relieving the human tragedies of poverty rather than proselytising, the dozen or so domestic missions set up around the country in the 1830s and 1840s stand as a symbol of the Unitarians' turning away from the systematic understandings and large-scale solutions of social and human problems that were typical of the Priestleyan generations to the primacy of individual example. The domestic mission was not concerned with natural law and its implementation, or even with education in its ordinary institutional sense – not, to borrow two twentieth-century terms, with social engineering but with casework: the bringing together of superior and inferior in a common humanity, the transmission of powerful moral influence in a one-on-one relationship, the action, as J. H. Thom put it, of 'heart acting on heart, conscience on conscience, soul on soul, man on man'.[3]

From his birth in 1805, William Gaskell was planted squarely in the main stream of Unitarian tradition. His father and uncle, leaders of the congregation at Warrington, were deeply persuaded of the truths of Unitarian Christianity in a difficult time and committed to spreading it abroad. Attendance at Glasgow University strengthened the views that William Gaskell had absorbed in Warrington, and in the 1820s they were further refined at Manchester College in York. At Cross Street Chapel in Manchester from 1828, Gaskell found many like-minded associates: the imposing but unadventurous senior minister during his first 20 years, J. G. Robberds; other ministers round about, among them John Relly Beard at the neighbouring chapel in Salford and an old friend from Glasgow, Henry Green, the minister at Knutsford; and members of his congregation with whom he had shared his college years.[4]

No manuscripts or lists of titles of Gaskell's unpublished sermons survive. But working from those sermons that did find their way into print or that were reported extensively in the press and from leading articles in the *Unitarian Herald* that can be identified with virtual certainty as Gaskell's, we can find clear indications of the quality of his Unitarianism.[5] A major preoccupation was justifying separation from the Church of England and establishing the higher moral ground that Dissent could claim. Gaskell was appalled by the Athanasian Creed, with its proclamation that salvation could be found only in the Holy Catholic Church. He repeatedly convicted Anglican clergyman of duplicity for subscribing to the creeds and the Thirty-Nine Articles, when their personal beliefs might differ – that 'miserable evasion and paltering with words' to be found among those 'who should be patterns of uprightness and integrity', while the Church continued to be riven into sects and its work impeded by profitless strife. Nor, in his view, was the cause of honest dealing helped by F. D. Maurice's 'marvellous power . . . of bending words in any direction which may best suit his own particular notions . . . '.[6]

Buf if the Church was guilty of evasion and moral cowardice, the case with orthodox Dissent was worse. Dissenters liked to insist that the Bible only was the religion of Protestants and loudly proclaimed the principle of private judgment, while rejecting any interpretation at variance with their own. Unitarians, on the other hand, had repeatedly stressed the importance of pursuing truth, wherever it might lead; indeed, Priestley was prepared to see Christianity itself fall before the tide of enquiry at some distantly future time. Here was an anchor of Unitarian commitment to toleration and religious liberty; here, too, was a key to Unitarian responsiveness to science. Gaskell was certain that each new disclosure of science would only reveal more fully the glory of the Creator, 'that the more we come to know of His working, the more clearly shall we see how marvellous it is, and the more profoundly be led to adore'. And he had a similar confidence on the doctrinal front. Though Unitarians rejected any exclusive doctrinal basis for salvation, they saw in their peculiar doctrines a release from fear, bitterness, and perplexity which required that they advocate their beliefs to others – a point Gaskell was making as fervently in sermons in 1875 as in those of the 1840s. Nor could Unitarians rest content with mere questioning or an agreement to differ. In 1860, in Manchester College, the very heart of the new school, where he was visitor from its removal to London in 1853 until his death, Gaskell told the students that those who maintained that Unitarians had 'no clear and settled belief' were wrong: they must have clear convictions and bear witness to them. And, though men could be truly moved only by an appeal to their emotions, though reason would not suffice and Unitarians had too often put too much stress on the intellect, there was no practical wisdom without speculative truth.[7]

Two years later, he returned to that theme in *Unitarian Christians Called to Bear Witness to the Truth*, one of his three sermons before the British and Foreign Unitarian Association – no other minister preached so many. In responding to it, the denomination's two newspapers made clear the gulf between them. 'There is', said the reviewer in the *Unitarian Herald*, 'a class of visionary theologians who are never sure of anything', who argue that truth is progressive, that the Bible is not yet fully revealed, and that human nature is scarcely known; who are not even certain of the uncertainty of all things and so have 'bewildered the weak, and justified the indifferent, and puffed up the contented' and have deflected Unitarians from their great work for humanity. In dealing a near-mortal blow to such arguments, the reviewer went on, Gaskell had armed the best elements in the denomination with his own positive sense of facts and truths 'divine in their origin, historical in their manifestation, human in their practical sanction, and personal in their application and value': he rested in the 'certainty of certainties'. The *Inquirer* dissented entirely from the assumption in the sermon that Unitarian theology was clearly defined in 'distinctly labelled precipitates from the metaphysical and philosophical admixtures in which Christianity has been diluted during the lapse of years', and refused to accept that there are 'a few grand essential residuary truths' set forth in the Gospel and in which all professing Christians could agree: the *Inquirer* would have none of Gaskell's 'certainty of certainties'. The great want of the age was a catholicity that could never be attained by the mere lateral extension foreseen in Gaskell's self-satisfaction, but only by increasing height, depth, consistence and richness to fill 'the whole range of the human spirit's wants'.[8]

No doubt, both defence and attack exaggerated Gaskell's position for polemical purposes as the denominational conflict rose to its peak. Gaskell was by nature an irenic man who shunned controversy. He worked intensely hard at doing good, within his denomination and out of it, accepting every invitation he possibly could to preach to other congregations than his own and on one occasion that could not have been unique making enormous efforts to attend a monthly meeting of ministers where, given his schedule, he was not expected. He was deeply involved with the work of domestic missions and helped John Relly Beard in founding the Unitarian Home Missionary Board (later Unitarian College Manchester) to train ministers as domestic missionaries. In 1883, Robert Spears, to whom Channing remained the fullest embodiment of Unitarian theology and morality, commented with heart-felt sympathy on the concluding words of Gaskell's address to a Sunday-school meeting in Manchester, that 'there is no blessing which can be conferred on any one that is at all comparable to a true and living faith in Christ', a faith that took many forms, in the work of Sunday school teachers and domestic missionaries or in politics. To be sure, Gaskell argued in 1858 in his memorial sermon for Sir John Potter, the great Manchester merchant and M.P., that Christians should not become 'noisy, brawling, rabid politicians', yet they could not be indifferent to forms of politics or wise administration and must constantly seek 'an enlightened regard to the good of the community, intelligence, public spirit, patriotism, and philanthropy'. But Potter's first priority had been 'to extend education among the poor, and afford them facilities for the cultivation of refining taste and improving pursuits . . . to improve and elevate the character, to lay deep in the soul those principles of moral and religious truth which in all circumstances will rule the life for good'. And of none of his activities was Gaskell prouder than of his lectures on literature to Manchester workingmen.[9] Was he not, then, at one with Martineau, Thom, and all the mid-century advocates of individual improvement and heightened example?

I have argued that this position was as compatible with the old as with the new school: Bache supported the domestic mission in Birmingham as fervently as did Martineau and Thom in Liverpool; Channing had detested Priestley's influence but he was profoundly admired by Harriet Martineau, a confirmed necessarian, and by Edward Tagart, a leader of the old school. Unfortunately for our purposes, it fell to Robberds to preach the commemorative sermon at Cross Street when Channing died in 1842, but Gaskell would have agreed fully in Robberds's tribute to the American preacher's intellectual gifts, the beauty and goodness of his thought, the stirring language, and his defence of the faith, but above all to his fearless championship of the oppressed and his efforts to bring men together.[10] In seeking Gaskell's theology, then, we must go beyond this broad consensus about practical Christianity.

From time to time the theology Gaskell had learned in his youth comes through unmistakably. In 1859 John Ashton Nicholls died; he was the Gaskells' friend and the very model of the Christian philanthropist. Gaskell's memorial sermon at Cross Street a few days later was, therefore, peculiarly personal and important.[11] In it are mingled biblically inspired confidence in resurrection and an essentially Priestleyan materialism and necessarianism touched with more recent scientific understandings. We are assured, Gaskell said, that no particle of matter is ever destroyed, that the body will change but never be annihilated, while Christianity adds to this scientific certainty confidence in the indestructibility of the spirit. Death is a change in mode and form of existence, achieved through suffering, like 'every other part of the plan of Divine Providence, which for our good, has placed us under a severe and painful system of discipline. It is by the same agency that we are trained for a new and higher condition of being'.

Certainly no sermon Gaskell ever preached could have matched in importance the one he gave on the occasion of his golden jubilee in 1878.[12] In looking back over his life, he found not only profound encouragement for the prosperity of Unitarianism but (in terms almost identical to Belsham's 60 years earlier) the certainty that evil was being alleviated and would be annihilated, under the government of fixed and intelligible principles.

Errors of plan are sure to be followed by defects of execution. Improper courses of conduct infallibly lead to mischievous consequences. Vice inevitably produces punishment, and virtue necessarily brings rewards and happiness. It the nature of things, it cannot be otherwise; if it might, the world would be a chaos, without law, without order, without object, without anything intelligible or certain – a mere wreck drifting blindly and hopelessly on to destruction and oblivion. As, however, in all its departments it is pervaded by universal relations and dependencies, their foundation is laid for our instruction and guidance. By these means the sciences are built up; by these means the ultimate object of the world's existence is discovered; and by these means we turn from the present to the past, and bring back to us lessons of an important and valuable kind.

To our moral guidance, he insisted, the pattern of certain succession of cause and effect is as the compass to the navigator, showing us our direction, the dangers we will encounter, and the way into safe harbour. We must, then,

make rigid inquiry into the moral character and natural consequences of our actions . . ., to trace our errors and vices to their issues and our miseries to their causes, to take warning and derive caution from the mistakes we have made and the perversion of which we have been guilty, and to bring the satisfaction and joy which we have experienced in the pursuit of truth and the practice of holiness to reinforce us in our efforts at patient continuance in well-doing.

These two revelations of continuity of theological belief stand out both in their explicitness and by their exceptionality in the corpus of William Gaskell's published work. One can be confident, however that had we heard his sermons, week in and week out, many more such acknowledgements would have occurred, not least because in writing sermons in the midst of a crushing burden of public and private obligations, Gaskell, like all of us, would have resorted to familiar, deeply held, and, so to speak, intellectually instinctive formulations. Committed though he was to practical improvement and eager though he was to avoid discord and controversy, the Priestleyan verities ran like a ground bass through all he did and said.

Mrs Gaskell's religion has been the subject of considerable scholarly attention.[13] But what that religion exactly was and how it informed her life and her novels are questions on which the confidence of successive pronouncements is not matched by precision and proportion. To some writers, her Unitarianism is pretty much summed up in terms like liberalism, humanitarianism, or even mere Christianity – the last a source of some ironic glee to me, as learned posterity accords to the Unitarians what so many orthodox Victorians were at pains to deny them: the Christian name. Dr Duthie, quite typically, emphasises the Unitarian tolerance in the novels and sees a steady concern to bring Christian faith and conduct into congruence through reverence for truth, rejection of hypocrisy and striving for charity and justice. For Dr Fryckstedt, Mrs Gaskell illustrates in *Ruth* 'the practical Christianity advocated by Unitarianism, which taught the fundamental goodness of man who could nevertheless stray and so commanded forgiveness'. Able to rely on pervasive awareness of Christian language and precepts in her audience, Mrs Gaskell could turn a moral purpose into a religious challenge to her age.[14]

Professor Wright, finding it 'extraordinarily difficult to give any precise definition of Unitarianism in the nineteenth century', places her 'fairly in the stream of evangelicalism in its broad, non-sectarian sense . . . one of the voices of the moral conscience of mid-Victorian England'. Eschewing all sectarianism, he insists, she was concerned with individual and social conduct, but 'it is the behaviour more than the religion which really interests her', and so religion itself becomes less important as in her later novels she moves away from the didactic mode of the earlier works. Professor Easson, like most critics, emphasises the 'direct, spiritual, and practical' nature of her religion as well as her tolerance and openness. He has characterised accurately and in some detail the conflict within the denomination and ends by suggesting that she was to be found on James Martineau's side. But Unitarianism is 'a presence rather than a force' in her novels; religion informs her novels, but she is not a religious novelist. Dr Cunningham contrasts her sensitive portrayal of a wide religious range with what he sees as the narrowness of the Cross Street congregation, and again identifies her with James Martineau's revolution: her 'openness and liberality' led to 'a merging of Dissent in the Church of England', to her fondness for Anglican heroines, to her close and comfortable identification with *Cranford*, where Dissent is not to be found, and to her tendency to portray (as in *Cousin Phillis*) an elegiac, 'rural and small-town Dissent, whose relaxed and generous world approximates closely to the Anglicanism of Cranford'.[15]

In trying to find a firmer footing, we may begin by striking out into the letters. Here the first, most obviously relevant feature is the impression, fragmented and tricky to interpret, that we can get of the community in which she lived. Within the constellation of Unitarian names that appear either as correspondents or as subjects of chat and gossip, the Gaskells' identification seems far stronger with Unitarians belonging to the old school or poised somewhere in the middle than with those identified with the new school. The Lalors, for example. Musical opportunity was a key factor in the decision to send Marianne to Mrs Lalor's school, but the Lalors had a wider presence than the school: they were seen on visits to London and John Lalor could be presumed upon for favours. He was a Dublin-born journalist who had converted from Catholicism around 1844 and who edited the *Inquirer* in 1847–9, when it was edging towards a middle position from the combative Priestleyanism of its early years under William Hincks. The long, intense correspondence with Eliza Fox ('Tottie') had much to do with Tottie's father; by that time, to be sure, W. J. Fox was scarcely Unitarian and had become far more interested in his secular, political pursuits. But he had left the orthodox Baptists to become an aggressive Priestleyan Unitarian, and it is significant that an equally long and intense correspondence with the whole Fox family was carried on by Harriet Martineau, who remained a necessarian to the end. Even more remarkable is the continued association with the Tagarts in London. Though Mrs Gaskell warned Marianne against the 'tone' of the household and their taste, there was constant visiting; Tagart, minister at Little Portland Street, was also secretary of the British and Foreign Unitarian Association, the author of a significantly timed book to reassert the centrality of Locke, and one of the most implacable opponents of Martineau's departures, as was Henry A. Bright, who appears as friend and correspondent, and who was one of those committed and theologically adept laymen who contributed to lively exchanges on doctrinal matters in the Unitarian press.[16]

The leaders of the new school were in the North – Martineau and J. J. Tayler until the College removed to London in 1853, Thom and Charles Wicksteed for their entire careers – but they play a surprisingly small part in the surviving letters. Tayler figures the most prominently. From time to time the Gaskells attended Tayler's chapel in Manchester, Tayler accompanied Meta on a journey from London to Manchester, William Gaskell stayed at his house in London, and he appears as one of many guests at a Robberds wedding, but that is all, at least in Mrs Gaskell's letters, except for the odd, bitchy passage about Mrs Tayler's concealed pregnancy and sudden delivery in Blackpool or the report of her strangely un-Unitarian objection to discussing Sir Walter Scott on a Sunday. There is, however, a long tribute by William Gaskell to Tayler, in his visitorial address to the students of the College at the end of the College term in which Tayler died. 'One of my best and oldest friends', Gaskell called him, and he praised Tayler's power as a teacher, his devoutness, his constantly questing intellect, and his reverence for truth, qualities that impressed others among Tayler's contemporaries (though not all) and that come through in his letters. But Gaskell was characteristically circumspect on the issues that had come to divide the old friends, more so than Tayler, who, in a memorial sermon, identified J. G. Robberds as belonging to the older phase of Unitarianism. Gaskell appears to have been more distant from James Martineau, a closer contemporary and a more difficult personality. At any rate, Mrs Gaskell tried without success to put Martineau off when he came to call in 1852 by pleading a deadline, and the next year when both families spent a day together in Wales, Mrs Gaskell wrote, 'I wish they weren't coming, – I like to range about ad libitum, & sit out looking at views &c; not talking sense by the yard'.[17]

This last can be taken as further evidence of Mrs Gaskell's lack of interest in theological matters. She described herself as a sermon-hater; was reported as rejecting one school for Marianne because it represented 'the very worst style of dogmatic hard Unitarianism, utilitarian to the backbone'; was delighted to see James Panton Ham, William Gaskell's assistant, depart for London, because what she wanted was 'some really spiritual devotional preaching instead of controversy about doctrines, – about whh I am more & more certain *we can never be certain* in this world' (but then Ham was a convert from Congregationalism, and doctrine mattered); and admired that very devotional quality in the preaching of Frederick Denison Maurice, whatever reservations her husband (and probably she herself) might have had about his message.[18]

Against all this, however, we must place a considerable weight of countervailing evidence. Even though she could say, only half in

jest, that she imagined heaven to be a place 'where we shan't have
any conscience, – and Hell vice versa', she was unquestionably ar
advocate of 'the real earnest Christianity which seeks to do as much
and as extensive good as it can'. But such heart-felt words only place
her firmly in the Channingite and philanthropic cross-currents that I
have suggested were central to understanding William Gaskell and
all the Victorian Unitarians. Her eagerness for good devotiona
preaching was widely shared as well: in a high romantic age, so
much of what was typical of eighteenth-century modes of thought
and reasoning (and of much Unitarian pulpit style) had come to
seem incapable of moving men's hearts. But these yearnings after
emotion and the eager, self-sacrificial pursuit of 'real earnest
Christianity' were quite compatible with strongly held and long-
established doctrinal positions.[19]

Despite her disclaimers, Mrs Gaskell was clearly able to talk a
length about theology and, it is easy to imagine, enjoyed it in a good
cause, as when she took Charles Bosanquet under her tutelage to
enlighten him about Unitarian views. And every once in a while she
turns deadly serious on a deeply held doctrinal point. In trying to
explain Marianne's disturbing flirtation with Roman Catholicism
she traced her daughter's vulnerability to her unresponsiveness to
ideas as a balance to her genius for practical things: she was
unselfish, sweet and meek, but without the toughness to know for
what she stood. Several years earlier, Mrs Gaskell was trying to
shore up Marianne's capacity to discriminate the grounds of her
inherited Dissent. For all the aesthetic pleasure Mrs Gaskell took in
the services of the Church, she was, she said, always pulled up shor
by parts of the liturgy, the opening of the Litany, for example, which
'did so completely go against my belief that it would be wrong to
deaden my sense of it's [sic] serious error by hearing it too often'.
Her advice was to go to chapel in the morning and to the Church in
the evening, when only the Doxology could offend against 'one's
sense of *truth*'. The Anglican liturgy reinforced the temptation not to
have a fixed belief,

> but I know it is wrong not to clear our minds as much as possible
> as to the nature of that God, and tender Saviour, whom we can
> not love properly unless we try and define them clearly to
> ourselves. . . . The one thing I *am* clear and sure about is this tha
> Jesus Christ was not equal to His father; that, however divine a
> being he was he was *not* God; and that worship as God addressed

to Him is therefore wrong in me; and that it is my duty to deny myself the gratification of constantly attending a service (like the morning service) in a part of which I thoroughly disagree.

This passage suggests how complicated was her protestation that she felt herself an Arian, a remark that may indicate only the nineteenth-century shift in emphasis (as in William Gaskell) from God the Father to Christ the Son or that may reject both the 'humanitarian' position of Priestley and that of contemporary Unitarian radicals.[20]

'Every young girl', Mrs Gaskell wrote, 'of seventeen or so, who is at all thoughtful, is very apt to make a Pope out of the first person who presents to her a new or larger system of duty than that by which she has been unconsciously guided hitherto' (*WD*, vol. VIII, pp. 166–7). Marianne was surely present to her mind when she thus caught Molly's awed response to Roger Hamley. But who might Elizabeth Stevenson's own pope have been? She was too young when she left her London home to have been affected by her father, and when she returned (at 17) to see him through his last illness, he could have had relatively little beyond a confirmatory effect on her religious views. Henry Green, who with his family became life-long friends, settled in Knutsford in 1827, too late to be formative, though the conversations on all those subsequent visits must have touched occasionally on denominational and doctrinal matters. The Misses Byerley were Unitarian in background and connection but nominally Anglican, and the girls in their school attended the parish church. Henry Green's predecessor at Knutsford was Joseph Ashton, a product of Manchester College York in its greatest period. He was, his obituarist wrote, greatly respected by his congregations (except for a quarrel over an organ at Whitby) though 'his manner wanted vivacity'. Diffident about publication, he left us only his account of the Whitby dispute and one sermon of 1845 (admirable for our purpose, though out of phase) on the text 'Buy the truth and sell it not' – buy it, he said, with arduous labour, but do not sell it for the good opinion of others. William Turner, in whose house Elizabeth Stevenson lived for parts of two years, is perhaps a better candidate. What printed sermons we have are of a practical bent, but in the answers to questions at his ordination in 1782 Turner avowed himself a Priestleyan and soon after his settlement at Newcastle undertook a rigorous programme of visiting and catechising. We can catch something of the aggressive Unitarian

tone at the Edinburgh chapel towards the end of her stay there from
the series of lectures undertaken by the new minister, B. T. Stannus,
though of course we do not know if she attended them, or the
chapel.[21]

She did not, I suspect, have a pope. But she lived her most
impressionable years in a closely-knit and homogeneous society in
which ministers from York and Glasgow and, as Henry Holland's
letters and many other sources show us, laymen from the same
background shared philosophical and ethical assumptions, a
vocabulary informed by those assumptions, and an intense
awareness of the beliefs and actions that those deeper assumptions
entailed in the moral and active life. Elizabeth Stevenson was, I
believe, thoroughly immersed in the dominant Unitarian thought of
the 1820s – it could scarcely have been otherwise – and William
Gaskell, her closest and most critical reader, confirmed what she
had already taken in and worked through with her the moral and
metaphysical dynamics and implications of her novels.

What effects, then, did her religious axioms have on her art? I
agree with the commentators that Mrs Gaskell's tolerance and
openness – virtues in which Unitarians left everyone else behind –
made her unusually sensitive to the varieties of religious experience,
though I might give even more credit to the wonderful 'ear' that
allowed her to render the differing religious accents of her
characters as impressively as she does their dialect. I am grateful,
too, for Dr Fryckstedt's discovery of Mrs Gaskell's obligations to and
literal borrowings from John Layhe's reports as domestic missionary
in Manchester in her painting of the condition of the poor in *Mary
Barton*.[22] There is, I am convinced, more to be done along this line,
for example, comparing Layhe's reports to those of other
missionaries, like the Rev. John Johns, who died at his post in
Liverpool in the cholera epidemic in 1849 and whose eloquence had
a galvanic effect on Liverpool charity. How much might such
reports be subject to the strictures that Mrs Gaskell herself visited
upon the reportage of the philanthropist Thomas Wright, whose
work in other respects she so much admired?[23] How far were all
such reports written to some literary standard or model as a
necessary technique of wringing support from busy or reluctant
people? Again, though she could 'never enter into *Sartor Resartus*',[24]
the Carlyle of *Chartism* suffuses *Mary Barton*, an influence that needs
closer analysis. And, as she could have had no direct experience of
the early trade unions, with their blood-curdling oaths and

extravagant rhetoric, a historian with a close knowledge of working-class movements in the 1840s and 1850s could surely find other sources that she used, as she used Layhe's reports, in bluebooks, newspaper accounts, trials and alarmist books like E. C. Tufnell's *Character, Object, and Effects of Trades' Unions*. Indeed, I suspect that too much can be made of Mrs Gaskell's immediate experience of the poor: though she taught in Sunday and day schools, invited her pupils to her house, and visited their homes, the domestic missions were deliberately engines of remote charity, the real work falling to specially recruited missionaries, and much of what she wrote to enlighten her ignorant and unfeeling audience she had to learn from reading.

Another point, puzzling and frustrating, has to do with the representation – or non-representation – of Unitarians in her novels. W. Arthur Boggs points out that nowhere is any form of the word Unitarian used.[25] Her own Unitarianism being common knowledge once her identity as the author of *Mary Barton* was revealed, one can understand why prudence might have dictated silence on the subject, if she were not to be known, with virtually certain results in the market, as a Unitarian novelist. But three major characters in the novels are ministers, and their plausible, though obscured, relationship to Unitarianism has caused much scholarly comment. I can add little to the general appreciation of Ebenezer Holman in *Cousin Phillis* other than to emphasise (what some writers have unaccountably missed) that he is offered as an Independent or Congregationalist and is consistent with that ascription. The Rev. Mr Hale in *North and South* is much more important. In general, Anglican clergymen in Mrs Gaskell's novels are portrayed unfavourably – as kindly and well-meaning, perhaps, but without great conviction, serving a kind of civic religion, compromising and excusing themselves in a way inescapable in an established church with a requirement of subscription, as we have seen William Gaskell arguing trenchantly. Even the evangelical Mr Gray in *My Lady Ludlow*, who has conviction to excess, comes through as a slightly comic, unworldly man who gets his qualified victories through well-intentioned but not well-educated obstinacy. Mr Hale stands out as an exception to all this doddering and dithering. He has his faults, yet he does sacrifice everything (perhaps, more accurately, everyone) on a point of conviction. Mrs Gaskell is deliberately inexplicit about his doubts, though they seem characteristically Unitarian; certainly Hale is not a sceptic but 'can resolve greatly about great things, and is capable of self-sacrifice in theory; but in the details of practice he is weak and vacillating'; he was modelled, she said, on a clergyman she knew who left the Church on principle, regretted it every day of his life, and would do it again.[26]

The most puzzling of the clerical portraits is the Rev. Thurstan Benson in *Ruth*. He is tied to a grand Unitarian theme, the power of truth, and his chapel is clearly Knutsford, lovingly detailed. But what goes on within that chapel is mystifying. Bradshaw is the type of powerful patron, habituated to command, known in all Dissenting denominations. But his tyranny over his family and his condemnation of Ruth and of Benson seem to arise from a conviction of original sin and belief in a judgemental God that would, I think, be impossible to find in a Unitarian congregation. Though the baptismal practice at Eccleston chapel – a service of thanksgiving and dedication at about six months of age – would fit with Unitarian custom, Benson's prayer on the occasion of Leonard's dedication would not: a long prayer in which 'thought followed thought, and fear crowded upon fear, and all were to be laid bare before God, and His aid and counsel asked' (*R*, vol. iii, p. 179). No more Unitarian were Benson's constant resort to evangelical language or his crying aloud, in his solitude, 'with almost morbid despair, "God be merciful to me a sinner!"' (*R*, vol. iii, p. 141).

At some point earlier in the century, Southwood Smith, for a time minister at Edinburgh and Yeovil before moving to London to begin his distinguished medical career, preached a sermon on James 3:9 against the concept of innate depravity, a point on which, as a former Baptist, he felt particular strongly. No one, he argued, becomes depraved suddenly, as the result of a single temptation, but only after a long course of indulgence in sin: 'a few repetitions may begin to rivet the adamantine choices of habit; one vice may induce a kindred vice, and the dominion of Sin, unchecked, be ever . . . enlarging on the mind, but the changes are gradual and progressive, not instantaneous and complete. Virtue lingers long, and submits not to an expulsion without many a struggle.' This view, more consistent with the depiction of Ruth's fall and redemption than Benson's preachings, is placed in the context of associationist psychology within the necessarian scheme.[27] And though Benson's radical democratic, and rationalist background (*R*, vol. iii, p. 184) might lead one to expect a similar allegiance, he reveals no such all-encompassing understanding of the physical and moral universe. He seems to be thinking his way into Ruth's moral catastrophe as if for the very first time – there was, we are told, no introspection or analysis of motive (*R*, vol. III, p. 141) – and he is content to wait patiently upon God. In contrast to his sister, whose name is Faith and who is capable of quick, decisive action, 'he deliberated and trembled, and often did wrong from his very deliberation, when his first instinct would have led him right' (*R*, vol. III, p. 203).

Perhaps Mrs Gaskell was so overwhelmed by the boldness of her subject, so uncertain of the reaction of her readers, that she had to suppress the reasoning that most educated Unitarians would have advanced and to surround her minister, despite some clear Unitarian lineaments, with a cloud of pious commonplaces. Certainly, Benson is one of the least successful of her creations, a ditherer in her best Anglican mode, led on by an almost accidental and certainly unreasoned expedient to do the right thing through the wrong methods. William Turner is often seen as a model for Benson, and there is something of the real minister in the fictional one – the transparent goodness, the likelihood that eagerness to do good might outrun judgment. But to triangulate from Benson's innocence and precipitousness to identifying him with Turner – a sophisticated, widely active, civic-minded, forthright urban man of the widest reputation, a devotional preacher but a theological Priestleyan – is a travesty. We are told that, in his retirement in Manchester, Turner read *Ruth* and recognised his Newcastle house in the description of Benson's residence in Eccleston. But he could never have recognised himself in the portrait of, as Harriet Martineau put it, 'such a nincompoop'.[28]

Mrs Gaskell's Unitarianism is not to be found in her characters but in the dynamics of her narratives and in her comments upon her characters' actions. To take an obvious Unitarian concern, education is one of the principal motifs of the novels. It can appear simply as a first step to higher things, as when Sylvia's dogged resistance to Philip's efforts to teach her gives way to painful efforts to learn to read under the biblically constricted tutelage of Alice Rose, 'for perhaps it might do me good; I'm noane so happy' (*SL*, vol. VI, p. 445). Mrs Gaskell had expressed her shock at discovering (through a book by Joseph Kay) how small was the proportion of educated children in England compared with the uneducated, but she certainly wanted education to do more than make people literate. She had welcomed Mrs Lalor's reputation for 'forming conscientious, thoughtful, earnest, independent characters' and later welcomed 'the enlargement of ideas' that Marianne had attained in the school. Much earlier, in *My Diary*, a journal that records evidence of the most scrupulous care for the intellectual and moral growth of her elder daughters, she had shown deep concern for the right rules of raising children, especially for the early inculcation of proper devotional and moral behaviour – a concern that was central in the Unitarian tradition and for which authority can be found in striking detail in Priestley. How far Sylvia fell short of that 'enlargement of ideas' may be suggested by the additional character that Mrs Gaskell considered for *North and South*, a rival to Margaret Hale for Mr Thornton's affections, but who, vetoed, survived (in my judgement) to become Sylvia – the daughter of an old friend of Mrs Thornton's in humble, retired country life on the borders of Lancashire: 'I know the kind of wild wayward character that grows up in lonesome places, which has a sort of Southern capacity of hating & loving. She shd not be what people call *educated*, but with strong sense.'[29]

One might also point to the intellectual growth that came from the partnership in learning of Phillis Holman, her father and Holdsworth, and that would certainly be resumed, following Phillis's recovery from her depressive illness, on her visit to Paul's family; or the integrating and softening of Thornton's vision that was the intended result of his tutoring in the classics by Mr Hale; or the transformation that comes over Ruth once she realises the infinitude of her ignorance, begins to exercise her intellectual powers and rises through study to a new comprehension of life and duty. By contrast, John Barton shows us that a little learning can be dangerous: 'The actions of the uneducated', Mrs Gaskell tells us, 'seem to me typified in those of Frankenstein, that monster of many human qualities ungifted with a soul, a knowledge of the difference between good and evil' (*MB*, vol. I, p. 196).[30] Barton had hankered after the right way, but 'it's a hard one for a poor man to find. No one learned me, and no one told me. When I was a little chap they taught me to read, and then they never gave me no books.' He had heard that the Bible was a good book, but that was worse than useless knowledge. He had not tried long 'to live Gospel-wise', though 'it was liker heaven than any other bit of earth has been': the talk of others about rights and his own response to the imperatives of love and suffering made him give up trying to square men's

actions with the texts. But 'from that time I've dropped down, down
– down' (*MB*, vol. II, pp. 430–1).

Job Legh is the foil, the self-educated man who has done it right,
the type of Manchester men who work the loom and read Newton
and who rise from science to broader views of everything (*MB*, vol.
I, p. 40). It is 'dear Job Legh' – from the last line of the novel – who
brings about the repentance and softening of Mr Carson. With many
expressions of self-doubt and inadequacy, Legh argues the real
merits of John Barton, deluded though he was through limited
vision and the horror of contrast between principle and practice,
between political economy and human needs and charity.

Another theme, central in Unitarian thinking and much remarked
on by scholars since, is truth. We have seen William Gaskell
preaching on the subject, following in the path of scores of Unitarian
ministers earlier in the century, and the word recurs in odd ways to
Mrs Gaskell's pen, for example, in her feeling that the Doxology
offended against her sense of truth, or her commendation of
Charlotte Brontë as 'truth itself'. Associated with the notion of truth
in Unitarian culture was the imperative of candour, in the double
sense of speaking out about truth and speaking with utter
frankness, witness William Gaskell's severity towards Anglican
compromising, and Harriet Martineau's astonishment that Mrs
Gaskell, in her life of Charlotte Brontë, could regret the publication
of the Atkinson letters through which Miss Martineau had
proclaimed her conversion to free thought: 'Clergymen's
daughters, (even though Protestants) know nothing of the
formation and publication of opinions; but Unitarians are supposed
to be thoroughly versed in the principle and have indeed no other
ground to stand on'.[31]

Truth, as has often been pointed out, is at issue even in small ways
in the novels – in the innocent deceptions, entirely understood,
about making cakes in *Cranford*, or in the 'perpetual lapses from
truth' in Mrs Gibson (*WD*, vol. VIII, p. 431), or in Cynthia's piteous
complaint that 'I've never lived with people with such a high
standard of conduct before', to which Molly candidly replies that
she must learn, for Roger's notions of right and wrong are quite
strict (*WD*, vol. VIII, pp. 475–6). At a profounder level, Mary
Barton suppresses evidence, and a lie sets up the central moral issue
in *Ruth*. In *North and South*, Mr Hale's bold action upon his doubts
sets a standard of fidelity to truth from which Margaret falls away in

the aftermath of the accidental encounters at Outwood station: it is almost as though Margaret Hale (whose name was Mrs Gaskell's preferred title for the novel) were the clergyman's daughter envisioned by Harriet Martineau, who had to learn the importance of fidelity to truth. In *Sylvia*, Philip Hepburn lies (or, more accurately, suppresses the truth) in a cause that seems arguably good, and presents the moral issue with a gravity and an awfulness of retribution not to be found, perhaps, prior to Conrad.

The consequences of violating truth are instances of the working of a larger principle, central to necessarian theology and, in Mrs Gaskell's novels, the certain succession of cause and effect. In his jubilee sermon, as we have seen, William Gaskell described it as our moral compass, a stimulus to inquiry into moral character and the sources, consequences and lessons of our errors and vices. The metaphor of the compass could have stood as epigraph to the collected edition of Mrs Gaskell's novels: only *Cranford*, a bringing together of charming sketches rather than a novel, escapes. And in the necessarian scheme, the inescapable effect of wrong formation of character or of deliberate or careless choice is suffering, for – again to quote William Gaskell's funeral sermon for John Ashton Nicholls – 'the plan of Divine Providence . . . for our good, has placed us under a severe and painful system of discipline', as preparation for 'a new and higher condition of being'.

Choices for illustration are many, in addition to the consequences of violation of truth already noted: the inevitable sequel of the indulgent upbringing of Mr Bellingham or the bitter tyranny of Mr Bradshaw; the fateful choices of Sylvia's father or the wretched Boucher, each but one victim among many. But I shall choose two. In the furor that erupted over *Mary Barton*, Mrs Gaskell thought her way back to the genesis of what she liked to call a 'tragic poem' in her notion of 'the seeming injustice of the inequalities of fortune' and her sense of the bewilderment they would pose for a man 'full of rude, illogical thought' and a correspondingly strong sympathy for those who suffered.

> I fancied I saw how all this might lead to a course of action which might appear right for a time to the bewildered mind of such a one, but that this course of action, violating the eternal laws of God, would bring with it its own punishment of an avenging conscience far more difficult to bear than any worldly privation.

John Barton is beyond the sort of prophylactic help that can flow from the accommodation arrived at between Thornton and Higgins, so far gone in the reinforcing psychology of habitual hatred that there remains only 'the Destroyer, Conscience', and death (*MB*, vol. I, p. 410). Facing death, John Barton comes to a profound sense of sin in the agony 'He sent as punishment', so 'thinking if I were but in that world where they say God is, He would, maybe, teach me right from wrong, even if it were with many stripes. I've been sore puzzled here. I would go through Hell-fire if I could but get free from sin at last' (*MB*, vol. I, p. 423). Elizabeth Gaskell had no doubt that in the life hereafter (and not in Hell-fire), John Barton, and all of us, would attain final salvation.

In *Wives and Daughters*, Mrs Gaskell's last novel, which some have seen as virtually devoid of religious influence, every major character, other than Molly, is a different incarnation of the law of cause and effect. With Squire Hamley and Mrs Gibson, we see the results of defective or limited upbringing: in the one case passion and prejudice impede communication between father and son, in the other, a combination of moral obtuseness, superficiality and snobbery threatens her new household and, more damagingly, creates a daughter who has grown up 'outside the pale of duty and "oughts"', who can never attain 'steady, every-day goodness' but alternates between effort and lassitude, 'a moral kangaroo' (*WD*, vol. VIII, pp. 254, 257). Mr Gibson, blinded by the dangers that might beset a motherless girl, chooses unwisely, sensing his error at the moment it becomes irrevocable, and in time he sees even Molly victimised by the connection. Osborne, overpraised and 'too indolent to keep an unassisted conscience' (*WD*, vol. VIII, p. 409), fails at the university and falls into 'the temptation, the stolen marriage, the consequent happiness, and alas! the consequent suffering' (*WD*, vol. VIII, p. 504), to which Roger, the clear-sighted scientist, provides an instructive counterpoint, though even he skirts disaster in the secret pledge to Cynthia. In the 'Concluding Remarks' added after Mrs Gaskell's death by Frederick Greenwood, the editor of *Cornhill Magazine*, we are told that Roger and Molly would have been married and of a few other probabilities in the unwritten closing chapters. Greenwood speaks of the brilliance of Mrs Gaskell's portraiture, of her delicacy and subtlety, and declares that the reader of the last three novels – *Sylvia's Lovers*, *Cousin Phillis* and *Wives and Daughters* – will feel displaced from a wicked world of selfishness and passion into one where, despite weakness, mistakes, and long and bitter suffering, people live calm and wholesome lives: the 'merely intellectual qualities' might need 20 years to come into their own, though he thought them clearly of secondary importance. But how might Mrs Gaskell really have drawn the moral from the skein of causality she had so admirably, centrally and, in the event, almost invisibly created?

Most commentators and most modern readers find difficulties with the climaxes of Mrs Gaskell's novels. To those who see *Mary Barton* and *North and South* as industrial novels and who bring to that perspective a conviction of the irreducibility of conflict between classes, the elaborately plotted reconciliations seem a violation of political reality and an authorial failure of nerve: the dying Barton and the vengeful Carson are joined together in a common anguish, and Carson undergoes inner reformation; Thornton and Higgins come together in realising their subjection to law, which must yet be humanised in their project (of quite disproportionate triviality) for a workmen's dining room. So, too, with the conclusion of the 'moral' novels, which to many readers must seem over-elaborate exercises in moral tidiness. Ruth goes through a succession of penances, in raising her child and in working as a nurse in a cholera epidemic that kills her; we see Philip, in the unlikely guise of a soldier, in heroics at Acre, in an expiatory sojourn in a hospital for decayed soldiers, and at last in the rescue of his child from drowning. Such improbable coincidences and extravagant action strike us as melodramatic and forced. They are certainly melodramatic. But in the necessarian economy they are more than that, bringing us squarely to face the idea of atonement, an extremely uncomfortable notion in our time.

'Many of the improvements now in practice in the system of employment in Manchester', Mrs Gaskell wrote towards the end of *Mary Barton*, 'owe their origin to short earnest sentences spoken by Mr Carson. Many and many yet to be carried into execution, take their birth from that stern, thoughtful mind, which submitted to be taught by suffering' (*MB*, vol. I, p. 451). As necessarians saw it, through suffering we learn the dictates of duty, to live to others, and to help them to the same end. How such thoughts fit into a wider Unitarian perspective is made clear in a sermon preached at the opening of the new Unitarian church in Sydney on 6 November 1853, by the Rev. G. H. Stanley, who had been trained at Manchester College in its last years in York and who had served two congregations in England before going out to Australia. Enjoining respect for the opinions of others, even when wrong or prejudiced,

Stanley deplored both the limiting effect of creeds and the danger of 'too great license of speculation' and called, as William Gaskell did, for 'well-grounded opinions, and well-defined views' as in 'the great leading truths of the Christian Revelation'. The greatest of these truths he saw as the unity and fatherhood of God, who chose the mission, life, death and resurrection of Jesus Christ as the *means* to secure the spiritual and eternal welfare of all men. Jesus suffered and died, not to change the mind of God, but the minds of men, to soften our hearts and to make us followers. Atonement, therefore, meant not expiatory sacrifice but its etymological derivation – at-one-ment, the reconciliation of all men with God and with each other.[32] The need to unite classes through awareness of common interests was a commonplace in the 1840s, and by the 1850s that unity seemed close to reality – the complete suffrage movement, the gradual eclipse of physical-force Chartism, the extraordinary events of 1848 were stages in that apparent consummation. A creature of that era, Mrs Gaskell thought it the depth of wickedness to set class against class, but bridging that gulf was only one work to be done in the broader quest for atonement, for reconciliation.

In the argument with which Job Legh persuades Carson to forgo his vengeance for quiet but powerful reforming, he declares his conviction that all the new, unsettling inventions come from God and that 'it is part of His plan to send suffering to bring out a higher good; but surely it's also a part of His plan that as much of the burden of the suffering as can be should be lightened by those whom it is His pleasure to make happy, and content in their own circumstances' (*MB*, vol. I, p. 448). That is pure Priestley, pure Belsham! It is revealing that this entire passage was not in the novel as Mrs Gaskell conceived it. When, after a long delay, the publisher found that the manuscript would fall short of the needed number of pages, Mrs Gaskell protested that she would rather give up some of her payment than interpolate anything. But interpolate she did, in what must have been a rush, and wrote from a ready stock of ideas a passage that made explicit the significance implicit in Barton's death in Carson's arms.[33] Suffering rooted in character or moral choice and worked out in reconciliation is the *leitmotif* of all the novels we have considered here. The explicitness to which Mrs Gaskell was forced in *Mary Barton* retreats behind the dramatic action that brings the other novels to an end, though the message varies not. How, in the quietest and subtlest of her novels, the philosophical circle might have been closed is a question that places the lost ending of

Wives and Daughters among the most tantalising and regrettable possibilities in the many works of art that death left unfinished.

Mrs Gaskell was not a religious novelist, but her Unitarianism gave her a world view so inclusive and so prescriptive that, when she set herself a social or moral task beyond mere tale-spinning, she was forced to be a philosophical novelist, worthy of being classed, if not ranked, with George Eliot, who among the Victorians has had that category almost to herself.

Notes

This paper was written largely during the tenure of a visiting fellowship at the Australian National University in Canberra. I should like particularly to thank Professor Oliver MacDonagh, whose reading of its first version led to extensive and beneficial changes and whose own work on Jane Austen (e.g. 'Highbury and Chawton: Social Convergence in *Emma*', *Historical Studies*, 18 (1978) pp. 37–51) is a model of what historians can do when confronting a novelist.

1. James Martineau, 'On the Life, Character, and Works of Dr. Priestley', in the *Monthly Repository* for 1833, reprinted with changes in his *Essays, Reviews and Addresses* (London, 1890–1) vol. I, pp. 1–42, esp. pp. 13–14.
2. R. K. Webb, 'The Unitarian Background', in Barbara Smith (ed.), *'Truth, & Liberty, & Religion': Essays Celebrating Two Hundred Years of Manchester College* (Oxford, 1986) pp. 1–30; and 'Flying Missionaries: Unitarian Journalists in Victorian England', in J. M. W. Bean (ed.), *The Political Culture of Modern Britain: Essays in Memory of Stephen Koss* (London, 1987) pp. 11–31.
3. J. H. Thom, *Religion, the Church, and the People* (London, 1849) p. 28.
4. On the elder Gaskells, see Thomas Asline Ward to Joseph Hunter, 9 March 1812, Sheffield Public Library. William Gaskell, *A Sermon on Occasion of the Death of the Rev. John Gooch Robberds* (London, 1854). The letters of Franklin Baker, Charles Wallace and Joseph Ashton, Unitarian College MSS C2⁹, John Rylands University Library of Manchester, make clear the common assumptions that underlay the close friendship of three of the area's ministers.
5. Gaskell's published works are listed in W. E. A. and Ernest Axon, *Gaskell Bibliography* (Manchester, 1895) pp. 16–20. Dr Williams's Library holds the minute books for the *Unitarian Herald* from 1861 to 1865; for the last two of those years, the minutes list the editor (the four were Gaskell, J. R. Beard, Brooke Herford and John Wright) responsible for the issue and the editor responsible for the leading article.
6. *Unitarian Herald* (hereafter cited as *UH*): 'A New View of the Athanasian

Creed', with the comment on Maurice, 15 July 1864; 'Infallible Fallibles', 13 January 1865; 'Subscription Altered, not Amended', 2 June 1865; 'Using Church Forms and Believing Them', 7 July 1865.

7. *UH*: 'What Would Orthodoxy Have?', 30 September 1864; 'Warrington Academy', 5 May 1865. See also *Protestant Practices Inconsistent with Protestant Principles* (London, 1836); *Some Evil Tendencies of the Popular Theology* (Wakefield, 1847); *Popular Doctrines that Obscure the Views which the New Testament Gives* (Manchester, 1875). The visitorial address is reported in *Christian Reformer* 16 (n.s.) (August 1860) 457–65.

8. *UH*, 23 August 1862; *Inquirer*, 16 August 1862.

9. Barbara Brill, *William Gaskell, 1805–1884* (Manchester, 1984). Gaskell remarks on his extramural preaching and his over-commitment in a letter to Thomas Holland, 19 April 1855, and in undated letters to J. R. Beard, Unitarian College MSS A2[1]. Henry Green's report on Gaskell's heroic efforts to attend the meeting are in a letter to John Gordon, 13 January 1863, in the same collection, C1[47]. Gaskell's irenic nature coupled with theological firmness is commented on by S. A. Steinthal in his memorial sermon (*UH*, 20 June 1884). Spears writes in *Christian Life*, 21 April 1883. Gaskell, *The Duties of the Individual to Society: A Sermon on the Death of Sir John Potter, M.P.* (Manchester, 1858).

10. Bache to Rees Lloyd, 17 October 1848, Unitarian College MSS A2[1], John Rylands Library; R. K. Webb, *Harriet Martineau: A Radical Victorian* (London, 1960) pp. 112, 144–5; Edward Tagart, *A Tribute to the Memory of William Ellery Channing* (London, 1842); and J. G. Robberds, *The Voice of the Dead* (London, 1842).

11. *Christian Views of Life and Death* (London, 1859). Mrs Gaskell was much distressed that prior commitments prevented her attending the funeral or the Sunday morning service at which the sermon was preached (J. A. V. Chapple and Arthur Pollard (eds), *The Letters of Mrs Gaskell* (Manchester, 1966) pp. 574–5: 20 September 1859).

12. *UH*, 9 August 1878.

13. References to Mrs Gaskell's novels are given in parentheses in the text following the quotations. The citations are to the Knutsford edition, edited by Sir A. W. Ward (London, 1906).

14. Enid L. Duthie, *The Themes of Elizabeth Gaskell* (London, 1980) pp. 150–76; Monica Correa Fryckstedt, *Elizabeth Gaskell's 'Mary Barton' and 'Ruth': A Challenge to Christian England* (Uppsala, 1982) pp. 54–86 and *passim*.

15. Edgar Wright, *Mrs Gaskell: the Basis for Reassessment* (London, 1965) pp. 23–50; Angus Easson, *Elizabeth Gaskell* (London, 1979) pp. 4–17; and Valentine Cunningham, *Everywhere Spoken Against: Dissent in the Victorian Novel* (Oxford, 1975) pp. 127–42.

16. *Gaskell Letters* (hereafter cited as *GL*) *passim* on the Lalors, Foxes, Tagarts and Bright. The Fox–Martineau correspondence is held by Dr R. S. Speck, San Francisco.

17. *GL*: on Thom, p. 846; on Wicksteed, p. 94; on the Taylers, pp. 63–4, 180, 186, 191, 510 and 600; on Martineau, pp. 177, 239. William Gaskell, *Address to the Students of Manchester New College, London, delivered . . . on June 23, 1869* (Manchester, 1869).

18. *GL*: as a sermon-hater, p. 492; on Unitarian dogmatism, p. 136; on Ham, p. 537; on Maurice, pp. 79, 117, 254–5.
19. *GL*: on conscience, pp. 109–10; on 'real earnest Christianity', p. 117.
20. *GL*: on Bosanquet, pp. 520, 647–51; on Marianne's difficulties, pp. 682–3, 687–8; on her 'Arianism', p. 648; on the liturgy, p. 860.
21. The typed memoir of William Stevenson in the Shorter Collection, Brotherton Library, University of Leeds, contains an extract from a letter from a friend describing Stevenson's college days at Daventry. On Ashton, *Inquirer* (1864) p. 461. On Turner's ordination, Philip Holland, *A Sermon delivered at Pudsey, in Yorkshire . . .* (Wakefield, 1782), to which are appended Turner's answers to questions; and Turner's *Address to the Members of the Society of Protestant Dissenters* (Newcastle, 1792). The Edinburgh lectures are listed in *Correspondence between the Rev. Dr John Ritchie . . . and the Rev. B. T. Stannus* (1831).
22. Fryckstedt, *'Mary Barton' and 'Ruth'*, pp. 90–7.
23. On Wright's playing fast and loose with facts, *GL*, p. 806.
24. *GL*, p. 117. *Mary Barton* (vol. I, p. 211) does, however, mention Herr Teufelsdreck (*sic*).
25. W. Arthur Boggs, 'Reflections of Unitarianism in Mrs Gaskell's Novels', unpublished dissertation (University of California, Berkeley, 1950) p. x, n. 2.
26. On Mr Hale, *GL*, p. 353.
27. The manuscript sermons of Southwood Smith, partly in shorthand, are in Dr Williams's Library, MS 12.60. Mrs Gaskell could have neither heard nor read this sermon, but its argument puts particularly well a commonplace of contemporary Unitarian thought.
28. Mrs Ellis H. Chadwick, *Mrs Gaskell, Homes and Haunts* (1910) pp. 149, 151. Harriet Martineau to Fanny Wedgwood, 11 April 1853, in Elizabeth Sanders Arbuckle (ed.), *Harriet Martineau's Letters to Fanny Wedgwood* (Stanford, Cal., 1983) p. 125.
29. *GL*: on the proportion of educated to uneducated, p. 230; on Mrs Lalor, p. 137; on the proto-Sylvia, p. 281. *My Diary* was published privately by Clement K. Shorter in 1923. Compare sections 11 and 12, 'Of Instructions in the Principles of Morals and Religion' and 'The Importance of Early Religious Instruction' in Priestley's *Miscellaneous Observations relating to Education* (1778), reprinted in J. T. Rutt (ed.), *The Theological and Miscellaneous Works of Joseph Priestley* (London, 1831) vol. XXV, pp. 43–52.
30. In his unpublished dissertation, 'Elizabeth Gaskell and Charles Kingsley: the Creative Artist's Interpretation of a Working Class World' (University of London, 1980), Dr John Simpson Cartwright deplores the metaphors of Frankenstein and of the collapsing room of the Borgias (vol. I, p. 194); because, he says, they depict Barton as a monster and deprive him of credibility as a character. But the metaphors are exact, given Mrs Gaskell's assumptions about cause and effect and the dangers of partial or no education.
31. *GL*: on the Doxology, p. 860; on Charlotte Brontë, p. 128. Harriet Martineau to Frances Julia Wedgwood, 4 May 1857, in Arbuckle, *Wedgwood Letters*, p. 153.

32. G. H. Stanley, *A Sermon, delivered at the Opening of the Unitarian Chapel
    . . . Sydney, November 6th 1853* (Sydney, 1853). See Joseph Priestley,
    section v on atonement in *A Familiar Illustration of Certain Passages of
    Scripture* (1791), in Rutt, *Works* (London, 1817) vol. I, pp. 472–80; Lant
    Carpenter, *Lectures on the Scripture Doctrine of Atonement, or Reconciliation*
    (London, 1843): or a little tract by John Wright on atonement in *Orthodox
    Doctrines Denied by Unitarians* (London, 1894), a series published by the
    British and Foreign Unitarian Association. According to the *New
    Catholic Encyclopedia*, 'atonement' is the only Anglo-Saxon word that
    has been used to indicate a theological doctrine.
33. Mrs Gaskell's account of the interpolation is in *GL*, p. 75. In the Shorter
    collection in Leeds is an unpublished review of *Mary Barton* by Emily
    Winkworth arguing that the conversation has 'the appearance of being
    dragged in because our authoress wanted to make them say what they
    did, and not because the story necessitated their saying it then, and
    there'. Miss Winkworth may well have known the truth of the
    situation. Dr Cartwright ('Elizabeth Gaskell and Charles Kingsley',
    pp. 206–7) insists that Mrs Gaskell, lacking the confidence to present
    Barton without compromise, could do no better than a contrived
    meeting of Barton and Carson and a subsequent, unconvincing
    reconciliation.

10

Peacock's Victorian Novel
MICHAEL SLATER

Gryll Grange was Peacock's only novel to appear during Victoria's reign. Unlike his earlier books, it came out first in serial form like most of the great Victorian novels, succeeding Whyte-Melville's *Holmby House: A Tale of Old Northamptonshire* in *Fraser's Magazine* in April 1860 and running until the December number. But the Victorianness of *Gryll Grange* is by no means restricted to its date and publication history. Despite superficial resemblances to Peacock's pre-Victorian 'novels of talk' with their idyllic country-house settings, *Gryll Grange* is really far closer in its essential nature to what we think of as characteristic of the Victorian novel than it is to *Headlong Hall* or *Crotchet Castle*.

Although modern critics have registered the difference of *Gryll Grange* from its predecessors,[1] contemporary reviewers treated it as if it were very much that Peacockian mixture as before. To them it was hardly recognisable as 'a novel pretty much like other novels':[2]

> The plot, as usual, is naught . . . he hardly even aims at probability. . . . His *dramatis personae* exist only as vehicles for the prevalent doctrines of the day; they have themselves no individuality, but are arbitrary lay figures . . . moved about by the author for the purposes of his satire.[3]

Other reviewers were more positive in their attitude towards this 'very strange book', enjoying its 'quaint, hearty, unostentatious Paganism' or its 'mellowness' of tone but they found in it very little in the way of conventional novel-interest. Peacock's characters 'are remarkable rather for what they say than for what they do, and are only interesting while they are saying it' and the 'thread of the tale' is found to be 'as slight as possible'. The *Spectator* notes, however, that some love interest is introduced for the sake of 'magazine readers' who cannot, apparently, dispense with such matter:

thus the various conversations and incidents tend to the ultimate tying of nine matrimonial nooses, which for so small a book would be extravagant but that seven girls go, as auctioneers say, 'in one lot'.[4]

Summing up Peacock's achievement in the *North British Review* eight months after his death, James Hannay rejoiced in the difference of his work from that of run-of-the-mill novelists but made no distinction between *Gryll Grange* and the earlier books:

We know what the fashionable novel of 1866 is – either a photograph of commonplace life by an artist who sets up his camera at the drawing-room door as mechanically as his brother artist at Mayall's; or a literary Chinese puzzle, made up of all imaginable complications of crimes committed by stupidly unnatural puppets fobbed off on us for characters. The Peacockian novel is something quite different. It is a sort of comedy in the form of a novel, making very little pretension to story or to subtle character-painting, but illustrating the intellectual opinions and fashions of the day in capital dialogues.[5]

We have to turn back to a much earlier Victorian assessment of Peacock, written in 1839 by Tennyson's admired fellow-Apostle, James Spedding, to find someone registering a sense of development in the novelist's art, a development that was carrying him towards the writing of a book like *Gryll Grange*:

In . . . *Headlong Hall* and *Melincourt*, the whole story might be stripped off, so as to leave a series of separate dialogues scarcely to be injured by the change. . . . In *Nightmare Abbey* this could not be so easily done. Without the successive situations which form the story the humour of *character* (which is more considerable in this than in the two foregoing tales) could hardly be brought out. Scythrop . . . Mr Glowry . . . and Mr Toobad . . . could hardly have been displayed in full character without the loves, jealousies and contradictions which it is the business of the narrative to develope [*sic*]. . . . In *Crotchet Castle*, the incidents are employed to bring out the humours of individual character.[6]

Spedding could hardly have foreseen that it would be over 20 years before a successor to *Crotchet Castle* would appear but, if he did eventually read *Gryll Grange*, he would certainly have recognised that Peacock's art had, despite the hiatus, continued to develop along the lines he had identified.

The reason for the long gap in Peacock's novelistic career was probably twofold. The death, in 1833, of his beloved mother whose intellectual companionship had meant so much to him was undoubtedly a severe blow to him as an artist as well as a man. 'He consulted her judgment on all that he wrote', Hannay records, 'and some time after her death, he remarked to a friend that he had never written with any zeal since'.[7] Also his 1836 promotion to the Chief Examinership of Correspondence at India House, in succession to James Mill, undoubtedly meant that his time became more fully occupied by his professional duties. Thackeray, meeting him in 1850, seems to have assumed that his writing days were over[8] and it was not until six years later, when he retired from the India Office, that Peacock publicly hinted at a new work. This was in a preface to a reissue of his second novel *Melincourt*: 'new questions have arisen which furnish abundant argument for similar conversations, and of which I may yet, perhaps, avail myself on some future occasion'. Fragmentary beginnings of stories found among Peacock's papers and dating, it would seem, from the late 1850s show evidence of a number of false starts before the rich tones of Theophilus Opimian, D.D., incumbent of Ashbrook-cum-Ferndale, Classical scholar and gourmet, inaugurated the first scene of *Gryll Grange* (after a *carpe diem* epigraph from Petronius):

> 'Palestine soup!' said the Reverend Doctor Opimiam, dining with his friend Squire Gryll; 'a curiously complicated misnomer. We have an excellent old vegetable, the artichoke, of which we eat the head; we have another of subsequent introduction, of which eat the root, and which we also call artichoke, because it resembles the first in flavour, although, *me judice*, a very inferior affair. This last is a species of the helianthus, or sunflower genus of the *Syngenesia frustranea* class of plants. It is therefore a girasol, or turn-to-the-sun. From this girasol we have made Jerusalem, and from the Jerusalem artichoke we make Palestine soup.'

Among the other novels that appeared during 1860/61 – *Great Expectations, The Woman in White, The Mill on the Floss, Lovel the Widower, Framley Parsonage, East Lynne, The Cloister and the Hearth* and Peacock's own son-in-law's *Evan Harrington* (to name only some of those that still survive as literature) – many had dramatic or startling openings but none, surely, that would have been quite so strange as this one for the contemporary novel-reader in quest of his or her 'picture of common life enlivened by humour and sweetened by pathos.'[9] Opimian's speech would have been surprising enough for such readers but Mr Gryll's rejoinder, bringing in what Byron would have called 'politics and ferocity',[10] would have been even more disconcerting:

> In my little experience I have found . . . that a man who successively betrays everybody that trusts him and abandons every principle he ever professed is a great statesman and a Conservative, forsooth, *a nil conservando*; that schemes for breeding pestilence are sanitary improvements [etc.].

The *Spectator* mocked novel-readers who were 'aggrieved' by the introduction of such matter:

> it confuses their minds, like having soup at the conclusion of dinner; they like novels to be novels, comedies to be comedies, and treatises on matters in general – if there must be such things – to be divided into their appropriate heads and published in the organ properly devoted to each species of observation.

Apart from his already-quoted jocose reference to the love-affairs in the book, however, this reviewer does not, as we have seen, go on to recognise just how much Peacock has now provided for his readers in the way of conventional novel-interest.

It is, of course, true that a number of the conversations in the book are, like the opening one, on 'matters in general'. It is also true that there are some touches of sheer fantasy in the book – more, perhaps, than in any of the earlier novels of talk, apart from some of the satirical strokes in *Melincourt*. Young Mr Falconer in his Tower with seven beautiful sisters as his own personal Vestal Virgins, regaling him with a nightly concert which always ends with a hymn to St Catherine, is presented in a situation decidedly more fantastic than young Scythrop in his owl-infested tower at Nightmare Abbey with its 'sliding panels and secret passages'. The happy-ending marriages of 'the Pleiades', Opimian's alternative name for the Vestals, with Harry Hedgerow and his six mates, 'all something to do with the land and the wood', have, as Marilyn Butler has well explicated, more to do with classical mythology than with 'common life' in the mid-Victorian New Forest.[11] And the 'mechanical pantomime' contrived by Lord Curryfin for the house-party's Aristophanic comedy – the dancing table and the chairs that chase characters off the stage – would tax the resources even of a modern Disneyland. The bulk of the novel, however, is characterised by an almost Trollopian 'realism' in its presentation of characters and their interactions with each other.

Of the book's 35 chapters only eight consist, wholly or primarily, of the kind of satirical conversations that constitute nearly all of *Headlong Hall* or *Crotchet Castle*. Most of them (21 out of the 35) are concerned with the establishment of a friendship between Opimian and Falconer, a young man after his own heart; with Falconer's struggle to remain content with his idealised bachelor life-style despite the attractions of the enchanting Morgana Gryll; and with Morgana's own dilemma, attended as she is by two highly congenial suitors neither of whom seems able either to withdraw or to propose. Although the only external obstacle to her marriage with Falconer, his Vestals, is removed in the manner of Shakespearian Romantic comedy, by Opimian's benign production of seven husbands for them, the presentation and analysis of feeling in the earlier episodes is very much what we might expect to find in a Trollope novel. This is also the case in the four remaining chapters of the book which deal with the brilliant and dynamic young Lord Curryfin and the way his growing fascination with the enigmatic Miss Niphet gradually overwhelms his initial feelings of attraction towards Morgana.

The contrast, both in technique and in focus of interest, with Peacock's earlier novels can be exemplified by comparing the presentation of Scythrop's emotional dilemma in *Nightmare Abbey* (ch. 10) with that of Falconer's. Here is Scythrop torn between Marionetta and Stella:

> He could not dissemble to himself that he was in love, at the same time, with two damsels of minds and habits as remote as the antipodes. The scale of predilection always inclined to the fair one who happened to be present; but the absent was never effectually outweighed, though the degrees of exaltation and depression varied according to accidental variations in the outward and visible signs of the inward and spiritual graces of his respective charmers. Passing and repassing several times a day from the

company of the one to that of the other, he was like a shuttle-cock
between two battle-dores, changing its direction as rapidly as the
oscillations of a pendulum, receiving many a hard knock on the
cork of a sensitive heart, and flying from point to point on the
feathers of a super-sublimated head. This was an awful state of
things. He had now as much mystery about him as any romantic
transcendentalist or transcendental romancer could desire. He
had his esoterical and his exoterical loves.

The style of this passage, its facetious references to the girls as
'damsels' and 'charmers', and its characteristically Peacockian wit in
the mock-pedantic elaboration of the cliché images of scales and
shuttle-cock, effectively prevent us from taking Scythrop's dilemma
at all seriously. We know we are reading light satire on the follies of
youth rather than being invited to sympathise with an inner conflict
in an individual young man. And the last two sentences remind us
also that Scythrop's dilemma is all an integral part of the sharply-
focussed overall literary satire of the book. Here, by contrast, is
Falconer in *his* dilemma:

> could he bear to see the fascinating Morgana metamorphosed into
> Lady Curryfin? The time had been when he had half wished it, as
> the means of restoring him to liberty. He felt now, that when in
> her society he could not bear the idea; but he still thought that in
> the midst of his domestic deities he might become reconciled to it.
>   . . . Impatience was always his companion: Impatience on his
> way to the Grange, to pass into the full attraction of the powerful
> spell by which he was drawn . . .; Impatience on his way to the
> Tower, to find himself again in the 'Regions mild of pure and
> serene air,' in which the seven sisters seemed to dwell . . . but it
> was with him as it is with many, perhaps with all: the two great
> enemies of tranquillity, Hope and Remembrance, would still
> intrude: not like a bubble and a spectre as in the beautiful lines of
> Coleridge . . . but their forces were not less disturbing, even in
> the presence of his earliest and most long and deeply cherished
> associations.   (ch. 20)

The personification of emotions here may make us think of
Charlotte Brontë rather than Trollope and the appeal to common
human experience recalls George Eliot but, whichever of the great
Victorian novelists we align Peacock with here, it is clear that the

writing is seeking to interest us in an individual dilemma. Even the literary allusions are highly appropriate to the particular character, for Falconer is a sensitive young man trying to live as much as possible in literature rather than in the very un-ideal real world, that 'mass of poverty and crime' that haunts his mind.

Gryll Grange is more fully dramatic than the earlier novels in that the characters talk to, and not just at, each other. Dr Folliott in *Crotchet Castle* holds forth on 'things in general' in much the same way whoever his interlocutors happen to be. Opimian, however, talks differently to his old friend, Squire Gryll, to his new young friend, Falconer, to his wife (Mrs Folliott is a mere off-stage joke but Mrs Opimian would clearly have been a match for Mrs Proudie; her redoubtable character and the excellent way in which the Opimians's marital relationship works is perfectly established in her one short scene), to Harry Hedgerow, and to his contemporary, old Miss Ilex. The lovers' dialogues of Captain Fitzchrome and Lady Clarinda, also in *Crotchet Castle*, are really only opportunities for the lady to demonstrate her sparkling proto-Wildean wit:

> CAPTAIN FITZCHROME. Is it come to this, that you make a jest of my poverty? Yet is my poverty only comparative. Many decent families are maintained on smaller means.
> LADY CLARINDA. Decent families: aye, decent is the distinction from respectable. Respectable means rich and decent means poor. I should die if I heard my family called decent.   (ch. 3)

In *Gryll Grange*, however, whether it is Morgana conveying secret hints and messages to the hesitant Falconer under cover of their animated discussion of Boiardo's *Orlando Innamorato* or Curryfin trying to get at Miss Niphet's feelings, there is always some genuine dramatic tension in the dialogue and often a strong sense of sub-text:

> The next morning Lord Curryfin said to Miss Niphet: 'You took no part in the conversation of last evening. You gave no opinion on the singleness and permanence of love.'
> MISS NIPHET. I mistrust the experience of others and I have none of my own.
> LORD CURRYFIN. Your experience, when it comes, cannot but confirm the theory. The love which once dwells on you can never turn to another.

MISS NIPHET. I do not know that I ought to wish to inspire such an attachment.

LORD CURRYFIN. Because you could not respond to it?

MISS NIPHET. On the contrary; because I think it possible I might respond to it too well.

She paused a moment, and then, afraid of trusting herself to carry on the dialogue, she said: 'Come into the hall and play at battledore and shuttlecock.' (ch. 29)[12]

The conveying to the reader of the feelings of this cool, self-possessed young woman as she is drawn more and more strongly towards Lord Curryfin is a triumph of understatement on Peacock's part. It is this statue-like figure that performs the most violent action in the book, an act which speaks volumes to us if not to Curryfin. After she has met him emerging from the water, having been capsized in using his newly-invented 'sail of infallible safety' (she exclaims 'in such a tone as he had never before heard, "Oh! my dear lord!"') she secretly arranges for the retrieval of boat and sail:

She returned in the evening, and finding the sail dry, she set it on fire. Lord Curryfin, coming down to look after his tackle, found the young lady meditating over the tinder. She said to him,
    'That sail will never put you under the water again.' (ch. 17)

Curryfin is touched by her 'kind interest in his safety' but at the end of the episode 'the young lady was still a mystery' to him.

It is not only his young lovers that Peacock succeeds in investing with a sense of vivid particularity – stronger than that achieved by Dickens for many of his *jeunes premiers*. Although Mr Gryll is little more than an amiable blank,[13] Dr Opimian's benevolence, whimsical scholarship, indulged prejudices against the modern world (prejudices which always yield, however, to the requirements of courtesy and civilised behaviour), together with his playing of the role of an 'innocent Iago' in trying to bring about the marriage on which he has set his heart, make him far more of a three-dimensional character than a mere talking head like Dr Folliott (whom, however, V. S. Pritchett strangely acclaims as 'perhaps the greatest of Peacock's characters'[14]). Still more refreshing to find in a mid-Victorian novel is Miss Ilex, an unmarried older woman intelligently interested in the arts and in social questions (she had 'on most issues an opinion of her own, for which she always had something to say'), described without any tinge of the usual bluestocking or busybody stereotyping. Nor is she at all presented as a man-hunting spinster, jealous of younger women, like Dickens's Rachel Wardle and her many successors in the Victorian novel. She is generously admiring of the handsome appearance made by Curryfin and Miss Niphet when they are skating together and, when asked, she gives advice both wise and kind to Morgana, even though the conversation pains her by reminding her of her own failure in love. Peacock makes us understand that this failure was the result of her following a mistaken model of feminine behaviour, a model that would have been familiar enough to his readers in the 1860s:

> I wrapped myself up in reserve. I thought it fitting that all advances should come from him: that I should at most show nothing more than willingness to hear, not even the semblance of anxiety to receive them. So nothing came of our love but remembrance and regret.   (ch. 27)

For all the greater character-interest of *Gryll Grange* there is a clear continuity between it and Peacock's earlier novels of talk in respect of his satirical targets: paper money, technological progress, the 'march of mind', Lord Brougham as the very incarnation of mischievous officiousness. New ones are added, like competitive examinations, Spiritualism and social science ('Pantopragmatics'), but most of his targets have been in Peacock's sights since the days of *Headlong Hall*. This aspect of his art is clearly still of great importance to him as a novelist but he has moved from one class of comic fiction, as defined by himself many years earlier, to another one. In an essay on 'French Comic Romances' published in the *London Review* in 1835[15] he made this distinction:

> In respect of presenting or embodying opinion, there are two very distinct classes of comic fiction: one in which the characters are abstractions or embodied classifications, and the implied or embodied opinions the main matter of the work; another in which the characters are individuals, and the events and actions those of actual life – the opinions, however prominent they may be made, being merely incidental. To the first of these classes belong the fictions of Aristophanes, Petronius Arbiter, Rabelais, Swift and Voltaire. . . .

To the latter class belong the writings of Pigault le Brun. His heroes and heroines are all genuine flesh and blood, and invest themselves with the opinions of the time as ordinary mortals do, carrying on the while the realities of everyday life. There is often extravagance both in the characters and the actions, but it is the mere exuberence of fancy [like Falconer's seven 'Vestals', for example?] and not like the hyperboles of Rabelais, subservient to a purpose.

The latter part of *Crotchet Castle* seems to be moving in the direction of Peacock's second class of comic fiction and *Gryll Grange* belongs entirely to it.

The difference of *Gryll Grange* from the earlier fiction is not, however, just a matter of transition from one mode of comic fiction to another, of humour replacing satire as being more acceptable to Victorian readers (as we have seen, contemporary readers seemed not to notice, in fact, the shift that had occurred in Peacock's art). *Gryll Grange* is like many other great Victorian novels in a sense we have not yet touched on, namely in its close relationship to the author's personal life. It has long been recognised that Dr Opimian is something of a self-portrait by Peacock and there are certainly strong points of resemblance between the fictional character and the character of Peacock in old age as sketched by his granddaughter.[16] The younger Peacock is recalled in Miss Ilex's description of her lover[17] and, more largely, in the character of Mr Falconer. Falconer, with his passion for Greek literature, his long rambles with his Newfoundland dog, his ardent idealism, and his home in a favourite haunt of Peacock's younger days,[18] seems to represent a blending of the young Peacock with reminiscence of his beloved friend at that time, Shelley, whose genius and extraordinary personality Peacock had just been recalling in some depth for his two-part 'Memoir' in *Fraser's Magazine*. Even Lord Curryfin with his busy involvement in public affairs, his intellectual curiosity and his inventive genius may perhaps be a reflection of the middle period of Peacock's life (between Falconer and Opimian, as it were) when he was the dedicated and innovative servant of the East India Company, personally supervising the construction of his 'iron chickens', the first steamships to ply between England and India.

This strongly personal element in *Gryll Grange* may well be one reason for its difference in mode from the earlier books. Writing out of his own response to experience of life, emotional as well as

intellectual, in a way that he had not done before, Peacock finds
himself investing his talkers with feelings and responses to life and
to each other that were not needed by their predecessors in his
fiction whose function was simply to dramatise his satire or to be the
agents of intellectual farce, like the characters in Wilde's *Importance
of Being Earnest.*

Given that it is such a personal book, *Gryll Grange* is a remarkably
serene one. Miss Ilex's story of missed happiness introduces a note
of sadness which is echoed in Morgana's song 'Youth and Age' but
the overall tone of the book is one of contentment and pleasure in
the good things of life: love, friendship, music and the other arts,
natural beauty, good food and wine. Marilyn Butler's title for her
chapter on *Gryll Grange*, 'The Satisfied Guest', is admirably
appropriate. Yet Peacock's personal life had certainly not been free
from sorrow, as J. B. Priestley pointed out in his 'English Men of
Letters' study of Peacock:

> his favourite child died when she was three; his wife became an
> invalid [and died in 1851]; his eldest daughter was quickly
> widowed and then made her tragic marriage with Meredith; his
> son was unstable and a constant source of anxiety; his youngest
> daughter [who had made a marriage he did not approve of] lost
> her two children and died herself not long afterwards; few men
> have known more misfortunes in their domestic life.[19]

Our knowledge of all this surely deepens our response to his last
novel. The septuagenarian Peacock who has always been faithful to
a true Epicurean approach to life, who has played a valuable and
honourable role in public life but found always his greatest
happiness in the private sphere, makes of his last book a great
affirmative gesture in spite of the sadnesses and disappointments
that have clouded his later years. He makes a distillation, as it were,
of all the literature that he has loved – the refreshing sanity of
Aristophanes and Petronius, the large humanity of Rabelais, the
festivity of the Greek lyric poets and the egregious Nonnus, the
romance of Boiardo and Ariosto – to create and celebrate a vision of
an ideal society, the world of *Gryll Grange.* The boisterous all-male
revelry accompanied by splendid drinking-songs that is such a
feature of the earlier books has no place here; instead, we have a far
more civilised version of social happiness in which women play just
as prominent a role as men. These two things – the lightly-carried

learning and the treatment of women – make *Gryll Grange* unusual among Victorian novels but in other ways it is, as I have tried to show, far more akin to them than it is to its predecessors in Peacock's fiction.

Notes

1. For example, David Garnett in his Introduction to *Gryll Grange* in *The Novels of Thomas Love Peacock* (London: Rupert Hart-Davies, 1948) p. 770: 'Almost for the first time we feel that we are in a company of real people, and not a few Characters and many Humours'; and Howard Mills: 'The book springs surprises that suggest Peacock was feeling his way towards a quite different kind of novel' (*Peacock: His Circle and His Age* (Cambridge: Cambridge University Press, 1969) p. 218). Not all modern critics have registered the difference however. Humphry House declared in 1949, 'his last novel is curiously like his first' (*The Listener*, XLII, pp. 997–8).
2. Bryan Burns, 'The Classicism of Peacock's *Gryll Grange*' in the special Peacock Number of the *Keats–Shelley Memorial Bulletin* (1985) no. XXXVI, p. 93.
3. *Westminster Review*, LXXV (April 1861).
4. *Saturday Review*, 16 March 1861; partially reprinted in *Peacock: The Satirical Novels: A Casebook*, ed. Lorna Sage (London: Macmillan, 1976) pp. 76–8; *Spectator*, 2 March 1861.
5. 'Recent Humorists: Aytoun, Peacock, Prout', *North British Review*, XLV (September 1866) 75–104.
6. 'Tales by the Author of *Headlong Hall*', *Edinburgh Review*, LXVIII (January 1839) 432–59; partially reprinted in Sage, *Casebook*, pp. 58–74.
7. *North British Review*, LXXXVI.
8. *Letters and Private Papers of William Makepeace Thackeray*, ed. Gordon N. Ray (London: Oxford University Press, 1945) vol. II, p. 718 (letter of 26 December 1850 to Mrs Brookfield): 'Peacock . . . a charming lyrical poet and Horatian satirist he was when a writer'; reprinted in Sage, *Casebook*, p. 75.
9. Trollope's definition of a novel in his *Autobiography*; quoted by Robin Gilmour in his *The Novel in the Victorian Age: A Modern Introduction* (London: Edward Arnold, 1986) p. 11.
10. *Byron's Letters and Journals*, ed. Leslie A. Marchand (London: John Murray, 1976) vol. VI, p. 9.
11. Marilyn Butler, *Peacock Displayed: A Satirist in his Context* (London: Routledge & Kegan Paul, 1979) pp. 251–2 and 268.
12. See ibid., pp. 256–8 where this passage is quoted in the context of an excellent discussion of the 'more vigorous and earthy wooing of Curryfin and Alice Niphet' contrasting with the indirect courtship of Falconer and Morgana.

13. Perhaps because Peacock was too concerned to make him quite inoffensive: 'He used to avow that in the character of Mr Gryll he had repaired the injustice with which he had hitherto treated the landed gentry' ([Sir Henry Cole], *Thomas Love Peacock: Biographical Notes*, unique copy in the British Library).
14. V. S. Pritchett, 'Thomas Love Peacock: the Proximity of Wine' (1944); reprinted in his *A Man of Letters* (London: Chatto & Windus, 1985).
15. Collected in *The Halliford Edition of the Works of Thomas Love Peacock*, ed. H. F. B. Brett-Smith and C. E. Jones (London: Constable, 1924–34) vol. ix, pp. 253–87. (Hereinafter cited as 'Halliford'.)
16. Halliford, vol. i, pp. ccvii–viii; partially reprinted in Sage, *Casebook*, pp. 86–7.
17. See Halliford, vol. i, p. civ.
18. See his description (Halliford, vol. viii, pp. 146 and 149) of 'the Dingle' in Windsor Forest and of the two- or three-storied tower nearby called 'The Clock-case' in his reminiscent essay, probably written just after *Gryll Grange*, 'The Last Day of Windsor Forest'. Falconer's favourite glade and his Tower (chs 12 and 4) seem clearly to be based on these places.
19. J. B. Priestley, *Thomas Love Peacock*, re-issue of 1927 edition (London: Macmillan, 1966) p. 103.

11

Thackeray: Novelist of Society

A. R. HUMPHREYS

I have recently been brooding on a problem which, though
seemingly far from the present topic, is in fact akin to it – the
problem of how Shakespeare's history plays render the historical
subjects they deal with. In what sense, with what complexity of
social and temporal perspectives, can one dramatise, or fictionalise,
history? How far can the past be made imaginatively present, with
what perspectives relating foreground figures to the society from
which they emerge? Whence comes, and with what power of
conviction, a sense of that manifold actuality felt as 'society', the
swarming supporting cast which gives a wide context to the main
actors? How nearly can historical drama or fictional narrative
approach the experience of being historically alive? It is in such a
light that I wish to look at Thackeray.

Of course, a novelist will relate his characters to some selection,
wide or narrow, of society, unless as with Defoe in *Robinson Crusoe* or
Melville in *Omoo* he concerns himself with the *isolato*. Is not this the
virtually inescapable condition of the novel, whether considered as
comprehensively as by Fielding or Scott, or as intimately as by
Richardson or Jane Austen, or as wide-spreading through family
and social history as in *Eugénie Grandet* or *Middlemarch*, *The Brothers
Karamazov* or *Buddenbrooks*, *A Passage to India* or *An American Tragedy*?
Is not this where Dickens's supreme success lies in *David Copperfield*
or *Little Dorrit* or *Bleak House*, Tolstoy's in *War and Peace* or *Anna
Karenina*, Henry James's in *Portrait of a Lady* or *The Ambassadors*?

Yet if this is virtually the indispensable condition of the novel,
Thackeray brings to its accomplishment very remarkable qualities.
George Saintsbury commented on 'that extraordinary fullness and
variety of living presentation which was to be . . . Thackeray's great
and almost unique attribute',[1] a most unusual range and balance of
envisaging. What I propose is to examine some of the means by

which, in his sense of time, place, social area and historical actuality, Thackeray achieves this 'extraordinary fullness', a fullness which, in respect of the novel in Britain, Saintsbury is right in calling 'almost unique'. Henry James wrote to William Dean Howells, in June 1879, to assert that 'it takes an old civilisation to set a novelist in motion' – an idea Howells had denied. On the contrary, James maintained, the proposition is 'so true as to be a truism', and he continued:

> It is on manners, customs, usages, habits, forms, upon all these things matured and established, that a novelist lives. . . . I shall feel refuted only when we [i.e. we Americans] have produced . . . a gentleman who strikes me as a novelist – as belonging to the company of Balzac and Thackeray.[2]

A commentator on *Vanity Fair*, Ioan Williams, has expressed what as readers we are likely to feel:

> One of the most fascinating aspects of *Vanity Fair* is the impression it gives of the interpenetration of the representational and the real. The title of the novel, the moral pattern involved, the system of contrasts, the persistent impulse towards typification revealed in the naming of characters – all these things are closely interwoven with the many references to topical events, social events, popular songs and performers and historical personages, . . . and exist in a context of human behaviour vividly realised.[3]

J. I. M. Stewart's introduction to the novel, in the Penguin English Library edition, speaks of

> an enormous canvas, not perhaps organised with any exceptional severity, but in which the major forms exist within an *ambiance* of extraordinary density, and every inch of which has been brilliantly animated by a fast and freely moving brush.[4]

Greatly though Shakespeare differs from Thackeray in temperament and tone, Thackeray's breadth and balance and ampleness, his ranging into complex perspectives, and the apparently effortless fertility of his actualising are qualities of a Shakespearian kind. As representative, and clearly as semi-autobiographical, one may consider part of the 47th chapter of

Pendennis ('Monseigneur s'Amuse'), when young Arthur has made his way to London:

> Mr Pen . . . was an exceedingly healthy young fellow, . . . with . . . a constant desire for society, which showed him to be anything but misanthropical. If he could not get a good dinner, he sate down to a bad one with perfect contentment; if he could not procure the company of witty or great or beautiful persons, he put up with any society that came to hand, and was perfectly satisfied in a tavern parlour or on board a Greenwich steamboat, or in a jaunt to Hampstead with Mr Finucane, his colleague at the *Pall Mall Gazette*, or in a visit to the summer theatres across the river, or to the Royal Gardens of Vauxhall, where he was on terms of friendship with the great Simpson and where he shook the principal comic singer or the lovely equestrian of the arena by the hand. And while he could watch the grimaces or the graces of these with a satirical humour that was not deprived of sympathy, he could look on with an eye of kindness at the lookers-on too: at the roystering youth bent upon enjoyment, and here taking it; at the honest parents, with their delighted children laughing and clapping their hands at the show; at the poor outcasts, whose laughter was less innocent though perhaps louder, and who brought their shame and their youth here, to dance and be merry till the dawn at least, and to get bread and drown care. Of this sympathy with all conditions of men Arthur often boasted: he was pleased to possess it; and said that he hoped thus to the last he should retain it. As another man has an ardour for art or music or natural science, Mr Pen said that anthropology was his favourite pursuit, and had his eyes always open to its infinite varieties and beauties.

Dickens would observe, and dramatise, all this, and more, but would do so with an eye not for general typification but for brilliant idiosyncrasy; a confirmed Dickensian may well find Thackeray too amiably indiscriminate. Yet however easy-going, even self-indulgent, Thackeray's air, his wide-ranging receptivity has valuably animating effects; it is, incidentally, engagingly akin to Victorian genre and social painting, now increasingly in favour – and that not only when it came from the hand of W. P. Frith. Relaxed and generalised though it is in the instance quoted, it can exert a striking weight of social registration, a weight well defined by

Dorothy Van Ghent, who sees, as the central subject of the novel,

> that node or intersection of extensive social and spiritua
> relationships constituted by Becky's activities: her relationship
> with a multitude of individuals – Jos and Amelia and George, olc
> Sir Pitt and Rawdon and Miss Crawley and the Bute Crawleys
> Lady Bare-acres, Lord Steyne, and so on – and, through these
> individuals, her relationships with large and significant blocks o
> a civilisation; with the middle-class Sedley block, that block which
> is in the process of physical destruction because of its lack o
> shrewdness in an acquisitive culture; with the other middle-class
> Osborne block, that block which has displaced the Sedley block
> through its own acquisitive shrewdness . . .; with the aristocrati
> Crawley block, in all its complexity of impotence and mac
> self-destruction . . .; with the ambiguous Steyne block, that is
> above the economic strife and therefore free of conventiona
> moral concerns, but in its social freedom 'stained' deeply ir
> nerves and blood.[5]

In chapter 62 of *Pendennis* ('The Way of the World') Thackera
provides an interesting account of Pen's frame of mind, interesting
because it reveals in Pen (and, by its unexpected earnestness o
engagement, in Thackeray himself) both scepticism about any fixec
points of view, and an awareness that all points of view are possible
Pen admits to a chameleon-like fluidity in political, religious anc
social opinions. Not, of course, that Pen, or Thackeray, was ar
immoralist; the most devastating portrayal of the immoralist ir
English fiction is, I suppose, Thackeray's own *Barry Lyndon* – Beck
Sharp is a model of propriety by comparison. As a moralist
Thackeray, within the context of mordant comedy, has ar
encyclopaedic eye for social and moral corruption, and forthrightl
condemns it. But, as Keats observed, what shocks the virtuou
moralist delights the chameleon poet. Flowing into and out of a
points of view, Thackeray shares in that paradox which unite
artists of the social comedy – the paradox that along with mora
judgement there goes an uncensorious empathy which enter
zestfully into good and bad alike – often, indeed, more zestfully into
the bad than the good. Unscrupulous Becky is vastly mor
interesting than virtuous Amelia. Nothing is to be rejected.

As Lord David Cecil observes, 'The dust lies thicker on Thackera
than on Dickens'.[6] One of the things, I suspect, that has told agains

Thackeray's reputation is this panoramic inclusiveness. Henry James, in the preface to *The Spoils of Poynton*, calls life 'all inclusion and confusion', art 'all discrimination and selection', and writing to Hugh Walpole (19 May 1912) he urged, 'Don't let any one persuade you . . . that strenuous selection and comparison are not the very essence of art'.[7] Such axioms are quite at odds with Thackeray's procedures. From a similar point of view to that of James, F. R. Leavis in *The Great Tradition* protests that Thackeray's art lacks significance:

> He has (apart from social history) nothing to offer the reader whose demand goes beyond the 'creation of characters' and so on. His attitudes, and the essential substance of interest, are so limited that (though, of course, he provides incident and plot) for the reader it is merely a matter of going on and on; nothing has been done by the close to justify the space taken.[8]

Yet in the wide panorama of the novels much more can properly be claimed than this. 'Social history' as such, however interesting, has nothing like the compulsive attraction which it takes on in Thackeray's novels. What social historian writes with anything like Thackeray's facility in richly communicative language, vital rhythms of presentation, or abundance of appreciated detail? To read of American colonial life, as rendered in *The Virginians*, for instance, is like living in the midst of it all. Thackeray's 'essential subject of interest' is limited only in that it is not very rewarding to the kind of demand Leavis so stimulatingly makes – the demand, that is, for moral discriminations subtly and maturely perceived. But it is almost unlimited if what one wants is the multiplicity and exuberance of human endeavour.

Writing to David Masson on 6 May 1851 Thackeray commented that Dickens (whom nevertheless he greatly admired) was too extravagant:

> I quarrel with his Art in many respects: wh[ich] I don't think represents Nature duly; for instance Micawber appears to me an exaggeration of a man, as his name is of a name. It is delightful and makes me laugh: but he is not more a real man than my friend Punch is: and in so far I protest against him – . . . holding that the Art of Novels *is* to represent Nature: to convey as strongly as possible the sentiment of reality.[9]

Fielding, whom Thackeray often refers to as the truest and most honest of novelists, had as he commenced *Tom Jones* proposed 'HUMAN NATURE' as providing 'prodigious variety', and in *Joseph Andrews* had undertaken to treat 'not men, but manners; not an individual, but a species'. Thackeray is in this respect Fielding's most notable successor. 'Nature' is the endlessly varied yet always representative portrayal of mankind; its mimesis involves such fictional likenesses as can merge into actual history, characterisations which stand for classes, scenes recognisable as those of the world at large, a verisimilitude of place and period which fits these into locational or historical reality, and commentary which generalises to the common human condition the codes of behaviour which the novel presents. Of all the Victorian novelists only Trollope rivals Thackeray in this range of qualities.

Without strain, with easy familiarity, Thackeray weaves his narratives as part of the continuum of actual history. *The Four Georges* opens with a characteristic personal link with the past (indeed, Philip Collins and I both knew an elderly gentleman who, as a child, had been dandled by an elderly lady who had seen Louis XVI and Marie Antoinette entering Paris in 1791). Here is Thackeray moving companionably into the society of his favourite century, in the opening of 'George the First':

> A very few years since, I knew familiarly a lady who had been asked in marriage by Horace Walpole, who had been patted on the head by George II. This lady had knocked at Dr Johnson's door, had been intimate with Fox, with the beautiful Georgiana of Devonshire, and with that brilliant Whig society of the reign of George III; had known the Duchess of Queensberry, the patron of Gay and Prior, the admired young beauty of the Court of Queen Anne. I often thought, as I took my kind old friend's hand, how with it I held on to the old society of wits and men of the world.

This sense of actual, living, relationship with the past is one of Thackeray's most attractive features. It is unpedantic, and free from archaeological rigour. If it has a fault, it is in the sentimentalised soft focus, typical of popular Victorian history, with which it viewed the past. (Thackeray could not bear Swift's supposed 'misanthropy', where this softening process did not work.) But that being said, the easy acclimatisation in the historical past is an enriching part of social awareness. Thackeray cannot lodge Arthur Pendennis in London's Temple Garden without surrounding him with its history – the mediaeval wars of York and Lancaster (the emblems of the rival factions, white and red roses, being by tradition plucked there); then, from his favourite eighteenth century, Addison and the *Spectator* and Sir Roger de Coverley, and Goldsmith and Boswell and Johnson. *Barry Lyndon*, the first of the really notable works, continues the rogue-biography precedents of Defoe and Fielding by immersing its hero in historical reality; like Barry's life the book is an absorbing confidence-trick. Or, in *Vanity Fair*, consider the role of the vicious Lord Steyne, modelled on the Marquis of Hertford who had died in 1842, five years before the novel appeared; his name identifies him with social and moral *stain*. The fictive biography of the end of chapter 64, ironically reciting the pompous rollcall of Steyne's home and foreign distinctions, resembles Hertford's obituary in *The Annual Register*: Geoffrey and Kathleen Tillotson give the details in their edition of the novel. As they observe, Steyne is 'completely assimilated to the action as ally and protagonist of Becky, and to the moral as a massive illustration of *Vanity Fair*';[10] Steyne, like many other elements in the novels, is fiction and history interchangeably. Gordon Ray remarks that Thackeray's was the last generation in which the aristocracy held its prestige, threatened already by the rise of industry (as, in their various ways, Disraeli's *Coningsby*, Mrs Gaskell's *North and South* and Dickens's *Hard Times* show it), but still dominant socially and politically, as it is likewise in Trollope's 'Palliser' series.[11] Steyne and his sombre mansion in Gaunt Square are strong expressions of an actual socio-historical situation. The finest interminglings of fact and fiction in the English novel are such episodes as Marlborough's Blenheim–Ramillies campaign in chapters 9 to 12 of *Henry Esmond*, Book II, and – a brilliant confidence-trick this in the same novel – the great sequence of fictional Beatrix Esmond's courtship by the historical Duke of Hamilton, the latter's killing by the historical Lord Mohun, and fictional Henry Esmond's share in the plot to restore the historical exiled Charles Stuart to the throne. These episodes, and those of the campaigns in America round the figure of George Washington, are done with exemplary assurance, and along with others, like the Battle of Waterloo episodes in *Vanity Fair*, they excite the mind to a quality of realisation which really enlarges experience and counters Leavis's reductive judgement.

What, though, has this to do with Thackeray and society? Like

Thackeray recalling his eighteenth-century lady, his fictional
Esmond remembers daily historical persons in their everyday
familiarity – Louis XIV, for instance, 'a wrinkled old man, pock-
marked, and with a great periwig and red heels to make him look
tall', and Queen Anne 'tearing down the Park slopes after her
stag-hounds, and driving her one-horse chaise, a hot, red-faced
woman'. If *Vanity Fair* is 'a novel without a hero', Gordon Ray
remarks, *The English Humorists* and *The Four Georges* portray a
century without a hero;[12] that, of course, is the point. In the first
paragraph of *Henry Esmond*, through the voice of Esmond,
Thackeray speaks for himself:

> I would have History familiar rather than heroic, and think Mr
> Hogarth and Mr Fielding will give our children a much better idea
> of the manners of the present age in England than the *Court
> Gazette* and the newspapers.

A society needs something of the heroic, no doubt, and Carlyle's
Heroes and Hero-Worship (1841) was having its influence. But
'History' is all that society lives through, its whole experience. So
The Virginians, written 20 years before Henry James developed his
Anglo-American themes, frames round such figures as General
Braddock the British leader and George Washington in America an
ample account of Virginian estate life, and around such figures as
Garrick and Johnson in England an appealing panorama of English
town and country life, tracing the international experience of the
young Warrington twins, George and Harry, in the context of a
crucial historical scene. George Warrington writes a novel which
Johnson commends; he sees Home's *Douglas* (that interesting
evidence of Scotland's literary renaissance) done at Covent Garden
theatre; he expects to meet Soame Jenyns, Horace Walpole,
Edmund Burke, and 'in fine, all the wits of Mr Dodsley's shop'. His
brother Harry serves under Lieutenant Colonel Richmond Webb,
nephew of the General Webb 'under whom my grandfather [Henry
Esmond] served in the great wars of Marlborough' (General Webb
was in fact a distant ancestor of Thackeray himself). Both brothers
fight, though on different sides, in the American War of
Independence, history and invention interweaving in a living
fabric, in environments validated by a convicting sense of social fact.

   Vanity Fair was at first subtitled 'Pen and Pencil Sketches of
English Society', later 'A Novel Without a Hero'. Not heroes but the
webs of social interaction are its subject. Both subtitles are

significant, though the first suggests a far slighter treatment than what we have, and the second puts its virtue negatively rather than positively. Social life must have its physical settings; of these Scott was the precedent master, Dickens the contemporary genius, limning with intense imagination the Dedlock mansion, Mrs Clennan's gloom-ridden refuge, the Veneerings' pretentious establishment, and the oppressive Marshalsea. Thackeray deals in no such atmospheric intensifications but in recognisable realities – realities so recognisable that we need the appreciative skill of his rendering before we see them as fully as we should. The great virtue of art, after all, is to make the new familiar and the familiar new. Here is his account of Clavering St Mary, in chapter 15 of *Pendennis*, based on Ottery St Mary in Devon and realising with the most engaged fidelity the aspect and nature of a settled old country town:

> Looking at the little old town of Clavering St Mary from the London road as it runs by the lodge at Fairoaks, and seeing the rapid and shining Brawl winding down from the town and skirting the woods of Clavering Park, and the ancient church tower and peaked roofs of the houses rising up amongst trees and old walls, behind which stretches a fair background of sunshiny hills that stretch from Clavering westwards towards the sea – the place looks so cheery and comfortable that many a traveller's heart must have yearned towards it from the coach-top. . . . On the south side of the market rises up the church, with its great grey towers, of which the sun illuminates the delicate carving; deepening the shadows of the huge buttresses, and gilding the glittering windows and flaming vanes. The image of the Patroness of the church was wrenched out of the porch centuries ago: such of the statues of the saints as were within reach of stones and hammer at that period of pious demolition are maimed and headless, and of those who were out of fire only Doctor Portman knows the names and history, for his curate Smirke is not much of an antiquarian. . . .
>
> The Rectory is a stout broad-shouldered house of the reign of Anne. It communicates with the church and market by different gates, and stands at the opening of Yewtree Lane, where the Grammar School (Rev. Wapshot) is; Yewtree Cottage (Miss Flather); the butcher's slaughtering-house, an old barn or brewhouse of the Abbey times; and the Misses Finucane's establishment for young ladies. The two schools had their pews in

the loft on each side of the organ until, the Abbey Church getting rather empty through the falling-off of the congregation, who were inveigled to the Heresy-shop in the lower town, the Doctor induced the Misses Finucane to bring their pretty little flock downstairs; and the young ladies' bonnets make a tolerable show in the rather vacant aisles. Nobody is in the great pew of the Clavering family, except the statues of defunct baronets and their ladies. There is Sir Poyntz Clavering, Knight and Baronet, kneeling in a square beard, opposite his wife in a ruff; a very fat lady, the Dame Rebecca Clavering, in alto-relievo, is borne up to Heaven by two little blue-veined angels, who seem to have a severe task – and so forth.

Thackeray was a skilful graphic artist as well as a writer, and Clive Newcome, in *The Newcomes*, reflects his artistic training. Thackeray's only rivals in this kind of scene-setting were George Eliot and Thomas Hardy. Hardy, an architect as Thackeray was a draughtsman, can be even more sharply vital and vivid – Casterbridge is memorably done. Yet it is done with an affectionate wryness, a curious sense of hauntedness alien to Thackeray's representative vision as though, keenly as it comes home upon the mind's eye, it does so mainly to form the scene for the freakish hostility of Fate – a sense even more evident in the Talbothays and Flintcombe Ash and, certainly, the Stonehenge scenes of *Tess of the d'Urbervilles*. George Eliot, who so finely gives the sense of St Oggs, in *The Mill on the Floss*, is nearer to Thackeray's appreciative fidelity, yet even she falls short of his many-layered topographical convinction. Thackeray offers his small south-country market town, fertilising the practical need for plot location until it blossoms into a total ecology – rector, curate, schoolmaster, schoolmistress, pupils, doctors, apothecaries, farmers; grey-towered Anglican church and new Dissenting chapel; with continuity and change from the Middle Ages; memorials mediaeval, Elizabethan, Georgian; rivalries of old Anglicanism, new Evangelicalism, dogged Dissent, and all shades of tolerance and intolerance.

Similarly with Brighton, the lively comic–fashionable watering-place of *Vanity Fair* and *The Newcomes*, as graphically coloured and holiday-spirited as any nineteenth-century social painting, and with London's legal Inns of Court richly freighted with historical associations, where Pendennis and Warrington read law (as Thackeray too had done), Paternoster Row and the publishers' establishments where Pen and Warrington hack themselves a pittance (as Thackeray too had done), and the shabby purlieus of their legal chambers in Shepherd's Inn. Local scenes like these grip Thackeray both as graphic artist and observer of social conditions. His subject is the whole interaction of people and places, people and events, people and professions, people and social mores, people and people, through an inexhaustible complex. The seventeenth chapter of *Barry Lyndon* is entitled 'I Appear as an Ornament of English Society', and Thackeray unrolls a wonderful web of social diplomacies as Barry is shown through London's coffee-houses and clubs, courted for his flashing style and equipages and entertainments, besieged by the needy hangers-on of his family, broken-down bogus noblemen, card-sharpers, shady lawyers and a rout of spongers who seem to have stepped out of the caricatures of Hogarth; Hogarth was indeed an artist Thackeray greatly admired not only for graphic power but for moral bite, zest for all sorts and conditions of life, and the power to project from visual detail whole vistas of social comment.

Though the Duke of Marlborough in *Henry Esmond* or Lord Steyne in *Vanity Fair* may – up to a point – ride the whirlwind and direct the storm, even such brilliant strategists as Beatrix in the former novel or Becky in the latter are swept along by life's unpredictabilities. What fascinates is the varied manners in which the self-seekers pursue their ends – the niggardly landowner Sir Pitt Crawley in *Vanity Fair*, his reckless, sporting parson brother the Reverend Bute Crawley with his domineering wife, the gross old businessman Mr Osborne and raffish young men-about-town like his son George, set against the less-disgraceful but still raffish self-centred Rawdon Crawley; the minor-nabob life of Jos Sedley and the military-Indian life of the O'Dowds (Thackeray was born in Calcutta); country gentlemen, creditable like Colonel Lambert or discreditable like Sir Miles Warrington, both of *The Virginians*; the lives of schoolboys, actors, actresses, hacks, budding lawyers, flunkeys, Irish adventurers, colonial estate-holders, worldly ecclesiasticis, worldlier clubmen headed by the unrivalled Major Pendennis – the panorama in town and country, at home and abroad, is inexhaustible. From any initial situation Thackeray's fertility creates an endless nexus of concurrent circumstances, not selectively in Jamesian fashion but inclusively; the value lies in the inclusiveness. In chapter 11 of *Vanity Fair* – 'Arcadian Simplicity' – Becky writes to Amelia Sedley about Sir Pitt Crawley's household, an impish letter introducing every concern which touches her malicious vision – her own desultory governessing, Sir Pitt's grasping farming and business, the visiting Dr Glauber and his proposal of marriage, wealthy Miss Crawley's arrival, the rivalry of the brothers Pitt and Bute for her favour, other Crawleys equally on the watch for her money, visits from neighbouring gentry, Rawdon's reckless dandyism – and we are never left unaware that it is Becky who writes, in words which to the guileless Amelia will sound only like epistolary chatter but which to us disclose every edge of her satiric intelligence.

The classic instances of this generic social topography, this drawing of the maps and cross-sections of social life, are the chapters (36–37) on 'How to Live Well on Nothing a Year', in *Vanity Fair*. They start with a companionable commentary surveying Vanity Fair and its stylish living and reflecting on the mysteries of bogus affluence – the carriage in Hyde Park, the grenadier footmen, the opulent dinners, the sons at Eton, the daughters with governesses, the Continental pleasure-jaunts, and all the rest, managed on an all-but-invisible income. Then Thackeray develops the Hogarthian comedy of Rawdon's and Becky's financial highwire performance, their acrobatic bank-balancing act – comedy with a black streak, for their self-indulgence ruins the honest landlord of their town house and the tradesmen who supply them. The pages glint through all the aspects of the Crawley pair's impudence – the showy entertainments, the refined façade, the suave elegances; Rawdon's gambling skill, and Becky's wit and audacity; their acquaintances sharply portrayed, along with the network of enveloping jealousies. Through 25 pages Thackeray keeps up the documentation, while at the same time developing the undertheme of the couple's degenerating personal relationship, Becky veering towards the glamour of high life, Rawdon towards the humiliation of being 'Mrs Crawley's husband', allies in deceit yet set on diverging courses, all revealed in a virtuoso piece of social analysis and dramatic psychology, of individual fates and representative truths.

Thackeray's authorial commentary is one of his more dubious procedures, yet since society and its practices are what he comments on it can, when not insulting the reader's intelligence, broaden the individual case into general experience. In chapter 3 of *Vanity Fair*, for instance, Thackeray invites us to agree that Becky's tricks to capture a husband are, since she has no mother to aid her, what society compels her to do. In chapter 5 of *Vanity Fair* and chapter 15 of *Pendennis*, respectively, the humiliations of Dobbin's humble childhood, and of young Pen's infatuation for the actress Miss Costigan, are broadened, by Thackeray's commentary, into a reminder of how vulnerable one is when young, and how for the young the pain of humiliation is fulsome. When Pen sets off for Oxbridge, Thackeray indulges his readers – indulges is the word – in a mock-sentimental harangue on what it means to the novice to be exposed to so new an environment. The patronising manner in which he does so is unhappy, but if we do not impatiently brush it off we may reflect on how vulnerable and uncasehardened adolescence really is.

My remaining words must go to some other procedures by which Thackeray weaves his social web. There is, for instance, his fascination with the nexus of gossip. Whatever the individual may do is spread around, accentuated, distorted and melodramatised. In *Vanity Fair* the expectation that Jos Sedley will marry Becky is aired initially in the Sedley family circle, but Amelia discusses it with Mrs Blenkinsop the housekeeper, and Mrs Blenkinsop with the lady's maid, and the lady's maid with the cook, and the cook with the tradesmen, until 'Mr Jos's marriage was now talked of by a very considerable number of personages in the Russell Square world'. When Becky refuses Sir Pitt Crawley's proposal, in chapters 15–16, this causes fervent speculation below stairs. The younger Pitt Crawley's ruses to become heir to his rich aunt, Miss Crawley, are reported all the way from fashionable Brighton, where they occur, to Hampshire where the Reverend Bute Crawley and his wife are scheming to similar ends. The servants at Lord Steyne's Gaunt House positively hum with discussion about Becky's visits there. One of the liveliest scenes in *Vanity Fair* is that in which, in Brussels, gossip has it that the British have been beaten at Waterloo, and the whole city seethes like a disturbed antheap. In *Pendennis* the Major owes much of his social knowhow to his valet Morgan, whose strategies prompt Thackeray to a discourse on how to 'get a knowledge of London society', namely, 'begin at the foundation, that is, at the kitchen floor' (ch. 37). Chapter 74 of *The Virginians* relates how England received the news of Wolfe's capture of Quebec, and his heroic death, three days after being plunged into gloom by reports of his hopeless situation:

The whole nation rose up and felt itself the stronger for Wolfe's victory. . . . Friends embraced each other when they met.

Coffee-houses and public places were thronged with people eager
to talk the news. Courtiers rushed to the King and the great
Minister by whose wisdom the campaign had been decreed.
When he showed himself, the people followed him with shouts
and blessings.

There is a touch of irony about Court adulation of the 'wisdom'
behind the campaign, for the previous paragraph is all about the
flukiness of military plans, yet Thackeray did prodigiously admire
William Pitt, the Minister in question, and the sense of general
exuberant involvement is enthusiastically conveyed.

Within the wide sweep of the novels the social milieux are richly
varied, to be visited not as museum specimens but as centres of
actual living. Theatres, pleasure-gardens, spas, taverns, law
chambers, schools and colleges, fields of hunting or battle, gaming-
dens; in *The Virginians*, the ecology of Virginian estate-life, and the
seemliness of Colonel Lambert's villa, in *Vanity Fair* the oppressive
grandeur of the Steyne mansion, the heavy materialism of the
Osborne house and the social frivolities of Continental Court-
capitals – all these are realised truly, convincingly, with apt artistic
appropriateness. Mr Osborne's study (*Vanity Fair*, ch. 24) is as
crushingly ungenial as its proprietor, heavy with leather chairs,
glazed bookcases, undisturbed rows of giltbound books, its
atmosphere grim with its master's bullying dominance and the
desolating assemblies for family prayers which he imposes. There is
not here much detail of architecture or décor (though elsewhere
Thackeray abounds in it, and he is skilful), yet it is a complete
symbolic rendering – that place for that man. Geoffrey Tillotson
observes of Thackeray that 'He has the gift for keeping the reader
assured that his personages occupy houses and rooms which
exist'.[13] They do, significantly. When we enter Osborne's 'genteel,
well-furnished drawing-room' in chapter 13 all we are specifically
given is the solemn clock over the fireplace, which figures again in
later chapters (23 and 42). Its subject is human sacrifice, Iphigenia
slain by her father Agamemnon, and its implications as to Osborne
family relationships are clear. We first hear of it as testy old Osborne
enters to his awaiting daughters in an utter silence 'only interrupted
by the alarmed ticking of the great French clock'. 'Alarmed' is
surprising and felicitous. Hardly applicable to the monumental
timepiece itself, the very essence of which is impassivity, it suggests

the taut nerves of those waiting, projecting on to the ticking their own overwroughtness. The passage continues:

> When that chronometer, which was surmounted by a cheerful brass group of the sacrifice of Iphigenia, tolled five in a heavy cathedral tone, Mr Osborne pulled the bell at his right hand violently.

How the passage resulted from revision is interestly examined in John Sutherland's *Thackeray at Work*.[14] Originally the group showed the biblical story of Jephthah sacrificing his daughter, but that was an act done unwillingly by an unhappy father, and so unsuited both to Osborne's heartlessness and his worldliness: moreover, the 'French' clock would be likelier to show a classical subject.

Thackeray's skill in representing a world of social significance is evident here in symbolic detail. More amply deployed, it displays itself *in extenso* in the gorgeous passage describing the high style of Lady Clavering's London reception rooms, in the 38th chapter of *Pendennis* ('In Which the Sylph Re-appears'), an exuberance of satiric relish:

> What could equal the chaste splendour of the drawing-rooms? The carpets were so magnificently fluffy that your foot made no more noise on them than your shadow; on their white ground bloomed roses and tulips as big as warming-pans; about the room were high chairs and low chairs, bandy-legged chairs, chairs so attenuated that it was a wonder any but a sylph could sit upon them, marqueterie tables covered with marvellous gimcracks, china ornaments of all ages and countries, bronzes, gilt daggers, Books of Beauty, yataghans, Turkish papooshes, and boxes of Parisian bonbons. Wherever you sate down there were Dresden shepherds and shepherdesses convenient at your elbow [one relishes that 'convenient']; there were, moreover, light-blue poodles and ducks and cocks and hens in porcelain; there were nymphs by Boucher, and shepherdesses by Greuze, very chaste indeed; there were muslin curtains and brocade curtains, gilt cages with paroquets and love-birds, two squealing cockatoos, each out-squealing and out-chattering the other; a clock singing tunes on a console table, and another booming the hours like Great Tom on the mantelpiece – there was, in a word, everything

that comfort could desire, and the most elegant taste devise. [One relishes 'comfort' and 'elegant'.] A London drawing-room fitted up without regard to expense is surely one of the noblest and most curious sights of the present day. The Romans of the Lower Empire, the dear Marchionesses and Countesses of Louis xv, could scarcely have had a finer taste than our modern folks exhibit; and everybody who saw Lady Clavering's reception-rooms was forced to confess [one relishes 'forced', too] that they were most elegant.

Through such marvellous accumulation of specification Thackeray defines the social ethos his characters represent, and to the ecology of which they fit by the same adaptive coloration as the fauna of nature. Acquisitors amid their acquisitions, gentry in mansions luxurious or delapidated, planters on their estates, roués at Brighton or jaunting to Continental watering-places (the 'Am Rhein' episode of *Vanity Fair* is delightfully exuberant about the whole business of fashionable excursions and the Weimar Thackeray himself so much enjoyed as a young man) – everyone has an environment of objects and tastes and occupations and acquaintances and reputation and class and customs and past perspectives and future prospects and historical antecedents. For Thackeray's 'extraordinary fullness and variety of living presentation', that 'great and almost unique attribute' – to echo Saintsbury again – we should be enormously grateful.

Notes

1. George Saintsbury, *A Consideration of Thackeray* (London: Oxford University Press, 1931) p. 67.
2. Quoted in F. O. Matthiessen, *The James Family* (New York: Alfred A. Knopf, 1947) p. 502.
3. Ioan M. Williams, *Thackeray* (London: Evans, 1968) p. 74.
4. *Vanity Fair* (Harmondsworth: Penguin, 1968) p. 10.
5. Dorothy Van Ghent, *The English Novel: Form and Function* (New York: Harper & Row, 1967) pp. 174–5.
6. David Cecil, *Early Victorian Novelists* (London: Constable, 1934) p. 67.
7. *Letters of Henry James*, selected and edited by Percy Lubbock (London: Macmillan, 1920) vol. ii, pp. 245–6.
8. F. R. Leavis, *The Great Tradition* (London: Chatto & Windus, 1948) p. 21.
9. *The Letters and Private Papers of William Makepeace Thackeray*, collected

and edited by Gordon N. Ray (London: Oxford University Press, 1945) vol. ɪɪ, p. 772.

10. *Vanity Fair*, ed. Geoffrey and Kathleen Tillotson (London: Methuen, 1963) p. xxxiii.

11. Gordon N. Ray, *Thackeray: The Age of Wisdom* (London: Oxford University Press, 1958) p. 26.

12. Ibid., p. 144.

13. Geoffrey Tillotson, *Thackeray the Novelist* (Cambridge: Cambridge University Press, 1954) p. 232.

14. See John Sutherland, *Thackeray at Work* (London: Athlone Press, 1974) pp. 11–15.

12

Heroines Adrift: George Eliot and the Victorian Ideology of Family

MICHAEL WOLFF

This essay is an initial attempt at fitting three of George Eliot's novels into a larger project about George Eliot and the excluded, George Eliot and others;[1] the others being all those who have not been governors – in this case primarily women whose governors were their husbands and fathers. The 'heroines adrift' of my title are Maggie of *The Mill on the Floss*, Romola of *Romola* and Gwendolen of *Daniel Deronda*, who each find themselves, at major turning points both in their own lives and in those of their novels, more or less helplessly afloat, having lost both their terrestrial and their moral moorings.

Maggie is 'Borne Along by the Tide' (Book VI, ch. 12), succumbing to her 'Great Temptation' (the title of Book VI) and gliding downstream with Stephen past the point of no return from which she nevertheless has to return. Romola, in chapter 61, 'Drifting Away', is leaving Florence a second time after she has lost the two men whose lives have made sense out of her life – her spiritual father, Savonarola, who has betrayed her godfather Bernardo, and Bernardo himself, who has been executed. And Gwendolen is alone with her hated husband and her murderous thoughts, first on the 'tiny plank-island of a yacht' in the Mediterranean and then in Genoa harbour in that 'stillness as in an island sanctuary' of a small boat before the squall which results in Grandcourt's drowning.[2] (The epigraph in the manuscript of that chapter of *Daniel Deronda* is from 'The Ancient Mariner': 'Alone, alone, all all alone / Alone on a wide wide sea! / And never a saint took pity on / My soul in agony'.)

Romola and Gwendolen, like Maggie, can see no way out of a moral impasse. And, although (unlike Maggie) they do survive their crises, they both come very close to death before they are saved. And again, they are rescued both from drowning and despair. Even

202

Maggie, although she does drown, drowns, so to speak, more or less under her own power and, if not rescued, is redeemed.

The Mill on the Floss, Romola and *Daniel Deronda* are also the only novels whose heroines are left at the end of the book with neither a husband nor children of their own, and this coincidence suggests that the drifting has some correlation with the ideology of family. I want to argue that these scenes in which the heroine drifts have a particular moral character and represent each heroine's move towards freedom and away from family, towards an, in the event, incomplete escape from those traditional constraints, which were, for George Eliot's readers, still the proper condition of women, and that such a move is also a sort of drift on George Eliot's part between daring and timidity.

So, first, let me offer some sweeping generalisations about family, and about the rise in the importance of the family as a symbolic institution from the turn of the nineteenth century on, so that even now 'family values' have the sort of sacrosanctity that G. M. Young said they had for the Victorians.[3]

The central generalisation is that the family has been, in effect, the only survivor of all those family-like groupings which were for centuries crucial to the traditional Catholic world-view. To live in that world was at every level to live in a family under the protection of a father or a lord – ultimately, of course, the Father and the Lord. The human meaning of the universe itself derived from the Fatherhood of God. Under Him were all those patriarchies and lordships from Adam and Abraham to the Trinity and the Holy Family and the Papacy; moreover, in secular life emperor, king and feudal lord were just as much reflections of God's Fatherhood as pope, bishop and priest. In theory, everyone all the time was either a father or a child.

That the human family was a microcosm of God's family was brought into everyday life most explicitly and routinely through St Paul's teaching that the love between husband and wife was an image of the love between Christ and His Church – the husband is head of the wife as Christ is Head of the Church – a doctrine at the heart of both the Catholic sacrament of marriage and the Anglican Solemnisation of Holy Matrimony. So, by the most sacred of traditions, all authorised intimacy between men and women (and, of course, between parents and children) is represented by family and is an imitation either of God's love for us or of our love for God, in the form of the loving authority of the father–husband or the loving obedience of the mother–wife.

This way of looking at things, perhaps never more than a vision, had, of course, begun to shrink and dissolve at least with the Reformation, when Church and State became officially national rather than universal. But, equally of course, the family as fact rather than metaphor survived, and with paterfamilias at its head and the others under obligation to defer to his rule, it constituted the memory and the hope of traditional authority and obedience. In *The Mill on the Floss*, the Anglo-Catholic clergyman, Dr Kenn, tells Maggie that 'the Church ought to represent the feeling of the community, so that every parish should be a family knit together by Christian brotherhood under a spiritual father'.[4]

For Dr Kenn the ideas of community, church and parish are intertwined with the ideas of brotherhood, father and family. Even for secularists, as we know, the momentum of family was such that for Comtists, Feuerbachians, organicists – all those who breathed the same cultural mixture as George Eliot – the ideological task was to find a metaphysic and an ethic that would permit humanity to see itself as a family without recourse to divinity.

For our purposes, two further generalisations now come into play. The first has to do with breaking down the cosmic family, the second with keeping up the domestic family.

First, because religious and secular hierarchies were steadily losing their intrinsic authority, people increasingly found themselves in a cultural vacuum. This vacuum had to be filled and was in practice filled by a new ideology of individualism – by the idea that, if there was no longer a reliable or desirable authority to depend on, one might as well make a virtue of independence, that is, of dependence on one's self. So self-expression and self-reliance, superficially at odds with family, begin to emerge as moral imperatives. Second, the division by gender inherent in traditional patriarchy was sustained in the family. Men (and only men) could now, in principle, lead unsupervised lives. Consider, for example, the Victorian resonance of the phrase 'self-made man' – a notion which has become a boast in the modern world, but which in a world truly fathered by God would be absurd as well as sinful. Consider also the dissonance of 'self-made woman' – 'We don't ask what a woman does', says Mr Wakem of Maggie, 'We ask whom she belongs to'.[5]

So, family continues to be a power because, for different reasons and for different people, it is compatible both with the old ideology of collective order and with the new ideology of personal freedom. It offers the double and mutually reinforcing promise of traditional security and modern autonomy. And it provides this satisfaction not only internally for its membership but externally for the culture at large. A nation of families is somehow less worrying than a nation of individuals. 'Family values' have become both a defence against and a support for the obligatory anarchy of *laissez-faire* and individualism.

In the shorthand of this essay, within the ideology of family, the ideology of person moves from soul to self. The soul, set in God's unchanging world, is placed and protected by Him, always reachable by love and grace. But the self is a law unto itself and ultimately alone, the autonomy and the aloneness giving it that freedom to be a self which modern ideology most cherishes.

While middle-class Victorian men had evolved into the condition of selves, women continued to be souls, embodying the old idea of family each in her place in the miniature hierarchy headed by paterfamilias. It was women, therefore, who were asked to guard and preserve 'family values' which the surrounding society had, in its commitment to the importance of self, implicitly disowned.

What we have then is a disguised ideological conflict between soul and self, family and freedom, represented in Victorian life by the extraordinary hopes and burdens placed by the society at large on the wife and mother and in George Eliot's fiction by the drift of Maggie, Romola and Gwendolen.

The fictional heroine is stereotypically a soul in that she is placed rather than free, either in a family or in a traditional setting within which she will find a family. It is when this situation becomes unbearable, and with it the apparent need to find some alternative to family, that the George Eliot heroine tries to escape from soul to self. Maggie, Romola and Gwendolen are each faced with such a situation, finding themselves displaced from their traditional settings and forced to try either to cope with the displacement, that is, to try to live as a self, free and alone, or to try to become re-placed in, that is, restored, to the family. The drifting that they undergo (or undertake) at this time becomes a metaphor of the dilemma of having to choose between soul and self, between family and freedom.

And the boats in the drifting episodes seem to be drifting without direction, almost without movement, and somehow outside of

time. It is not only that time seems to be suspended. Ordinary
thought seems impossible. It is in abeyance for Maggie or Romola
and obsessive for Gwendolen. So there is neither action nor
inaction, but instead a half-awake, half-asleep spiritual drift, as
though between life and death. Maggie, for instance, feels the boat
might well go on forever, Romola allows herself the more than
passing thought that, once in the boat, she might sleep forever and
Gwendolen compares herself and Grandcourt to the Flying
Dutchman who must sail forever.[6]

Unlike the classic male journeys of odyssey or pilgrimage or
picaresque, these driftings foresee no end or, at best, an end without
achievement. On the water Maggie does not will an elopement,
Romola does not actually seek her own death, nor does Gwendolen
seek Grandcourt's. And yet part of what it means to be in the boat is
that they do nevertheless wish to elope, to die, to murder.

Maggie does die; Romola and Gwendolen are fixed in their
widowhood. They have been suspended outside of or beside
society, without families of their own. Each, it is true, is rescued
from the immediate consequence of her drift. Maggie does not have
to marry Stephen and sever herself from Tom; indeed she is, though
fatally, to be restored to him. Romola does not have to die or
disappear; she has the restorative fantasy of saving the plague-
ridden village and then, at the end, of stationing herself with
marginal responsibilities on the edge of the reality of Florence.
Gwendolen does not have to go on suffering her murderous
thoughts within Grandcourt's paralysing grip; she emerges from
her drift to be restored to Deronda, then to lose him, then to survive
that loss. Each hopes, after her trauma, for the most modest, one
might say minimal, version of the womanly life. And, though
without her own family, each stays at the moral centre of her book.

When the heroines submit to the flow of the water, they also
submit to permanent exile from family and the tradition or, what
amounts to the same thing, to burial within it.

Maggie, one might argue, has always been adrift, certainly since
the loss of her father's protection and, because she has no
opportunity to marry, she cannot be put back in her place except
with her brother. Her fantasy of herself as a little queen who looks
like Lucy, her running away to be Queen of the Gypsies,[7] are
childish anticipations of the adult escapade with Stephen in that the
point is not so much that Maggie is moving towards an elopement

with Stephen but rather that she is trying to get away, to live on her own behalf, to claim freedom and a chance at pleasure.

But her move towards freedom is hardly in itself a free act. The first time she and Stephen are alone together Maggie is aware of pleasure and drift but not capable of thought or moral resistance. 'Under the charm of her new pleasures, Maggie . . . was ceasing to think . . . of her future lot', and 'in spite of her resistance, . . . was borne along by a wave too strong for her'. And this is well before the chapter called 'Borne Along by the Tide', at the beginning of which Philip has said that she 'will be selling her soul to that ghostly boatman who haunts the Floss – only for the sake of being drifted in a boat for ever'. Once actually on the river, Maggie seems to have no will; 'memory was excluded'; 'thought belonged to the past and the future lay outside the haze in which they were enveloped'. She loses all sense of time and place and obligation in the name of a love which is as much the effect of a new sense of herself as of any charm exerted by Stephen.[8]

Maggie's 'Great Temptation' is the impulse towards freedom and self-expression and away from privation and self-repression. And this is how she herself later characterises what she sees as an act for which she must take responsibility: 'she had rent the ties that give meaning to duty, and had made herself an outlawed soul, with no guide but the wayward choice of her own passion. . . . [S]he must forever sink and wander vaguely, driven by uncertain impulse; for she had let go the clue of life'.[9]

There is a notable repetition when Dr Kenn later characterises St Ogg's. I have already quoted his belief that the parish should be like a family. He adds that in contemporary society 'At present everything seems tending towards the relaxation of ties – towards the substitution of wayward choice for the adherence to obligation'.[10] 'Wayward choice' is both Dr Kenn's and Maggie's phrase for 'freedom to be a self'. Its opposite for both of them is 'the tie that gives meaning to duty', the obligation represented by family and community.

Kenn's idea of community is matched by Aunt Glegg's idea of clan. Both are traditional positions which would willingly restore Maggie to the social family. On the other hand Tom cannot receive Maggie because for him family feeling has been modernised so that it is no longer a matter of clan but of 'personal pride'. Moreover, Maggie has also paradoxically insisted on her right to stay as an outcast in St Ogg's because to leave would be to continue to drift: 'I should have no stay. I should feel like a lonely wanderer, cut off from the past.'[11]

So it is not only that Tom's personal pride refuses her her place in the family and that St Ogg's, in its rejection of Christian brotherhood, refuses her her place in the community, but her own refusal of dependence denies her her aunt's offer of her place in the clan.

When Maggie returns to St Ogg's, she returns not from a rebellion but from a drifting which never fully takes her outside the tradition, in which she has never fully committed herself to the assault on family represented by Stephen and her own lapse into selfishness. The condition of drift in which she is both agent and victim and yet neither begins before she entrusts herself to the water and continues after her return through that crucial point where she prays for strength to endure a life whose purpose seems to have reduced itself to the blessing and comforting of others.

The flood comes and Maggie, no longer drifting, is swept away into a water-journey in which she is no longer a dependent soul, but rather a free self determined to show her brother that, in rescuing him, she can superimpose on the womanly behaviour of loving submission an unwomanly act of freedom and initiative.

Maggie cannot survive her last burst of self-assertion. But in death she becomes for a time self-determining and, after her death, her grave bcomes a shrine for Philip and Stephen, her two other lovers. It is not clear, however, whether they are worshipping Maggie as a self, a woman who has fought free of family, or as a soul, a woman who has fought her way back into the family.

Romola drifts away when she escapes totally, not only from the loss of family, but from a collapse of all traditional ties. She had once before tried just such an escape when, her father and brother having already died, the death of her marriage to Tito had seemed as death to her soul and the end of all those bonds which gave her old life cohesion. Her response then had been to cast off the past, in particular by taking off her betrothal ring, and to leave her home and city for a vague new life. For a brief moment, in the emphatic last words of the chapter (and of a part of the original serial), 'She was free and alone'.[12]

But, three chapters later she has been turned back. A chance encounter with Savonarola restores her to tradition and family when he insists that her marriage cannot be arbitrarily dissolved and that she must also reassume the role of daughter both of the Church and Florence. She does this through the fatherhood of Savonarola himself and of her godfather Bernardo, who has always been, in her own words, 'her second father'. Her first attempt to live without a family has thus been shortlived and, from the start, morally suspect. But this second family is also shattered when she is forced, by the egoism of Savonarola's political theology, to separate herself from him, 'to stand outside' his version of 'God's kingdom', and to witness Bernardo's execution.[13] Romola has no more men to cling to, no more family to belong to, no more womanly relationship to shape her identity, and, in the words immediately before the chapter 'Drifting Away', Romola's 'thought was that all clinging was at end for her and that she must escape the grasp under which she was shuddering'.[14] (The end of 'clinging' here is the same as the end of 'obligation' in *The Mill on the Floss*; the urge to 'escape' is the same as Maggie's 'wayward choice'.)

Her move from clinging to attempted escape is the move from family to freedom, from soul to self. Her story has, properly enough for such a woman, been, up to now, precisely one of clinging, first to her father, then to Tito, then to her father's memory, then to Savonarola and Bernardo, her new spiritual and secular fathers.

Romola is now once again apparently free of family, free of obligation, and thus free to move. But as a woman she has no clear use for freedom. She can and does escape, but, since she seems to escape from everything which gives her life meaning, there is literally nothing left for her to escape to. And so she travels to the coast with some apparent sense of purpose, but once there she wraps herself in her cloak as in a shroud, lies down in her boat as in a coffin, and commits herself to the emptiness of the sea, and to drifting away in deathlike sleep (ch. 61).

However, Romola does not, after her all-but-suicidal drifting away, die (though in the serial version it took two months for readers to find this out).[15] She wakes to a fantasy-romance in which she is restored not only to her community but to spiritual authority over the mock-family of Tito's mistress and children. But before she can settle into that she has had to drift in a strange twilight freedom of the same dream-like quality that washes over Maggie's time with Stephen. As with Maggie, the drifting staves off a return which is seen to be inevitable because, in the end, there is no place for a woman in Dodsonian or Florentine culture that is not defined by its family name. At the end of *Romola*, Romola is not, strictly speaking, daughter, sister, wife or mother. But she has chosen obligations that make her a bit of each and thus on balance more a madonna than a free woman.

In her 'fierceness of maidenhood', in her dislike of being touched, Gwendolen is already trying to insist that she is a free self, not a captive soul. She begins adult life with the impossible wish (perhaps gratified after the ordeal of her narrative) that she might avoid clinging altogether, either by being an independent self, or, if society will not permit that, by lording it over her husband. She hopes to be more than a spoiled child or a princess in exile. She aims at empire and at playing empress either without an emperor or with a submissive one.[16]

By the opening scene of *Daniel Deronda*, she has already discovered that young women are not allowed selves, and that there are no submissive emperors. Her trip to Leubronn, like Romola's first flight to Florence, is her first attempt to escape the clinging that she feels is being forced on her. Her conflict is that, although marriage to Grandcourt had seemed at first to promise freedom from the trammels of tradition and family, she has begun to fear that he represents rather the pathology of family, that to belong to him will indeed be punishment for her version of Maggie's 'wayward choice' (Book IV). 'Gwendolen Gets Her Choice' is the title of the book in which she marries; marriage to Grandcourt comes to mean imprisonment with him on the yacht which, for him, was a time of 'dreamy, do-nothing absolutism', while for her, 'the tiny plank-island' was 'the domain of a husband to whom she felt she had sold herself'. For Gwendolen the ideology of family is as much political as it is domestic – her lost freedom can only be regained by Grandcourt's assassination.[17]

For her the dream of being adrift was not as dreamy as it had been for Maggie and Romola. For her the 'floating gently-wafted existence . . . was becoming as bad as a nightmare. . . . She had made up her mind to a length of yachting that she could not see beyond.' Nor was it a release from captivity. In the sailboat, 'she could do nothing but sit there like a galley-slave'. Romola had gone from 'clinging' to 'escape'. For Gwendolen it is more complicated. 'The strife within her seemed like her own effort to escape from herself. She clung to the thought of Deronda.'[18]

Her drift, while structurally similar to Maggie's and Romola's appears to be the moral opposite – she has Deronda to cling to and wants to escape from rather than for her self. She is not alone or with a lover; she is with a man whom she wants to murder. He drowns and she says that she sees her wish outside her, and in that very wish is the assertion of self, the move towards freedom that she shares with Maggie and Romola.[19]

The dream (or nightmare) of murdering Grandcourt is the most strenuous attack on family by any of George Eliot's heroines just as Deronda's insistence that Gwendolen cultivate self-disapproval and let her terror be of her own soul is the most subtle defence of the tradition.[20] As with the condition of drift itself, the situation is full of ambiguity.

What differentiates Gwendolen from the adult Maggie and from Romola is that from the start she has seen herself as 'a self'. She arrives at her condition of moral drift through Deronda's teaching her what it means to be 'a soul'. And she is ready to give up her new freedom because the cost of asserting it against Grandcourt (and against Mrs Glasher) has been just too great.

Although Gwendolen follows Maggie and Romola in her intention to be the sort of woman who blesses and comforts those around her, her last words to Daniel can be read as being more for his sake than for hers. Perhaps more final is her cry that she will live, that she means to live, for this book does not, according to me, end with family, despite those who talk of Gwendolen's restoration to her mother's home, but with a self who, unlike Maggie or Romola, has at least the option of being free and alone.[21]

But from another perspective it is rather a measure of her desolation that the most Gwendolen can claim for her future is survival itself, unaccompanied by any of the blessings which surround Maggie's death and Romola's life. In any event, none of them is given any clear alternative to the traditional obligations of sex-typed family role, not even while they are adrift.

My point, however, is that George Eliot is not content to have her heroines merely succumb to their confinement. Escape has been a real option – it's just that it could not be permanent. Gwendolen may, however, be an exception – she is allowed, at least for some readers, to hover between family and freedom. Her suspension outlasts the book, she is adrift at the end, witness to George Eliot's hopeful uncertainty about some *tertium quid* that might save women from the inadequacy both of being tied to a family and a past in which they are subordinated souls and of being freed of a family and a present in which they are alienated selves.

Each heroine emerges from her escape, her flight to freedom, her wayward choice, her drift, a more powerful woman. It appears that she uses that new power in the interest of family and the tradition, Maggie by reconciling herself with Tom and Stephen and Philip, Romola by returning to a peaceful home outside the hubbub of Florence, Gwendolen by accepting the loss of Deronda. But the endings are, I believe, ambiguous, especially Gwendolen's, and one could argue that the drifting does go on forever, and that Maggie, Romola and Gwendolen, despite their assimilation into the conclusions of their books, never fully give up their sense of self. And it is in this way that George Eliot – at least in these novels – struggled against as well as for the Victorian ideology of family.

I have spoken in this essay as though the problem of being adrift in this way, that is, of needing some new familial and social role, is peculiar to Victorian middle-class women. But it has been hard, it seems to me, for any of us, men or women, Victorians or post-Victorians, to see our way clear to versions of family or community which permit the personal freedom we are now reluctant to give up.

The double and paradoxical duty which the modern family has had to perform, of satisfying the soul while permitting the self, has provoked the very tension which it was designed to avoid. For many Victorians (and for how many of us still?), the ideological dogma of family only thinly disguises how anachronistic it has become.

On this matter George Eliot was herself appropriately adrift. Her bewilderment was, I think, over being apparently unable to reconcile her belief that motherhood completes womanhood, and that society depends on those ties for which family provides the model, with her discomfort over the patriarchal authority with which the very idea of family had been imprinted.

And she was also, surely, aware that there were delusions about the alternative of a free and independent self somehow immune from the damage which comes to all selves in the course of separation and disconnection from the fathers and mothers and which can only be repaired by some sort of reconnection. We all want both independence and connection – freedom and family. For me, the masculine posture of aggressive self-reliance denies this inevitable damage. The more coerced feminine condition has at least the negative virtue of acknowledging the damage.

How to combine freedom and family, how to avoid choosing between them, is the problem. Not being able to choose is what I have called 'drifting'.

So, it is on behalf of all who have to live with the complexities of this question that George Eliot's heroines drift between the 'ties' of 'obligation' and 'wayward choice', between 'clinging' and 'escape', between family and freedom. Perhaps, as with Maggie, Romola and Gwendolen, we have no recourse but to drift.

Notes

1. See also my 'George Eliot, Other-Wise Marian Evans' in *Victorian Women and Men, Browning Institute Studies*, vol. xiii (1985) pp. 25–44. I wish to thank Pat Kennedy, Lee Edwards and Sara Wolff for help with this essay.
2. George Eliot, *Daniel Deronda*, ed. B. Hardy (Harmondsworth: Penguin, 1967) ch. 54, pp. 733 and 746 (all page references are to Penguin editions).
3. G. M. Young, *Portrait of an Age* (Oxford: Oxford University Press, 1953) pp. 150–2.
4. George Eliot, *The Mill on the Floss*, ed. A. S. Byatt (Harmondsworth: Penguin, 1979) Book vii, ch. 2, pp. 624–5.
5. *MF*, bk vi, ch. viii, pp. 542–3.
6. *MF*, bk vi, ch. xiii, *passim*; *Romola*, ch. 61, p. 528; *DD*, ch. 54, p. 746.
7. *MF*, bk i, ch. vii, p. 117; bk i, ch. ix, p. 173.
8. *MF*, bk vi, ch. vi, p. 515; ch. vii, p. 534; ch. xiii, p. 584; ch. xiii, p. 589.
9. *MF*, bk vi, ch. xiv, p. 597.
10. *MF*, bk vii, ch. ii, p. 625.
11. *MF*, bk vii, ch. iii, p. 631; bk vii, ch. ii, p. 626.
12. George Eliot, *Romola*, ed. Andrew Sanders (Harmondsworth: Penguin, 1980) Part vi, ch. 37, p. 401.
13. *Romola*, ch. 59, p. 678 and ch. 60.
14. *Romola*, ch. 60, p. 585.
15. Chapter 61 ends Part xii; ch. 68, 'Romola's Waking', begins Part xiv.
16. Chapter 7, pp. 102, 115; ch. 4, pp. 68–9, 71.
17. *DD*, ch. 54, pp. 732, 733; e.g. ch. 56, p. 756.
18. *DD*, ch. 54, pp. 738–9; ch. 56, p. 760; ch. 54, p, 746.
19. *DD*, ch. 56, p. 761.
20. *DD*, ch. 36, p. 509; ch. 56, p. 762; and see epigraph to *DD*.
21. *DD*, ch. 70, p. 882; ch. 69, p. 879.

13

The Victorians in Virginia Woolf: 1832–1941

GILLIAN BEER

Where did Victorian writing go? What happened to those piled sentences of Ruskin's, those Carlylean metaphors, the lyrical grotesqueries of Dickens, aspirated for the speaking voice but lodged between covers? One answer is that they went into the writing of Virginia Woolf – and some very strange things happened to them there.

In May 1882 Adeline Virginia Stephen was born into what she later described as that 'complete model of Victorian society', the family of Leslie Stephen, editor of the *Cornhill Magazine* and of the *Dictionary of National Biography*, literary essayist, mountaineer and Victorian man of letters and intellectual *par excellence*.[1] In that same year of 1882 (the last of his editorship of the *Cornhill*) there appeared, among articles on 'The Sun as a Perpetual Machine' and 'The World's End', an anonymous piece on 'The Decay of Literature', which looked back to the great days of Dickens and Thackeray, Elizabeth Gaskell and Kingsley, failed even once to mention George Eliot, and bemoaned the decline in novelistic achievement of the years between 1850 and 1880. The writer does unbend a little after observing that realism does not suit the English genius:

> We can only say in the vaguest way that in the mental as in the physical world there are periods of sudden blossoming, when the vital forces of nature are manifested in the production of exquisite flowers, after which it again passes into a latent stage. . . . Perhaps the Shakespeare of the twentieth century is already learning the rudiments of infantile speech, and some of us may live to greet his appearance, and probably . . . to lament the inferiority of the generation which accepts him.[2]

214

If the writer of that essay had any immediate family hopes it might have been of his son Thoby, then rising two and 'learning the rudiments of infantile speech'. As it turned out, the gender and the model are wrong (Shakespeare is not quite the fitting comparison). Like Dombey and Son, Stephen and Son (for Leslie Stephen was the writer) proved to be Stephen and Daughter after all.

Leslie Stephen, who was born in 1832, died in 1904, only just outliving the Victorian age. He did not live to see the emergence of Adeline Stephen as Virginia Woolf, who in November 1928 mused in her diary: '1928–1832. Father's birthday. He would have been 96, 96, yes, today; and could have been 96, like other people one has known: but mercifully was not. His life would have entirely ended mine. What would have happened? No writing, no books; – inconceivable.' But despite the gloom of that judgement she realises in the next paragraph that her own writing has changed her relationship to her parents, freeing them as well as her. The burden of the parental is laid aside and she can respond to the previous generation anew, as contemporaries: 'I used to think of him and mother daily; but writing the Lighthouse laid them in my mind. And now he comes back sometimes, but differently. . . . He comes back now more as a contemporary.'[3] This process of resistance, exorcisement, transformation and a new levelling relationship expresses also Woolf's relations with Victorian culture and writing.

The Victorians are not simply represented (or re-presented) in her novels (and in her last novels The Years and Between the Acts they are so with peculiar intensity); the Victorians are also in Virginia Woolf. They are internalised, inseparable, as well as held at arm's length. They are mimicked with an art of parody so indebted to its material that it sometimes, as in Orlando, seems at a loss to measure the extent of its own subversion or acquiescence. Wrestling with the angel in the house is a more protracted struggle even than that of the biblical wrestling match of Joseph and the angel.[4] For this angel is indoors, inside the self, a maternal figure whose worsting and expulsion might prove to have an intolerable creative cost. In The Pargiters Virginia Woolf acknowledges that dilemma and distinguishes the woman writer from the hero.

Virginia Woolf grew up a Victorian. She was already a young adult before the twentieth century. One of the tropes of modernism is its insistence on its own novelty, its disconnection from the past. 'In 1910 human nature changed', as Virginia Woolf asserted. But that assertion should not mislead us: Woolf did not simply reject the

Victorians and their concerns, or renounce them. Instead she persistingly rewrote them. Surviving our parents is a hard lesson to learn (parent-texts as well as parent-people), but essential if we are to survive at all. One way is ignore them, another way is elegy, a third is to liberate them so that they become elements in a discourse and an experience which, bound in their historical moment, they could not have foreseen. Rewriting sustains and disperses, dispels, restores and interrupts. The five preceding sentences have already appeared in another essay I have written, 'Virginia Woolf and Pre-history', which examined her responses to evolutionary theory.[5] They are essential also to my current enterprise of tracking Woolf's argument with the culture within which she grew, out of which she grew, and which she never quite grew out of.

Virginia Woolf grew up imbued with the literary culture of late Victorian life, familiar with the major writers as books, acquaintance and, in some cases, kin. But she was always peripheralised educationally. She had the run of her father's library, supplemented by the books he brought home for her from the London Library, but she did not – unlike her brothers – go to school or university. She rightly and profoundly resented this exclusion. She did not take part in the early history of the women's colleges. She was never a student at Girton or Newnham and took a wry look at them only in her middle age. She had no experience of institutions. The school scenes in *The Waves* are as distant from her own autobiographical experience as are the university scenes. Writing to Vita Sackville-West, Woolf suggests that she has missed therefore, not learning, but the slapstick of ordinary experience: 'But then think how I was brought up; mooning about alone among my father's books; never any chance to pick up all that goes on in schools – throwing balls; ragging, slang; vulgarity; scenes; jealousy.'[6]

In her essay on Elizabeth Barrett Browning the summary that Woolf offers of Barrett Browning's early life has an undertow of self-reference, a suppressed congruity from which she must break free.

> Her mother died when she was a child; she read profusely and privately; her favourite brother was drowned; her health broke down; she had been immured by the tyranny of her father in almost conventual seclusion in a bedroom in Wimpole Street.[7]

Virginia Woolf's mother died when she was 12; her brother Thoby died of typhoid on a visit to Greece; her health repeatedly broke down; and, although the tyranny was of a different kind, any reader of Stephen's *Mausoleum Book* and of Virginia Woolf's own accounts will recognise the tyrannical tenderness of the husband–father. It is not surprising that the Barrett Browning letters Woolf chooses to quote include one where Elizabeth Barrett Browning complains that her upbringing has made her too inward, too inexperienced in human nature. One task that Virginia Woolf set herself was necessarily that of how to escape from the education described by Aurora Leigh, Barrett Browning's first-person woman poet. Aurora remarks that women's rapid insight and fine attitude is approved:

> As long as they keep quiet by the fire
> And never say 'no' when the world says 'ay',
> For that is fatal, – their angelic reach
> Of virtue, chiefly used to sit and darn,
> And fatten household sinners, – their, in brief,
> Potential faculty in everything
> Of abdicating power in it.[8]

The description seems more apt, perhaps, to Julia Stephen, Virginia's mother, or to Mrs Ramsay (in *To the Lighthouse*), than to Virginia herself. But she is obliged to repeat the rebellion already described in *Aurora Leigh* in the 1850s and to pry apart that fatal compacting of 'potential', 'abdication' and 'power'. This she had to do in her writing. 'Power' is a word she very rarely uses in her own work. Instead she peripheralises many of the imposing categorisations of narrative and renders frail and absurd those claims to authority which emanate from family or past literature.

In his severe obituary of Leslie Stephen for the *Cornhill*, Frederic Harrison, after setting Stephen alongside the mid-Victorian masters, ends by emphasising his limitations: he wrote without much poetry, only of literature; he was really only interested in the eighteenth and nineteenth centuries; he had no awareness at all of the Middle Ages and he was incorrigibly English in his preferences – never wrote of Dante or Molière or Goethe or other great European writers.[9] Woolf explored many of the writers who lay outside her father's sympathies: she had a particular responsiveness to the incandescent intelligence of Elizabethan and seventeenth-century language; she read Dante 'in the place of honour' while her mind was still red-hot at the end of each day's work on *The Waves*;

probably she too did not read Goethe, to judge by the nature of her allusions to him.[10] Isa, in *Between the Acts*, is haunted by the line from Racine's *Phèdre*: 'Venus toute entière a sa proie attaché'. But Woolf did not eschew her father's pleasures, reading Sterne particularly with admiration. To them, she added the roll, the rise, the carol, the creation (though Hopkins is a poet she only twice and passingly refers to, however closely her feeling for the 'thisness' of things runs to his). All this is to say that she had a more shifting and scintillating sense of the fugitive presences of literature in our experience than had her father. Yet she shared the fascination of her parents' generation with 'Englishness', even if the definition differs.

Despite her abhorrence of the imperialism and patriarchy of English society past and present – and particularly of their forms as she experienced them in late-Victorian England – she is yet attracted by the idea of English history and of England. She tries to find a distance from which it will be possible to observe what is unmarred by disagreeable opinions or out of date politics, to find a language and a rhythm by which to measure what persists without faltering in land and people.

From our present vantage-point, which emphasises the invention of tradition and the fictionality of all celebrated pasts, this enterprise may seem as romantically unprincipled as any imperialist dream, but it is nevertheless one to which Woolf brought the instruments of linguistic analysis and recall in all their refinement. To find a linguistic rhythm by which to express England without false patriotism she must work through parody and pastiche, fracturing and conjuring the verbal traces of the past – as we see particularly in *To the Lighthouse*, *Orlando*, *Flush*, *The Pargiters* and *The Years* and *Between the Acts*. She works, too, through what is communal: architecture, clouds, cows, street-scenes. She is appalled by permanence when it is the permanence of heavy objects or relationship. She is heartened by the permanence of shifting and fleeting manifestations which recur: the day passing; cows bellowing; clouds; the sound of voices and of feet brushing the pavement; and writing, which again and again lends itself to fresh reading.

Looking back on her own early family life she emphasised its seeming permanence and bruising enclosure. The house 'seemed tangled and matted with emotion. . . . It seemed as if the house and the family which had lived in it, thrown together as they were by so many deaths, so many emotions, so many traditions, must endure for ever. And then suddenly in one night both vanished'.[11] Loss and freedom became hard to distinguish. Everyday life, whose familiarity makes it seem permanent, vanishes even fecklessly, the heavy furniture more fleeting than the residual forces of emotion. In another passage Woolf expresses her relations to Victorian society in terms which invoke the Gradgrinds and the horseriders in Dickens's *Hard Times*, where Mr Gradgrind comes upon his children, 'his own metallurgical Louisa' and 'his own mathematical Thomas' 'abasing' themselves to peep into the circus tent. Woolf writes:

> I felt as a tramp or a gypsy must feel who stands at the flap of the tent and sees the circus going on inside. Victorian society was in full swing. George was the acrobat who jumped through the hoops and Vanessa and I beheld the spectacle. We had good seats at the show, but we were not allowed to take part in it. We applauded, we obeyed – that was all.[12]

The circus has here become the central image for society, instead of representing an alternative world of amusement and skill opposed to the regulated workaday one. In this passage Virginia Woolf first figures herself as tramp or gypsy, but then – more prosaically – as bourgeois spectator: 'we had good seats'. The peeping Thomas and Louisa have been given good seats at the circus and required to admire its self-congratulatory and competitive antics. Sissie Jupe was a worker in the circus family, but the Stephen daughters were kept outside the ring. By a rearrangement of Dickensian hyperbole Woolf condenses the garish Grand Guignol of family and public life as circus. This impacting yields a comic image of Victorian society at its exercise.

Woolf's writing, indeed, everywhere suggests that hyperbole was the principal stylistic and psychological mode of Victorian experience, despite their dowdy surface. It was manifested in their hubristic desire to run the world in imperialism, in their uncontrolled procreativity, and in the besotted plenitude of their natural world:

> And just as the ivy and evergreen rioted in the damp earth outside, so did the same fertility show itself within. The life of the average woman was a succession of childbirths. She married at nineteen and had fifteen or eighteen children by the time she was thirty; for twins abounded. Thus the British Empire came into existence; and thus – for there is no stopping damp; it gets into the

inkpot as it gets into the woodwork – sentences swelled, adjectives multiplied, lyrics became epics, and little trifles that had been essays a column long were now encyclopaedias in ten or twenty volumes.[13]

Like, one may say, the assembled volumes of Leslie Stephen's *Dictionary of National Biography*, the nation's memorial boast of its curious and manifold distinction.

With hyperbole goes promiscuity, so that a statue of Queen Victoria is transmogrified by a sunbeam into 'a conglomeration . . . of the most heterogeneous and ill-assorted objects, piled higgledy-piggledy in a vast mound . . . seemingly calculated to last for ever'. 'The incongruity of the objects, the association of the fully clothed and the partly draped, the garishness of the different colours and their plaid-like juxtapositions afflicted Orlando with the most profound dismay' (p. 209). Woolf's technique is to display the obverse of the Victorian ideal intellectual fiction of *synthesis*. As she demonstrates, synthesis more often founders as clutter than discovers true relations. Its intellectual acquisitiveness becomes indistinguishable from material greed.

Yet the medium for the opening of her satire on the Victorian age in *Orlando* is a version of Ruskin's prose: Ruskin both represents the idealistic mode of Victorian polymathism and the Victorian response to the particular. Of Ruskin's writing she said elsewhere: '*Modern Painters* takes our breath away. We find ourselves marvelling at the words, as if all the fountains of the English language had been set playing in the sunlight for our pleasure, but it seems scarcely fitting to ask what meaning they have for us'.[14] In *Orlando* she takes up Ruskin's late sad vision of 'the storm-cloud of the nineteenth century' and interpenetrates it with the language of chapter 26 of *Modern Painters*, 'Of Modern Landscape'. The most striking thing about modern landscapes argues Ruskin, 'is their *cloudiness*'.

Out of perfect light and motionless air, we find ourselves on a sudden brought under sombre skies, and into drifting wind; and, with fickle sunbeams flashing on our face, or utterly drenched with sweep of rain, we are reduced to track the changes of the shadows on the grass, or watch the rents of twilight through angry cloud. . . . The aspects of sunset and sunrise, with all their attendant phenomena of cloud and mist, are watchfully delineated; and in ordinary daylight landscape, the sky is considered of so much importance, that a principal mass of foliage, or a whole foreground, is unhesitatingly thrown into shade merely to bring out the form of a white cloud. So that, if a general and characteristic name were needed for modern landscape art, none better could be invented that 'the service of clouds'.[15]

To Ruskin 'the service of clouds' brings with it the loss of *'stability, definiteness*, and *luminousness*, we are expected to rejoice in darkness, and triumph in mutability'. Woolf opens her chapter thus:

The great cloud which hung, not only over London, but over the whole of the British Isles on the first day of the nineteenth century stayed, or rather, did not stay, for it was buffeted about constantly by blustering gales, long enough to have extraordinary consequences upon those who lived beneath its shadow. A change seemed to have come over the climate of England. Rain fell frequently, but only in fitful gusts, which were no sooner over than they began again. The sun shone, of course, but it was so girt about with clouds and the air was so saturated with water, that its beams were discoloured and purples, oranges, and reds of a dull sort took the place of the more positive landscapes of the eighteenth century. (p. 205)

Woolf sympathetically appropriates Ruskin's analysis, but to his afflicted, creatively agitated description she adds a single term: damp. Whereas in Ruskin's account words like 'flashing', 'drenched', 'angry' suggest the drama of extremes, Woolf continues her description thus:

But what was worse, damp began to make its way into every house – damp, which is the most insidious of all enemies . . . damp steals in while we sleep; damp is silent, imperceptible, ubiquitous. Damp swells the wood, furs the kettle, rusts the iron, rots the stone. So gradual is the process, that it is not until we pick up some chest of drawers, or coal scuttle, and the whole thing drops to pieces in our hands, that we suspect even that the disease is at work. (pp. 205–6)

In Woolf's comic version of Ruskin the transacting words are 'insidious', 'silent', 'imperceptible', 'gradual'. Instead of turmoil and dash, she expresses the dowdiness of swollen continuity which at last, in a new hyperbole, simply 'drops to pieces in our hands': the traditional phrase attributed by the middle classes to hapless servant girls who have broken valuable objects. Here, the (absurd) explanation is given: damp. The lexical play is extreme: objects have lost all weight ('we pick up some chest of drawers, or coal scuttle') even while they are permeated with chill damp.

So the passage functions as pastiche: she brings out the repressed humdrum, 'damp', to supplement and undermine the mythic aggrandised account of Victorian weather in Ruskin, what he later calls, quoting Aristophanes, 'the coronation of the whirlwind'. But the passage functions also as collusion and celebration. Ruskin attracts her as the writerly medium for expressing the Victorian age perhaps because of his antagonistic relationship to the powers of his society, as well as, I think, his capacity for self-contradiction. She opens her essay on Ruskin by enquiring 'What did our fathers in the nineteenth century do to deserve so much scolding?' and she observes the teacherly tone which so often takes over from poet or prophet in Carlyle and Ruskin. But another reason for her responsiveness to Ruskin is his countervailing immersion in the specific: his joyous zeal in particularising gives life to his writing in the modernist era, particularly to Virginia Woolf in her search for the 'moment', both evanescent and fully known. Ruskin's hyperaesthesia matched Woolf's own: his helpless openness to the sensory world alternated with a severe and minatory closing of the self against the follies and injustices of the age. He is askance from his generation, even while we take him as typifying much in Victorian literature and society. The fountainous and the crabbed alternated in his writing, often within a sentence.

Perhaps, too, Virginia Woolf appreciated the androgynous in Ruskin. He was never merely a patriarchal figure, though his fatal over-identification with women had results as disastrous to his happiness as his ignorant idealising of them. It will be remembered that the Victorian husband of Orlando, Shelmerdine, is 'really' a woman, to the degree that she is 'really' a man. Seeking the woman's sentence, as Woolf did, she might have glimpsed it among the Victorians in the agglomerative, impressionistic, ranging movement of Ruskin's sentences. In her re-writing of that sentence she interrupted its hyperbolic drive, scissored its afflatus, and yet, as in *The Waves*, swam with its tide. His emphasis on change and sameness in his description of waves and his metaphors certainly accord with Woolf's project in *The Waves*:

> Most people think of waves as rising and falling. But if they look at the sea carefully, they will perceive that the waves do not rise and fall. They change. Change both place and form but they do not fall; one wave goes on, and on, and still on; now lower, now higher, now tossing its mane like a horse, now building itself together like a wall, now shaking, now steady but still the same wave till at last it seems struck by something; changes, one knows not how, becomes another wave.   (*Modern Painters*, vol. III, part IV, p. 161)

Fortunately, in the whimsical good sense of the unconscious, fathers can be mothers, so that when she thinks back through her mothers as she says women must do, Ruskin may be among them. Perry Meisel, in *The Absent Father*, has made a case for Pater as her obliterated kin and I have argued the case for Darwin in 'Virginia Woolf and Pre-history'.[16] There is no contradiction in such multiplicity. In literary relationships parents are not restricted to two, nor need their gender be stable. Moreover, they may be most valuable when they come back as contemporaries. Despite his moralism, Ruskin represents a world alive to Woolf, opposed to that of Arnold – a world of acute sensation, of passionate involvement with the anonymous life of unrecorded people: as she puts it, 'an eagerness about everything in the world'.[17] His effects can sometimes even be seen, perhaps, in that condescension, the opening of *The Years* (though even here it is difficult to mark how far the plurals are parodic). Equally, though, he provides an example of 'impassioned prose' where there is nothing 'unfused, unwrought, incongruous, and casting ridicule upon the rest'. Seeking 'saturation' in her own writing in *The Waves* she finds it in Ruskin, as she could find also a description of the action of waves which answers to her own need for the *permanently changing*, the untransformed.

The hyperbole in Ruskin's writing both amuses and empowers her; his feeling for detail lies alongside her own, yet it is distanced from hers by his nostalgic preference for the discrete and stable particularity of medieval observation, where acorns, fishes, faces, each are given their full record in the picture. Though this is Ruskin's declared preference, Woolf's writing has learnt more from the shifty evanescence of detail in Ruskin's prose, even while he seeks to analyse in fullest spectrum all the changes of colour and to list their sequences.

Ruskin's struggle to record and value 'life' through language, to render the visual world through the symbolism of letters, offered Woolf also a displaced understanding, a place from which to assess her own project. It would be a mistake to read the figure of Orlando as a self-portrait. Orlando is her hero-ine, not herself. Orlando is close to Vita Sackville-West and participates in the swashbuckling inertia of the landed classes who survive, not greatly changed by historical forces or even by simple onward movement of time. Virginia Woolf, on the other hand, is the writer whose hyperaesthesia forces her close into the welter of circumstance, and who controls that closeness by appropriating and recasting writing of the past as pastiche and celebration. In *Orlando*, in particular, her writing of others' writing is audacious. She can clutch, jettison, repossess those sombre, turgid sentences of the Victorians. The panache of *Orlando* helps her to break out of those 'seclusions' which she shares with Elizabeth Barrett Browning and which result, according to her description of Barrett Browning, in another form of hyperaesthetic hyperbole:

> The tap of ivy on the pane became the thrash of trees in a gale. Every sound was enlarged, every incident exaggerated, for the silence of the sick-room was profound and the monotony of Wimpole Street was intense. . . . Ordinary daylight, current gossip, the usual traffic of human beings left her exhausted, ecstatic, and dazzled into a state where she saw so much and felt so much that she did not altogether know what she felt or what she saw.[18]

This reading of Elizabeth Barrett Browning seems self-admonitory; it certainly does not pay sufficient attention to the wit of *Aurora Leigh*. It is by means of wit that Barrett Browning channelled heightened observation into often caustic poetry, as in her account of the over-interpretative scrutiny of Aurora's slightest acts as the household waits upon the outcome of her rejection of Romney. The humour both of Barrett Browning and of Woolf becomes much more marked when read aloud. On the page the eye glides without incongruity from level to level of discourse. Read aloud, the same passage registers the awkwardness of a syntax which seeks to yoke unlike, the collusive asides muttered within the public sentence. It is in the light of her endangering kinship with Barrett Browning (the sensibility of the sick room, the writer's recalcitrance too quick consumed, the unstaunched lyric effusion) that we should measure also Woolf's admiration for this poet who was a woman, and thereby trod across the categories of expectation, and who had for company her own creation, 'Aurora Leigh', a women poet, and Flush, a spaniel. Virginia Woolf's choice of a dog as her second subject for biography, after the man/woman of *Orlando*, and before Roger Fry, has been a source of puzzlement, not to say embarrassment, to many of her professional readers.

In *Flush* Woolf finds a new means of measuring and limiting Victorian hyperaesthesia and hyperbole. Flush's doggyness means that the early Victorian age is experienced through different senses, its description made strange through hearing, touch, but particularly through smells. Woolf relishes the new configurations which emerge from the Browning letters when the encounters they record are re-perceived as a racy mixture of coarse and delicate textures yielding smells, scents, stench, odours. She brings out playfully the censored version of the past we usually accept as true by offering us supplementarily a smell-repertoire. It is impossible, this method paradoxically suggests, to regain the physical welter of life. Even the subtle naming of smells cannot communicate their pungency:

> Mixing with the smell of food were further smells – smells of cedarwood and sandalwood and mahogany; scents of male bodies and female bodies; of men servants and maid servants; of coats and trousers; of crinolines and mantles; of curtains of tapestry, of curtains of plush; of coal dust and fog; of wine and cigars. Each room as he passed it – dining-room, drawing-room, library, bedroom – wafted out its own contribution to the general stew.[19]

The bourgeois world stinks and so does the world of the poor.

Flush, like Elizabeth Barrett, like Adeline Virginia Stephen, is a prisoner always on the edge of escape in Victorian bourgeois society. When he is stolen and his mistress goes to Whitechapel to rescue him, she sees for the first time the world of the poor:

> They were in a world where cows were herded under bedroom

floors, where whole families sleep in rooms with broken
windows; in a world where water is turned on only twice a week,
in a world where vice and poverty breed vice and poverty. . . .
They had come to a region unknown to respectable cab-drivers.
. . . Here lived a woman like herself; while she lay on her sofa,
reading, writing, they lived thus.

The next sentence reads: 'But the cab was now trundling along
between four-storeyed houses again' (p. 89). This episode alone is
shown through the eyes of Miss Barrett, rather than those of Flush,
as though Woolf needed to move outside the arch device of the
animal observer (whose subversiveness is limited by its quaintness)
and to observe human chagrin more directly, though still through
that securing and mocking device of the carriage-window within
which the reader trundles safely through the dangers of Victorian
London.

It would probably be too much to claim on Woolf's behalf any
specific project in *Flush* of socially disquieting her reader about
conditions still current in England. Rather, this small and lightly
learned work suggests the fictionality of our imagined Victorian
England, even by its use of documents and known personages. The
spaniel's nose and eyes and ears yield us intimacies with the sensory
material of that past world but it remains fictional, irrecoverable. In
her essay on 'Geraldine and Jane' (Geraldine Jewsbury and Jane
Carlyle) Woolf presents a poignant appreciation of the impossibility
of knowing other people fully. Knowing them across time in letters
sometimes gives the illusion of full intimacy but she ends by quoting
Geraldine Jewsbury:

> Oh, my dear (she wrote to Mrs Carlyle), if you and I are drowned,
> or die, what would become of us if any superior person were to go
> and write our 'life and errors?' What a precious mess a 'truthful
> person' would go and make of us, and how very different to what
> we really are or were![20]

Virginia Woolf's method in her quasi-biographies is to suggest that
we can know the past and its people best, not through opinions, but
through textures, sounds, smells, sight (though rarely taste),
through bodily impersonation – a method which, at the same time,
shows up the absurd though necessary mismatch between writing
and being. Her methods mock the ponderously achieved apparatus

of the 'life and opinions' biography, and the assumption that the individual's success is the criterion for making record worthwhile, which is harboured by much Victorian biography.

Woolf enjoyed reading biography, and, especially, autobiography. Her own method mocked the hagiographic style of many Victorian 'lives and letters', the summary accounting of the *Dictionary of National Biography*. She repudiated the insistence on action and event as the biographer's main resource. But she abjured equally the demystifying iconoclasm of Lytton Strachey. She liked delicately to bring to the surface mislaid lives, particularly those of women, excluded from historical record.

In her essay 'I am Christina Rossetti' she remarks on the fascination of reading biographies:

> Here is the past and all its inhabitants miraculously sealed as in a magic tank; all we have to do is to look and listen and to listen and to look and soon the little figures – for they are rather under life size – will begin to move and to speak, and as they move we shall arrange them in all sorts of patterns of which they were ignorant, for they thought when they were alive that they could go where they liked.[21]

The image of the controlling biographer and the knowing reader surveying the belittled figures of the past 'sealed as in a magic tank' seems aimed at Lytton Strachey and his accounts of Victorian figures. Strachey, indeed, had remarked in a letter to Maynard Keynes in 1906 that the Victorian age was one in which people 'were enclosed in glass'. He adds: 'it's damned difficult to copulate through a glass case'.[22] Woolf suggests that the glass is a product of the biographer's distance and it is he, not his subjects, who finds it difficult to copulate. (Strachey's formulation revealingly suggests his baulked desire sexually to invade his subjects.) In Woolf's judgement the biographer, like the realist novelist, claims too much authority – an authority which stifles their awareness of the spontaneity and aimlessness of life: 'as they move we shall arrange them in all sorts of patterns'. The joke at Strachey's expense grew sad when he died while she was in the midst of writing *Flush* in which she demonstrates how to release the Victorians from the stodginess of self-approval without simply transferring that self-approval into modernist knowingness.

In 1929, in 'Women and Fiction', she remarks that future women

writers will 'be less absorbed in facts. . . . They will look beyond the
personal and political relationships to the wider questions which the
poet tries to solve – of our destiny and the meaning of life'.[23] Woolf is
seeking an impersonality which will not be alienation and a
permanence which will not be stasis. Frederic Harrison, in his
obituary of Leslie Stephen, singled out for praise Stephen's essay
'Sunset on Mont Blanc' (1873). The essay opens thus: 'Does not
science teach us more and more emphatically that nothing which is
natural can be alien to us who are part of Nature? Where does Mont
Blanc end, where do I begin?'[24] This is certainly a grandiose and
emphatic way of presenting the problem of the frontiers of identity.
But put in less massive, less hyperbolic style it is a question that
Woolf's writing, like that of her father, constantly poses. And
Victorian scientific writing presented her, as much as him, with a
language in which to muse upon such issues.

In *Mrs Dalloway* Peter meditates with whimsical recollection on
Clarissa's possible thoughts, 'possibly she said to herself, as we are a
doomed race, chained to a sinking ship (her favourite reading as a
girl was Huxley and Tyndall, and they were fond of these nautical
metaphors)'.[25] Let us take up the hint that this passage's allusion
offers us and consider the reading that Woolf must herself have had
in her background to make the point here. The problem of 'where
Mont Blanc ends and I begin' was presented by Huxley in a way
which seems much closer than Stephen's formulation to Virginia
Woolf's language, with its rapid shifts of scale and perturbation
between metaphor and substance. Huxley is arguing, against
appearance, for 'community of faculty' between living organisms
quite unlike in complexity and scale: between 'the brightly-coloured
lichen' and the painter and botanist.

> Again, think of the microscope fungus – a mere infinitesimal
> ovoid particular, which finds space and duration enough to
> multiply into countless millions in the body of a living fly; and
> then of the wealth of foliage, the luxuriance of flower and fruit,
> which lies between this bald sketch of a plant and the giant pine of
> California, towering to the dimensions of a cathedral spire, or the
> Indian fig, which covers acres with its profound shadow, and
> endures while nations and empires come and go around its vast
> circumference. Or, turning to the other half of the world of life,
> picture to yourselves the great Finner whale, hugest of beasts that
> live, or have lived, disporting his eighty or ninety feet of bone,

muscle, and blubber, with easy roll, among waves in which the stoutest ship that ever left dockyard would flounder hopelessly; and contrast him with the invisible animalcules – mere gelatinous specks, multitudes of which could, in fact, dance upon the point of a needle with the same ease as the angels of the Schoolmen could, in imagination.[26]

These alternations imply unity by proposing only diversities: 'what is there in common between the dense and resisting mass of the oak, or the strong fabric of the tortoise, and those broad disks of glassy jelly which may be seen pulsating through the waters of a calm sea, but which drain away to mere films in the hand which raises them out of their element?' The word 'pulsating', set with faintly shocking energy between words indicating stability and immoveability ('disks', 'glassy', 'calm'), is typical of the imaginative allure of Huxley's style which here finds its point of intervention in the tactile: the hand enters the water and changes pulsating life to 'mere films'. The fibrous connectedness of bodily life and physical world, the recognition of other forms as our 'unacted parts', which inform this and other Huxley passages, may be compared to the language of self-discovery in the childhood section of *The Waves*: 'My body is a stalk'. Rhoda rocks her petals as boats in a basin: 'On we sail alone. That is my ship. It sails into icy caverns where the sea-bear barks and stalactites swing green chains. The waves rise; their crests curl; look at the lights on the mastheads. They have scattered, they have foundered, all except my ship which mounts the wave.'[27] The 1927 commentary in *Orlando* ponders with some element of pastiche of the earnest enquiring Victorians: 'even now (the first of November 1927) we know not why we go upstairs, or why we come down again, our most daily movements are like the passage of a ship on an unknown sea, and the sailors at the mast-head ask, pointing their glasses to the horizon: "Is there land or is there none?"' Froude in his life of Carlyle describes the Victorian age as one with 'the compasses all awry and nothing left to steer by but the stars'.[28] 'A doomed race, chained to a sinking ship': Clarissa's supposed images of empire and of degeneration register the darkest thoughts of the Victorians about themselves – and of Virginia Woolf's quarrel with them. At the heart of that quarrel was her rejection of their masculinism, their Mont Blanc self-image.

But within Victorian scientific writing was to be found release from such glacial impersonality. It is signalled in that other favoured name in *Mrs Dalloway*: John Tyndall. Tyndall's principal scientific work was on radiant heat and he wrote at large concerning the 'use of the imagination in science', not only in the essay of that title but in his lectures on light, on heat and on sound. Waves compose the universe and are endlessly in motion, as light-waves, heat-waves, water-waves, sound-waves.

> Darkness might then be defined as ether at rest; light as ether in motion. But in reality the ether is never at rest, for in the absence of light-waves we have heat-waves always speeding through it. In the spaces of the universe both classes of undulations incessantly commingle. Here the waves issuing from uncounted centres cross, coincide, oppose, and pass through each other, without confusion or ultimate extinction. . . . Its waves mingle in space without disorder, each being endowed with an individuality as indestructible as if it alone had disturbed the universal repose.[29]

In such a theory individuality is indestructible but part of an endlessly fleeting pattern of coincidental crossing of waves. Interpretation rather than interaction is emphasised, and motion and stasis are hard to distinguish. The individual particles remain, the form changes. As Tyndall wrote in *On Light* of wave-motion: 'The propagation of a wave is the propagation of a *form*, and not the transference of the substance which constitutes the wave.'[30] Thus we have simultaneously form and dissolution, onward motion and vertical rocking. The parallels with the community of life-histories in the *The Waves* are striking. The passage is worth quoting in full:

> The central difficulty of the subject was, to distinguish between the motion of the wave itself, and the motion of the particles which at any moment constitute the wave. Stand upon the sea-shore and observe the advancing rollers before they are distorted by the friction of the bottom. Every wave has a back and front, and, if you clearly seize the image of the moving wave, you will see that every particle of water along the front of the wave is in the act of rising, while every particle along its back is in the act of sinking. The particles in front reach in succession the crest of the wave, and as soon as the crest is passed they begin to fall. They then reach the furrow or sinus of the wave, and can sink no further. Immediately afterwards they become the front of the succeeding wave, rise again until they reach the crest, and then

sink as before. Thus, while the waves pass onward horizontally, the individual particles are simply lifted up and down vertically. Observe a sea-fowl, or, if you are a swimmer, abandon yourself to the action of the waves; you are not carried forward, but simply rocked up and down. The propagation of a wave is the propagation of a form, and not the transference of the substance which constitutes the wave.

Tyndall, too, it was who in 'The Use of the Imagination in Science' brought to public knowledge that the blue of the sky was distance, not colour: and this assertion of his provoked considerable hostility in the 1870s. We know that the Tyndalls were friends of the Stephens. More important, Tyndall's exercise of the imagination in the oceans of the universe continued to have meaning for Woolf through to the end of her writing life. Near the beginning of *Between the Acts* she describes the 'blue that has escaped registration' in words close to those of Tyndall.[31]

When we consider Virginia Woolf's relations to the Victorians we scant their meaning if we fail to recognise how widely imaginative was her continuous reading and her rewriting, how broad a knowledge she drew on. Victorian physics may have come more strongly to her mind again in the 1930s because of the intervention of Einstein's theories, which fascinated her, and her reading of Eddington and Jeans. I have discussed that probability elsewhere. The Victorian reading bases of her imagination were not simply expunged, outdated by modernist writing and science. They were, as probably, reawakened by such interventions.[32]

In *Between the Acts* Victorian England re-emerges as a not-quite-dislodged present no longer represented, as in *The Years*, as past family and national history. Instead, *Between the Acts* is preoccupied with synchrony as a new form (perhaps the only feasible remaining form) for permanence. When she wrote this work Woolf was nearing 60 years old, closer in age to the old people in the book than the young. Isa looks 'at Mrs Swithin as if she had been a dinosaur or a very diminutive mammoth. Extinct she must be, since she had lived in the reign of Queen Victoria'.[33] As had Virginia Stephen.

In *Between the Acts* she shows the whole community of England poised, only half-aware, on the brink of national disaster (it is an afternoon of mid-June, 1939). In the village pageant the past is summoned up, in the form of caricature, celebration and reminiscence. 'Home' and "Ome' epitomises Victorian expansion and repression together.

> BUDGE . . . Home, gentlemen; home, ladies, it's time to pack up and go home. Don't I see the fire (he pointed: one window blazed red) blazing ever higher? In kitchen; and nursery; drawing-room and library? That's the fire of 'Ome. And see! Our Jane has brought the tea. Now children where's the toys? Mama, your knitting, quick. For here (he swept his truncheon at Cobbet of Cobbs Corner) comes the bread-winner, home from the city, home from the counter, home from the shop. 'Mama, a cup o' tea'. 'Children, gather round my knee. I will read aloud. Which shall it be? Sinbad the sailor? Or some simple tale from the Scriptures? And show you the pictures? What none of 'em? Then out with the bricks.'   (pp. 200–1)

Budge, the constable, guards 'respectability', 'prosperity', 'the purity of Victoria's land'. But it is 'going home': giving way like an old garment. Mrs Lynn Jones, watching the representation of Victorian family life, protests inwardly against the parody, but muses:

> Was there, she mused, . . . something – not impure, that wasn't the word – but perhaps 'unhygienic' about the home? Like a bit of meat gone sour, with whiskers, as the servants called it? Or why had it perished?   (p. 202)

Does the past simply 'go off', like a piece of meat, too closely connected to appetite to endure? Was the Victorian home particularly corruptible? Woolf here moves in on our irremediable confusions between language and body. She separates out for attention the word 'unhygienic', itself a Victorian coinage and crucial to the anxieties of that culture. So 'perished' exhibits both the sense of irremediable individual death and of technical material decay which operate within different linguistic registers. ('We perish each alone', we recollect, but rubber perishes.)

Mrs Jones continues her musing, considering the different modes of time: circular, and onward.

> If they had met with no resistance, she mused, nothing wrong, they'd still be going round and round and round. The Home

would have remained; and Papa's beard, she thought, would have
grown and grown; and Mama's knitting O what did she do with
all her knitting? – Change had to come, she said to herself, or
there'd have been yards and yards of Papa's beard, of Mama's
knitting. Nowadays her son-in-law was clean shaven. Her
daughter had a refrigerator.   (p. 203)

Death, mercifully, prevents the entire filling of the world with
beard and knitting ('1928–1832. Father's birthday. He would have
been 96, 96, yes today. . . . What would have happened? No
writing, no books; – inconceivable'). So I return to my opening
question: 'Where did Victorian writing go?' Did it perish with the
Home? That seems to be the force of the jest here: the key
rhyme-words within the passage are 'Fire' and 'Tea'. But Mrs Lynn
Jones is followed by Isa thinking that Mrs Swithin must be extinct.
We know better, as readers, since the shifty lexical play of the book
finds its periods of mediated perception chiefly through the mind of
Mrs Swithin who now answers Isa's questions 'Were they like that?'

'The Victorians', Mrs Swithin mused. 'I don't believe' she said
with her odd little smile, 'that there ever were such people. Only
you and me and William dressed differently'. 'You don't believe
in history', said William.   (p. 203)

The old imperialist Bart and the Christian lady Mrs Swithin, by
virtue of old age, live in a shifting time in which pre-history, the
Victorian age and the present are all in synchrony, but as 'orts,
scraps, and fragments'. Woolf places all her people this time in a
possible final moment (as she wrote the book the bombers moved
overhead and the boats set out for their rescue mission to Dunkirk
just across the water). Budge's gesture towards Pointz Hall has a
double meaning: 'Don't I see the fire (he pointed: one window
blazed red) blazing ever higher.'
    It is sunset, the war is about to begin. She shows a group who
seem to go back uninterrupted to pre-history, but the constant
references to the History of Civilisation and the dinosaurs remind
us, lightly, that civilisations end and the dinosaurs are no more.
    She changes the image of 'orts, scraps, and fragments' from its
signification in *Troilus and Cressida* as the greasy remains of a meal,
into an archaeological image of vestiges, shards. The scraps of the
communal and personal past are recuperable only *as* gossip and

pastiche, a flotsam of significant fragments. The fragments, significantly, never collapse again into 'synthesis', that Victorian ideal of mind and writing. She jostles Victorian language into new patterns, establishing her separation from them. And that makes it possible for her to acknowledge them as kin.

Notes

1. For discussion of Woolf's Victorian upbringing, see Noel Annan, *Leslie Stephen: The Godless Victorian* (London: Weidenfeld & Nicolson, 1984) and Phyllis Rose, *Woman of Letters: A Life of Virginia Woolf* (Oxford: Oxford University Press, 1978). Woolf was called Adeline after her mother's sister, Adeline Vaughan, who died the year before Virginia's birth: see Leslie Stephen, *The Mausoleum Book*, ed. A. Bell (Oxford: Clarendon Press, 1977) pp. 59, 66–70. 1832 is the year of Stephen's birth, 1941 of Woolf's death.
2. *Cornhill Magazine*, xlv (1882) 585–93, 481–90; xlvi (1882) 602–12 (quotation from pp. 611–12).
3. *The Diary of Virginia Woolf*, ed. Anne Olivier Bell (London: Hogarth Press, 1980) vol. iii, p. 208.
4. Woolf uses Coventry Patmore's title, *The Angel in the House*, for her own oppositional purposes. See *The Death of the Moth* (London: Hogarth Press, 1942) pp. 150–1, where a close relation between her mother and the angel is suggested.
5. Gillian Beer, 'Virginia Woolf and Pre-history', in *Virginia Woolf: A Centenary Perspective*, ed. Eric Warner (London: Mamillan, 1984) pp. 99–123 (quotation from p. 100).
6. Quoted in Annan, *Leslie Stephen*, p. 119.
7. Virginia Woolf, *Collected Essays* (London: Hogarth Press, 1966) vol. i, pp. 212–13.
8. Elizabeth Barrett Browning, *Aurora Leigh* (London, 1857) bk i, l. 426.
9. Frederic Harrison, in the *Cornhill Magazine*, xvi (n.s.) (1904) 432–43.
10. *The Diary of Virginia Woolf* (1982) vol. iv, p. 5; *Virginia Woolf's Reading Notebooks*, ed. Brenda Silver (Princeton, N.J.: Princeton University Press, 1983) li, p. 243 and lviii, pp. 255–73.
11. *Moments of Being: Unpublished Autobiographical Writings*, ed. Jeanne Schulkind (Brighton: Sussex University Press, 1976) p. 161; see also 'Since the War', in *A Haunted House and other Short Stories* (London: Hogarth Press, 1943) p. 44, where she remarks that it was 'shocking and wonderful to discover' that these 'real things, Sunday luncheons, Sunday walks, country houses, and tablecloths, were not entirely real, were indeed half phantoms'.
12. 'A Sketch of the Past', in *Moments of Being*, p. 132.
13. *Orlando* (London: Hogarth Press, 1928) p. 207. Further page references are included in the text.

14. *Collected Essays*, vol. I, p. 206.
15. *Modern Painters* (New York, 1881) vol. III, containing Part IV, 'Of Many Things', pp. 248–9.
16. Perry Meisel, *The Absent Father: Virginia Woolf and Walter Pater* (New Haven, Conn., and London: Yale University Press, 1980); Beer, 'Virginia Woolf and Pre-history'.
17. *Collected Essays*, vol. I, pp. 206–7.
18. *Collected Essays*, vol. I, p. 214.
19. Virginia Woolf, *Flush: A Biography* (London, Hogarth Press, 1940) p. 19. Further page references are included in the text. Woolf's most rumbustious representation of chosen Victorians is *Freshwater: A Comedy* (London: Hogarth Press, 1976).
20. *Collected Essays*, vol. IV, p. 39.
21. Ibid., p. 54.
22. Quoted in Michael Holroyd, *Lytton Strachey: A Biography* (London: Heinemann, 1970) p. 312.
23. Virginia Woolf, 'Women and Fiction', in *Granite and Rainbow* (London, 1958) p. 83.
24. Frederic Harrison, *Cornhill Magazine*.
25. Virginia Woolf, *Mrs Dalloway* (London, 1925) p. 88.
26. Thomas Henry Huxley, 'On the Physical Basis of Life', *Lay Sermons, Addresses and Reviews* (London, 1870) pp. 104–27 (quotation from pp. 105–6). Huxley's volume is dedicated to John Tyndall.
27. Virginia Woolf, *The Waves* (London, 1931) p. 8.
28. James A. Froude, *Thomas Carlyle: A History of his Life in London, 1834–1881* (London, 1884) vol. I, pp. 289–91.
29. John Tyndall, *On Radiation* (London, 1865) pp. 9–10.
30. John Tyndall, *Six Lectures on Light* (London, 1873) p. 53.
31. See, for example, 'The Scientific Use of the Imagination' in John Tyndall, *Use and Limit of the Imagination in Science* (London, 1870) p. 26, and the responses collected in this volume, for example, *The Times*, 19 September 1870.
32. For a rather general discussion of the possible effects of Woolf's reading in twentieth-century popular physics see Alan J. Friedman and Carol C. Donley, *Einstein as Myth and Muse* (Cambridge: Cambridge University Press, 1985).
33. Virginia Woolf, *Between the Acts* (London: Hogarth Press, 1941) p. 203. Further page references are included in the text.

Index

Ouida (Marie Louise de la Ramée), 113
Our Mutual Friend, 3, 61, 72, 114; characters: Fledgeby, 34; Bradley Headstone, 65; Betty Higden, 72
Owen, Richard, 5–7
Owen, Robert, 67

paedophilia/paedophobia, 28–9, 31, 76
Page, Norman, 60
'Pallette, Peter' (illustrator), 102
Palmerston, Henry John Temple, 3rd Viscount, 71–2
Parsons, Mary, 63n12
Pater, Walter, 223
Patmore, Coventry: *The Angel in the House*, 234n4
Patten, Robert, 98
Paul, St, 203
Paul Periwinkle or the Pressgang, 102–3
Peacock, Thomas Love, 174, 182; *Crotchet Castle*, 172–3, 176, 178, 181; 'French Comic Romances', 180; *Gryll Grange*: serialised, 172; Victorianness, 172; reception, 172–5; technique and character of, 175–83; *Headlong Hall*, 172–3, 176, 180; 'The Last Day of Windsor Forest', 184n18; *Melincourt*, 173–5; 'Memoir' on Shelley, 181; *Nightmare Abbey*, 173, 176
Peckham, Morse, 129
Peel, Sir Robert, 67
Penguin Books, 60–1
Phillips, Watts: *The Dead Heart*, 37
'Phiz' *see* Browne, Hablot K.
Pickwick Papers: success, 26; and social reform, 57; criticism of Chancery, 69; serial publication, 98–101; sales, 101; imitators, 102–3; characters: Count Smorltork, 51n28; Rachel Wardle, 180
Pitt, William, 198
Pollock, Sir Jonathan Frederick (Chief Baron), 69
Potter, Sir John, 150
Priestley, J. B., 182

Priestley, Joseph, 144–6, 148, 157, 162, 167
Pritchett, V. S., 179
Pueckler-Muskau, Hermann L. H., Prince von, 45
Punch, 105–9

Racine, Jean, 217–18
Ravenscourt, Edward (publisher), 103
Ray, Gordon, 191–2
Reach, Angus: *Clement Lorimer*, 111–12
Reade, Charles, 113
Rector's Progress, The (by 'Clericus'), 103
Reid, Captain Mayne: *The Headless Horseman*, 113
Revolution (1848), 66
Reynolds, G. W. M.: *Mysteries of London*, 106; *Pickwick Abroad*, 103
Riouffe, Honoré de, 48
Robberds, J. G., 148, 155
Rodwell, G. Herbert: *Woman's Love*, 106–7
Roland, Mme Marie Jeanne, 48
Rossetti, Christina, 129, 227
Rotch, Benjamin, 61
Rousseau, Jean-Jacques: *Confessions*, 45–7; *Rêveries du Promeneur Solitaire*, 45
Routledge (publishers), 113
Rowland Bradshaw, or the Way to Fame ('by the author of Raby Rattler', i.e. Thomas Hall), 106
Ruby, George, 55, 59
Rue, Emile de la, 70
Ruskin, John, 5, 64n12, 220–4; *Modern Painters*, 220, 223

Sackville-West, Vita, 216, 224
Sadleir, Michael, 100
St John, Percy B.: *The Miser's Will*, 106–7
Saint-Martin, Louis-Claude de, 44
Saintsbury, George, 185–6, 200
Sampson Low (publishers), 116
Sams, W. R. (publisher), 106
Saunders & Otley (publishers), 100